THE FLAVOR OF THE SOUTH

THE FLAVOR OF THE SOUTH

Delicacies and Staples of Southern Cuisine

JEANNE A. VOLTZ

ILLUSTRATED BY MEL KLAPHOLZ

WINGS BOOKS
NEW YORK • AVENEL, NEW JERSEY

DESIGNED BY LAURENCE ALEXANDER

This 1993 edition is published by Wings Books,
distributed by Outlet Book Company, Inc., a Random House Company,
40 Engelhard Avenue, Avenel, New Jersey 07001,
by arrangement with Jeanne A. Voltz.

Random House
New York • Toronto • London • Sydney • Auckland

Printed and bound in the United States of America

Library of Congress Cataloging-in-Publication Data
Voltz, Jeanne.
   The flavor of the South : delicacies and staples of southern
cuisine / Jeanne A. Voltz : illustrated by Mel Klapholz.
      p.   cm.
   Originally published: 1st ed. Garden City, N.Y. : Doubleday, 1977.
   Includes index.
   ISBN 0-517-41303-5
   1. Cookery. American—Southern style.   I. Title.
TX715.2.S68V65   1993   93-3290
641.5975—dc20   CIP

8 7 6 5 4 3

To the memory of

MARIE SEWELL APPLETON, who had the nerve to let a curious child invade her kitchen

and

JAMES LAMAR APPLETON, who taught the child to taste

Contents

NOTE:
Whenever an asterisk precedes the name of a dish, the recipe for that dish is included elsewhere in the book. Consult Index for page numbers.

INTRODUCTION

Southern cooking has been romanticized beyond all proportion to reality by Stars and Bars waving rebels. It has been slandered unfairly by thousands introduced to the mediocre brand of food dished up in highway restaurants whose major virtue seems to be gaudy signboards screaming, "Homemade Pecan Pie" or "Southern Fried Chicken."

Yet southern cooking is unique, the only culinary style in the country that might be regarded as a cuisine. It is honest food, capitalizing on an abundance of fresh foods provided by fertile land and sea and year-round mild climate. It is simple cookery, with distinctive style but not stylized food.

Anthropologists classify diets in various ways—by breadstuffs, for example. The southern diet is based on corn and rice. Hot biscuits are the magnificent wheaten exception, but in some parts of the South more corn bread and rice are consumed than wheat. Or the principal protein food is used as the key to a diet—beef in the United States, veal in France, lamb in England, legumes in India and parts of Africa, dairy products in northern Europe. Southern cookery employs some of all these, plus generous portions of pork and seafood. But Southerners are the world's champion chicken eaters. They like it fried, baked, stewed, barbecued—any way you can cook it.

Other intellectuals judge a cuisine by its flavors. The flavor of the South is a heady mixture of onions, celery, sweet and hot peppers, tomatoes, cumin, horseradish, chili powder, mustard, cinnamon, nutmeg, allspice, cloves, ginger, and the distinctive contribution of the Indians, filé, powdered leaves of native sassafras.

Southern cooking is sensual, not intellectual. The most damning description a Southerner born and bred to Brunswick stew, gumbos, and hot biscuits with home-milled cane syrup can accord a food is, "It doesn't have any taste!" Southerners cook and eat to enjoy. The simplest foods, fresh tendergreens and pot liquor with corn bread or fried pan fish and hush puppies, are cooked with painstaking care.

Only in the South and California do home cooks insist on fresh produce of a quality almost forgotten in other areas. Supermarkets have taken over food distribution in the South, as everywhere, but farm markets, fresh produce and seafood peddlers, and roadside stands still purvey fresh foods in beautiful seasonal array. In the South an old-fashioned vegetable dinner is still possible—even probable for summer noon.

Southern cuisine is influenced by diverse food styles, American Indian, English, Irish and Scotch, African, French, Spanish, Mexican, representing every flag planted on the soil, no matter how briefly. More recently, Cuban Spanish and Puerto Rican Spanish people have brought their food customs to Florida. Middle European Jews have also put their stamp on the cuisine.

Historically southern cooking relied on servants. These culinary geniuses have vanished to mill and office jobs, along with their ex-mistresses. The supply lines from garden to table have lengthened in the South. Meals are simpler. More elaborate dishes are reserved for special occasions. Heavy cream and fresh cane syrup don't flow so freely as a generation ago. But food is still a major concern in southern homes.

This selection of recipes is personal, drawn from my earliest gastronomic experiences at the table of a mother and grandmothers who spent much time and energy preparing food to the taste of demanding families. But they, too, updated their cooking as times and supplies demanded. This is food they might serve if they still lived today. These recipes represent the best of the old, some simplified to more modern, foolproof methods, with the most delectable of the new.

JEANNE VOLTZ
New York, N.Y.

BEVERAGES

Southern thirsts are legendary—and so are the thirst quenchers. They run from Coca-Cola, its numerous imitators, iced tea, and fruit punches to native corn whiskey (fine spirits indeed when it is good, white lightning one wouldn't care to have strike the palate twice when it is crude), *Ramos Gin Fizz, and *Mint Juleps. Coffee in the South is likely to be strong and fragrant, an eye-opening brew. Receptions dot social calendars in such cities as Tallahassee, where *Coffee Frappé has been ladled from huge punch bowls for generations. Tea also is a party brew, spiced, laced with sherry, rum, or fruit juice. Iced tea predominates in summer.

Prohibition, and local and state beverage control laws that followed, almost wrecked the southern use of good wines. But the grape is rising again. By the mid-1970s a choice of table wines was available in many state liquor stores and supermarkets where sale of wines is allowed. In cities some excellent wines are served, and men and women are forming wine tasting and buying groups, as in other areas of the country. The South's most celebrated gourmet, Thomas Jefferson, maintained a fine wine cellar in the White House, and many southern gentlemen were connoisseurs of good wines. A Mr. Habersham (or Habisham, depending on the writer), of Savannah, reputedly developed an especially fine madeira, called Rainwater. He had casks of madeira shipped for his table, had it filtered and clarified to produce this clear light madeira, which is now produced by many bottlers.

CAFÉ BRULOT

Cut orange peel in continuous spiral, peeling off as much white pith as possible. Place in bowl or 2-cup measure. Add cloves, cinnamon, and brandy. Let stand 2–3 hours. Pour brandy with orange spiral and spices over sugar in chafing dish. Mash sugar with back of a silver ladle to dissolve it. Ignite brandy and gradually pour in hot coffee to extinguish the flame. Ladle into demitasse or Café Brulot cups. MAKES 8 SERVINGS.

Peel of 1 medium orange
7 whole cloves
3 cinnamon sticks, broken
¾ cup brandy
10 lumps sugar
3 cups hot Louisiana coffee or dark roast coffee

TALLAHASSEE COFFEE FRAPPÉ

Combine hot coffee, milk, and sugar and stir until sugar is dissolved. Cool. Pour in punch bowl, add ice cream and whipped cream, and stir to give a swirled effect. Ladle into punch cups. MAKES 16–18 PUNCH CUP SERVINGS.

1 quart hot strong coffee (6 servings)
1 cup milk
1 cup sugar
1 pint coffee, vanilla, or chocolate ice cream
½ pint heavy cream, whipped

VIEUX CARRÉ CAFÉ AU LAIT

Brew coffee in any preferred manner, though a drip coffee maker with filter gives less muddy coffee with full flavor. Don't skimp on ground coffee. Use a coffee measure (2 tablespoons) for each 6 ounces (¾ cup) water. Heat milk over moderate heat, just until bubbles form at edge.

Customarily hot coffee and hot milk are served in separate pots, then poured half and half at table, though coffee and milk may be poured into cups in the kitchen. Pass sugar for those who want it, though New Orleanians prefer café au lait unsweetened. MAKES 6 CUPS.

2 cups hot Louisiana-style coffee (with chicory)
2 cups milk
Sugar

CLASSIC ICED TEA

Bring 1 quart freshly drawn water in saucepan to a full rolling boil. Remove from heat and immediately add tea. Stir and let stand 5 minutes. Pour remaining cold water in pitcher. Stir brewed tea and strain into pitcher of water. Serve at once, pouring tea over ice cubes in tall glasses, or cover and store at room temperature until ready to serve. Place a sprig of mint in each glass if desired. Pass sugar and lemon. MAKES 10–12 SERVINGS.

2 quarts water
15 tea bags or ⅓ cup loose tea
Ice cubes
Mint sprigs (optional)
Sugar
Lemon wedges

REFRIGERATOR TEA

Pour water in pitcher. Add tea. Cover loosely and let stand in refrigerator overnight. Remove tea bags or strain into another pitcher. To serve, pour over ice cubes in tall glasses. Place a sprig of mint in each glass if desired. Pass sugar and lemon. MAKES 5–6 SERVINGS.

1 quart cold tap water
8–10 tea bags (tags removed) or 3 tablespoons loose tea
Ice cubes
Mint sprigs (optional)
Sugar
Lemon wedges

SPICED TEA

Combine tea, cloves, cinnamon, lemon and orange peels in large teapot or enamelware or stainless-steel pan. Add boiling water, cover, and steep 5 minutes. Strain, add lemon and orange juices. Serve at once or keep hot over warmer. Pass lemon and sugar to flavor and sweeten as desired. MAKES 12 SERVINGS.

3 tablespoons loose tea or 8 tea bags
½ teaspoon whole cloves
2 cinnamon sticks, broken
Grated peel of 1 lemon
Grated peel of 2 oranges
8 cups boiling water
½ cup lemon juice
½ cup orange juice
Lemon slices studded with whole cloves
Lump sugar

SUMMER SPICED TEA

Combine water, sugar, salt, cloves, 2 crumbled cinnamon sticks, and nutmeg in saucepan. Bring to a boil, cover, and simmer 20 minutes. Strain into tea. Cool. Fill tall glasses with ice cubes and place a whole cinnamon stick in each. Fill with spiced tea mixture and garnish with lemon or lime slices. MAKES 6 SERVINGS.

¾ cup water
½ cup sugar
Dash salt
1 teaspoon whole cloves
8 cinnamon sticks
Dash nutmeg
5 cups brewed tea
Ice cubes
Lemon or lime slices

CHABLIS CHAMPAGNE PUNCH

Cut peel of orange in thick spiral, cutting slightly into pulp, and leave attached to orange. Place orange in small punch bowl. Add chablis and let stand 15 minutes. Add ice cubes and champagne. Remove orange, detach peel, and let spiral of peel float in punch. Serve at once. MAKES 20 PUNCH CUP SERVINGS.

1 small orange
2 fifths chablis, chilled
2 or 3 trays ice cubes
1 fifth dry champagne, chilled

CHRISTMAS EGGNOG

Egg whites will have larger volume if warmed to room temperature before beating. Beat egg whites until soft peaks form. Add sugar a tablespoonful at a time and beat until stiff peaks form. Set aside. Beat egg yolks until thick and light-colored. Stir 1 cup Bourbon into egg yolks. Fold yolks into whites. Stir in remaining Bourbon, rum, milk, and whipped cream. Cover and chill several hours or overnight. Stir to blend, pour into a chilled punch bowl or individual cups, and serve. Splash a drop or two of Pernod on each cupful for those who like it. Dust with nutmeg. MAKES 15–18 PUNCH CUP SERVINGS.

6 eggs, separated
¼ cup sugar
2 cups Bourbon
1 ounce dark rum (2 tablespoons)
2 cups milk
1 pint heavy cream, whipped
Pernod, Herbsaint, or anisette
Nutmeg, preferably ground at table

FLORIDA SUNBURST

Peel mango, remove seed, and slice fruit into blender Add orange concentrate and water or orange juice. Blend at high speed until mango is puréed. Pour 1 ounce vodka in each 6–8-ounce wineglass and fill with orange juice mixture. MAKES 6–8 SERVNGS.

NOTE: A canned mango and pineapple or mango and orange nectar may be purchased in some areas of the country. This may be used in the Sunburst in place of the mango and orange juice.

1 medium mango
1 6-ounce can frozen orange concentrate, liquefied as directed on label, or 1½ cups orange juice
Vodka, chilled

MINT JULEP

Preparing a mint julep is more ritual than recipe and controversies rage over the fine points. This procedure produces a well-frosted tumbler filled with a smooth drink appropriate for Derby Day or anytime.

Chill julep cup, a straight-sided 10-ounce tumbler of silver or other metal, in refrigerator for 2–3 hours. A double old-fashioned glass can be used, but glass will not frost as well as silver. Clip a handful of well-leafed mint stems, wash under cold running water, dry in paper towels, and chill in vegetable crisper. Tear 6 or 8 leaves into chilled julep cup and bruise well with plastic or glass muddler. Work in sugar and a splash of water to form a syrup. Pack ice in cup, fill with Bourbon, and stir. Stick a sprig of mint in the ice. MAKES 1 SERVING.

NOTE: Some julep makers insert a straw in the cup, trimmed short so the drinker smells the mint, but the julep then becomes more powerful, so others insist a julep is imbibed without straw so that each sip passes through the ice.

6 or 8 large mint leaves
2 teaspoons confectioners' sugar
Water
Crushed ice
3 ounces (approximately) Bourbon
1 mint sprig

PINK CHAMPAGNE PUNCH

Combine lemon juice, grenadine, and sugar in punch bowl which will hold at least 8 quarts. (If bowl is not large enough, make a half recipe at a time.) Stir until sugar is dissolved. Place ice in bowl. Add champagne, sauterne, and club soda. Stir gently to mix. Float lemon and orange slices on punch. MAKES ABOUT 40 PUNCH CUP SERVINGS.

Juice of 1 lemon
½ cup grenadine syrup
½ cup sugar
1 large block ice
2 fifths champagne, chilled
2 fifths dry sauterne or other dry white wine, chilled
2 28-ounce bottles club soda, chilled
Sliced lemon and orange for garnish

PITCHER BLOODY MARY

Mix salt, lemon juice and pepper sauce in pitcher. Add tomato juice. Chill at least 1 hour. Place 4 or 5 ice cubes in each tall glass. Add 1½ ounces vodka to each and fill with tomato juice mixture. Stir. Place a celery stick stirrer in each. MAKES 6 SERVINGS.

⅛ teaspoon salt
Juice of 2 lemons
4 drops hot pepper sauce
3 cups tomato juice
Ice cubes
9 ounces vodka
6 celery sticks with leaves

RAMOS GIN FIZZ

Place ice cubes in blender with sugar, orange flower water, lemon and lime juices. Blend until almost smooth. Add egg white, gin, and milk and blend until foamy. Pour in tall glasses. MAKES 2 SERVINGS.

NOTE: For parties, the host may keep 2 or 3 blenders busy making Ramos Fizzes. The egg white and milk mixture can be premeasured and set out in small glasses and the lemon and lime juices presqueezed.

4 or 5 ice cubes
2 teaspoons confectioners' sugar
⅛ teaspoon orange flower water
2 tablespoons lemon juice
1 tablespoon lime juice, preferably Key lime
1 egg white
¼ cup gin (2 ounces)
½ cup milk

APPETIZERS
AND CANAPES

Southerners persist in calling a cocktail party a "reception." This is the principal means of entertaining lots of people—more prevalent, even, than the fabled barbecue. Hostesses call anything served with cocktails canapés, though the true canapé is rarely served. More often such tidbits as *Benne Wafers, *Cheese Pecan Wafers, and *Hot Sausage Bites are served. The ultimate is tissue-thin slices of country ham in tiny hot biscuits. Recipes for the biscuits and the ham are in the bread and meat chapters respectively. A huge bowl of iced shrimp, if the host and hostess can afford it, and cocktail sauce for a dip (both these recipes in their appropriate chapters) is peculiarly southern.

An appetizer at table means just two words, shrimp cocktail, served frosty cold in stemmed glasses. Freshly opened oysters or crab have fans, too. Fresh fruit cocktail and a half grapefruit, well iced, and some of the ready-made cocktails start important dinners here, as well.

AVOCADO BUTTER

Peel and seed avocado. Slice into bowl or blender. Add salt and lemon juice. Mash or blend until smooth. Mix in mayonnaise. Serve as spread for toast, hot breads, or crackers. MAKES 1 CUP.

1 small or ½ large soft avocado
¼ teaspoon salt
2 tablespoons lemon or lime juice
2 tablespoons mayonnaise

BAYOU MEAT TART

Chill pastry while preparing filling. Preheat oven to 400°. Mix oil and flour in heavy skillet; cook and stir until browned. Add onion, celery, green pepper, and garlic and cook until onion is golden, stirring often. Add water, ground beef, salt, red pepper, and lemon juice. Break up meat with fork so it is crumbly and simmer 15–20 minutes, stirring 2 or 3 times. Roll out pastry very thin. Fit into 9-inch pie plate or tart shells or cut in 4-inch circles and press into 2½-inch muffin cups to form shallow tart shells. Fill with meat mixture. Bake until pastry is golden, about 40 minutes for 9-inch pie, 30 minutes for tarts, or 20 minutes for miniature tarts. Serve warm as a main course, warm or at room temperature as hors d'oeuvre. MAKES 1 9-INCH PIE, 6–7 5-INCH TARTS, OR 2 DOZEN 2-INCH TARTS.

Egg Yolk Pastry (see following page)
¼ cup oil
¼ cup flour
1 small onion, chopped
1 rib celery, chopped
½ green pepper, chopped
1 clove garlic, minced
½ cup water
1 pound lean ground beef
1 teaspoon salt
½ teaspoon crushed dried red pepper
Juice of ½ lemon

EGG YOLK PASTRY

Combine flour and salt in bowl. Add lard and cut in with pastry blender or 2 knives until mealy. With fork, blend in egg yolks, then water to form a dough that clings together. Roll out on lightly floured surface to ⅛ inch. MAKES ENOUGH FOR 1 9-INCH PIE SHELL, 6 5-INCH TART SHELLS, OR 2 DOZEN 2-INCH TARTLET SHELLS.

NOTE: Pastry can be mixed in a food processor, but may require slightly less water. Pastry is easier to handle if chilled 30 minutes or longer before rolling.

2 cups flour
1 teaspoon salt
½ cup lard, cut in pieces
2 egg yolks
⅓ cup (approximately) cold water

BENNE WAFERS

Spread sesame seeds in large shallow baking pan and toast in 350° oven until deep golden, 12–15 minutes. Stir or shake pan 2 or 3 times while toasting. Cool. Reduce oven temperature to 325°. Combine flour, salt, baking powder, and cayenne in bowl. Add shortening and butter and cut in with pastry blender or 2 knives until particles are like meal. Add water a tablespoon at a time and blend with fork until dough clings together. Add toasted seeds and knead in thoroughly. Turn out on lightly floured surface and knead a few strokes, working in any loose seeds. Roll out to ⅛ inch. Cut with floured 1¾-inch round cutter. Place ½ inch apart on lightly greased cookie sheets. Bake 15–20 minutes, until dry on top and beginning to brown at edges. Cool on racks and store in tightly covered container. MAKES 4–4½ DOZEN.

NOTE: Benne Wafer dough can be mixed in a food processor, but will require slightly less water. Use just enough to make dough cling together in a ball.

1 cup sesame (benne) seeds (2¼–2¾ ounces)
1 cup flour
½ teaspoon salt
½ teaspoon baking powder
⅛ teaspoon cayenne or hot pepper sauce
¼ cup vegetable shortening
2 tablespoons butter or margarine, cut in pieces
3–4 tablespoons ice water

CAVIAR MOLD

Pour broth into 2-cup measure and add water to make 2 cups. Pour ½ cup of the broth mixture into small saucepan. Sprinkle gelatin over it and let soften. Stir over low heat until gelatin is dissolved. Stir in remaining broth and lemon juice. Keep mixture at room temperature while assembling mold. Spoon caviar into 1-quart or into 2 1-pint molds (ring molds or fluted molds) which have been oiled or sprayed with nonstick coating. Work gently to prevent breaking caviar. Carefully pour enough gelatin mixture over caviar so it barely floats. Shake lightly to level. Refrigerate until just set, 20–25 minutes. Meanwhile, mash egg whites and yolks separately. Mash onion into whites and parsley into yolks. Carefully spoon whites over caviar layer. Add broth so whites barely float. Shake gently to level. Refrigerate until just set. Add yolks and remaining broth. Chill until firm. Loosen edges of mold with tip of knife, then dip mold in very warm water. Turn out on plate. Garnish with watercress or lettuce leaves. Slice and serve with crackers or melba toast. MAKES 8–10 APPETIZERS.

1 10¾-ounce can condensed chicken broth
Water
2 envelopes unflavored gelatin
Juice of ½ lemon
1 3½-ounce jar caviar (or more to taste)
3 hard-cooked eggs
1 small onion, minced
1 teaspoon minced parsley
Watercress or small lettuce leaves
Crackers or melba toast

TEXAS CAVIAR (PICKLED BLACK-EYED PEAS)

Drain peas and combine with green pepper, onions, oil, vinegar, pepper, and salt. Mix well. Spear pieces of garlic on wood picks and push down into liquid. Cover and refrigerate overnight. Remove garlic, cover, and refrigerate until ready to serve, up to 2 weeks. Transfer to relish dish and serve with slotted relish spoon to drain off juice. Guests need small plates and forks for this hors d'oeuvre. Any leftovers may be tossed with greens to serve as salad. MAKES 10–12 APPETIZER SERVINGS.

1 16-ounce can cooked dried black-eyed peas.
½ green pepper, seeded and thinly sliced
3–4 green onions, thinly sliced
½ cup oil
¼ cup vinegar
⅛ teaspoon crushed dried red pepper
¼ teaspoon salt
1 clove garlic, split

CHEESE PECAN WAFERS

Cream together butter and cheese until well blended, using electric mixer at medium speed or sturdy wooden spoon. Work in flour, salt, and cayenne with spoon until well blended. Work in pecans. Shape into rolls 1½ inches in diameter on waxed paper. Wrap paper, rounding dough as paper is rolled. Flatten ends and twist ends of paper. Refrigerate overnight. From the roll, cut ¼-inch-thick slices and place ½ inch apart on ungreased cookie sheets. Bake at 350° 15 minutes or until edges begin to turn golden. Cool on wire racks and store in tightly covered containers. MAKES 8–9 DOZEN.

1 cup butter or margarine, softened
2 cups shredded extra sharp Cheddar cheese (½ pound)
1½ cups flour
½ teaspoon salt
¼ teaspoon cayenne or hot pepper sauce
1 cup finely chopped pecans

GARLIC CHEESE

Combine cream and Cheddar cheeses and garlic in large bowl. Mix at low speed of electric mixer or knead by hand until well blended. Work in Worcestershire, cayenne, and pecans. Liberally sprinkle the centers of 4 sheets of plastic wrap with paprika. With plastic spatula or wooden paddle, scoop cheese onto paprika on plastic wrap. Shape cheese in rolls about 1½ inches in diameter, rolling and shaping with hands or plastic wrap. Twist ends of wrap around each roll and refrigerate overnight or longer. Slice thin and serve on round crackers or melba toast. MAKES ABOUT 60 CANAPÉS.

1 8-ounce package cream cheese, softened
4 cups shredded sharp Cheddar cheese (1 pound)
3–4 cloves garlic, minced
1 teaspoon Worcestershire sauce
Dash cayenne
¼ cup finely chopped pecans
Paprika

PIMIENTO CHEESE

Combine cheese and pimiento with liquid. Mash together with fork until pimiento is in small pieces and well mixed with cheese. Add mayonnaise and mix well. If not moist enough, add more mayonnaise to taste. Cover and chill at least 1 hour to blend flavors. Use as a spread for sandwiches or crackers. MAKES ABOUT 1½ CUPS, ENOUGH FOR 6 SANDWICHES OR 2 DOZEN COCKTAIL CRACKERS.

2 cups shredded sharp Cheddar cheese (½ pound)
1 2-ounce can or jar pimiento
¼ cup mayonnaise

SEWING CLUB CHEESE STRAWS

Preheat oven to 400°. Roll out pastry on floured surface to ⅛ inch, keeping it more or less rectangular. Sprinkle half the sheet of pastry with cheese, using 2–3 tablespoons for a 4×8-inch area. Sprinkle lightly with cayenne. Fold other half over cheese. Roll out pastry again, sprinkle half with cheese and cayenne, fold and repeat 2 or 3 times, sprinkling with cheese and folding. Finally, fold, roll out thin, and cut in strips with sharp knife or pastry wheel. I prefer cheese straws about ⅓ inch wide and 2–3 inches long, though they may be narrower or wider, longer or shorter. Place on greased baking sheet. Cheese straws may be twisted and ends pressed to the baking sheets to anchor them. Bake 8–10 minutes, until pale golden. Remove from cookie sheet, cool and store in tightly covered container. Serve as snack with soft drinks, cocktails, or as an accompaniment to salads or soups.

Pie pastry scraps
Shredded sharp Cheddar cheese
Cayenne

CAROLINA CHICKEN DRUMLETS

With kitchen scissors cut off meaty joint of wing. Reserve remaining joints for broth or other uses. Salt meaty sections generously and sprinkle with pepper. Coat well with flour. Heat about ½ inch oil or shortening in heavy skillet. Add wings, being careful not to crowd, and fry over medium heat until golden brown. Test with skewer at the meaty end of a drumlet. Drain on absorbent paper. Place in shallow baking dish, cover with foil, and keep warm until ready to serve or reheat 10 minutes in preheated moderate oven (325°–350°). Arrange on plate with bowl of barbecue sauce for dipping in center. MAKES 6–8 HORS D'OEUVRE SERVINGS.

12–16 chicken wings
Salt
Pepper
Flour
Oil or shortening for frying
Barbecue sauce (commercial or homemade)

CORN MEAL PUFFS

Preheat oven to 375°. Combine water, butter, and salt in medium-size saucepan. Bring to a boil. Add corn meal and flour all at once. Stir rapidly over heat until mixture leaves sides of pan and forms a compact ball. Continue to cook 3 minutes, mashing dough with spoon against sides of pan. Remove from heat, turn dough into small bowl of electric mixer, and beat about 1 minute to cool slightly. Or beat with sturdy wooden spoon to cool slightly. Beat in eggs 1 at a time. Continue beating until dough is smooth and has a satiny look. Drop dough by tablespoonfuls or teaspoonfuls on ungreased baking sheet, swirling tops to round off puffs. Space large puffs 2 inches apart, small puffs 1½ inches apart. Bake 50 minutes. Slit each puff with knife point and return to oven for 10 minutes to crisp centers. Cool and fill with chicken, tuna, shrimp, or crab salad or cocktail spreads to serve as luncheon entrees or party snacks. MAKES 10–12 LARGE PUFFS OR 2½–3 DOZEN COCKTAIL SIZE.

1 cup water
½ cup butter or margarine
¼ teaspoon salt
½ cup corn meal
¾ cup flour
4 eggs

HOT SAUSAGE BITES

Let sausage meat stand at room temperature until pliable. Preheat oven to 350°. Add cheese, baking mix, and pepper to meat. Knead with hands until well blended. Roll into balls about ¾ inch in diameter. Place 1½ inches apart on ungreased baking sheet. Bake 18 minutes or until lightly browned. Balls will become somewhat irregular in shape while baking, but they do not spread much. Serve immediately or cool and reheat at 400° for 5 minutes before serving. Unbaked bites can be frozen and baked just before serving. Allow 25–30 minutes baking for frozen bites. MAKES 6 DOZEN.

1 pound pork sausage meat, preferably hot
1¼ cups finely shredded sharp Cheddar cheese (10 ounces)
3½ cups buttermilk baking mix
¼–½ teaspoon crushed dried red pepper

HORSERADISH MEAT SPREAD

Blend potted meat, horseradish, and Worcestershire until smooth. Cover and chill at least 1 hour. Pile in small bowl and serve with crackers or melba toast. MAKES 8–10 CANAPÉS.

1 3-ounce can potted meat
2 tablespoons prepared horseradish
1 teaspoon Worcestershire sauce or to taste
Crackers or melba toast

MINTED MELON CUP

Combine sugar and water. Stir over low heat until sugar is dissolved. Bring to a boil and boil uncovered until syrupy. Remove from heat and stir in peppermint extract. Cool thoroughly. Combine melon balls. Pour mint syrup over melon, cover, and refrigerate 2–3 hours. Spoon melon into stemmed glasses, adding some of the syrup to each. Garnish with mint sprigs. Serve as appetizer or dessert. MAKES 6 SERVINGS.

NOTE: A similar melon cup can be prepared with frozen melon balls. Open 2 10-ounce packages, turn into bowl, and sprinkle with peppermint extract. Peppermint flavor will permeate melon balls as they thaw. Serve while still frosty.

1½ cups sugar
1 cup water
⅛–¼ teaspoon peppermint extract
1 cup watermelon balls
1 cup honeydew balls
1 cup cantaloupe or Key melon balls
Mint sprigs

SALTED PECANS

Preheat oven to 250°. Roast pecans in large shallow pan such as broiler pan or jelly-roll pan until shiny, about 15 minutes. Add butter, mix well, and return to oven. Roast about 20 minutes longer (or until nuts are crunchy), stirring 2 or 3 times. Stir in salt. Cool on paper towels to absorb any excess butter. Store in tightly covered container. MAKES 1 QUART.

1 pound shelled pecan halves (4 cups)
½ cup butter or margarine
1½ teaspoons salt, seasoned salt, or onion salt

SHRIMP RÉMOULADE

Combine paprika, pepper, oil, mustard, vinegar, and horseradish in blender and blend until well mixed. Add parsley and celery and blend until all ingredients are chopped fine and blended. Add sauce to shrimp, mix lightly, cover, and chill several hours or overnight. Pile in bowl and garnish with a few celery leaves in center or at edges. Or serve as salad on greens. MAKES 8 APPETIZER OR 6 SALAD SERVINGS.

NOTE: If Creole mustard is not available, use Dijon-style mustard and increase horseradish to 1 tablespoon.

1 tablespoon paprika
½ teaspoon pepper
⅓ cup olive oil
2 tablespoons Creole mustard
2 tablespoons vinegar
½ teaspoon prepared horseradish
½ cup parsley sprigs, packed
½ cup diced celery heart (1 small)
2 pounds shrimp, cleaned and cooked
Celery leaves

SEAFOOD AVOCADO COCKTAIL

Pick over crab meat and remove any cartilage or shell. Peel and seed avocado. Cut in cubes and toss with lemon or lime juice. Divide avocado cubes into 4 cocktail glasses or small bowls. Pile crab or shrimp on the avocado. Serve with Garlic Mayonnaise or other dressing. MAKES 4 SERVINGS.

½ pound crab meat or cleaned cooked
   small shrimp
1 small or ½ large avocado
Juice of 1 lemon or lime
*Garlic Mayonnaise, Russian or Thousand
   Island Dressing

SOUPS

Soups of the South reflect every culinary influence that has been incorporated into the cuisine. Vegetable soups are loaded with fresh fine things from home gardens. Seafood soups are inevitable along the coastline. Creole, Spanish, French, and Old English influences are tasted in other soups. Soup with corn bread, the country staple, makes a meal, with buttermilk or sweet milk by the pitcherful and fruit pie for dessert. In some homes vegetable soup is served with fiery hot pepper vinegar. In others, the soup is "creamed." Each person pours in sweet milk to suit his taste, thereby cooling off the steaming-hot soup.

AVOCADO CREAM SOUP

In a saucepan, cook onion in butter until tender but not browned. Stir in flour, salt, pepper sauce, milk, and broth. Cook and stir until smooth and soup comes to boil. Simmer uncovered about 10 minutes. Meanwhile, peel and seed avocado, cut into chunks, and place in blender or mixing bowl. Add lemon juice and blend or mash until puréed. Add 1 cup of the soup, cover blender, and blend until smooth. Return avocado mixture to soup, add food color to tint delicately if desired, heat, and serve, floating an avocado crescent on each serving. Or chill, thin to desired consistency with cream or milk, and serve cold. MAKES 4 SERVINGS.

2 tablespoons minced onion
2 tablespoons butter or margarine
2 tablespoons flour
1 teaspoon salt
3 drops hot pepper sauce or dash cayenne
1 cup milk
1½ cups chicken broth
1 soft avocado
1 tablespoon lemon juice
Green and yellow food color (optional)
Avocado crescents

SPANISH BEAN SOUP

Combine bones, water, 1 onion, salt, and pepper in large kettle. Cover and simmer 1 hour or until a rich broth is formed. Add potatoes and simmer 15 minutes. Remove bones. Meanwhile, cook remaining onion and garlic in oil until tender but not browned. Add to broth. Add saffron to a ladleful of broth and steam over boiling soup about 30 seconds. Stir dissolved saffron into soup. Add chick-peas and bring to a boil. Cover and simmer 5 minutes. Add food color if a deeper color is wanted. Add chorizo and bring to a boil. Ladle into soup plates and sprinkle with parsley. Serve with thick slices of Cuban or French bread. MAKES 4–6 SERVINGS.

1–1½ pounds beef bones
6 cups water
2 onions, chopped
2 teaspoons salt
¼ teaspoon pepper
2 large potatoes, peeled and cubed (about 1 pound)
1 clove garlic, crushed
2 tablespoons oil
3 or 4 threads saffron
1 16–20-ounce can chick-peas
Yellow food color (optional)
1 small chorizo (Spanish sausage) or 2 ounces smoked sausage, sliced
Minced parsley

CHICKEN BONUS SOUP

Combine chicken, water, celery, carrot, onion, salt, pepper, and bay leaf. Bring to a boil, cover, and simmer 45 minutes or until chicken bits are falling off bones. Remove bones from soup, strip off meat, and return meat to soup. Taste and add more salt if needed. Add rice, cover, and simmer 30 minutes. MAKES 4 SERVINGS.

6 or 8 chicken necks, wing tips, backbones, or carcass, preferably with bits of meat
1 quart water
1 rib celery, chopped
1 carrot, peeled and sliced
1 onion, peeled and studded with 2 whole cloves
1 teaspoon salt
½ teaspoon pepper
1 bay leaf, crumbled
4–5 tablespoons rice

GROUPER CHOWDER

Wash fish heads and place in large skillet with water to cover. Add bay leaves, salt, and pepper. Cover and simmer 20 minutes to make stock. Strain, discarding fish heads. Reserve 3 cups stock for chowder. Remainder can be refrigerated or frozen for other uses. Cut grouper into chunks about 1 inch square and set aside. Combine potatoes, onions, and 3 cups stock in large kettle. Cover and simmer 15 minutes or until potatoes are almost tender. Add fish. Cover and simmer until fish is opaque, about 10 minutes. Add milk and heat well. Add nutmeg, taste, and add more salt and pepper if needed. Ladle into hot bowls and serve with crackers, garlic bread, or corn sticks. MAKES 6 SERVINGS.

2 or 3 fish heads
Water
3 bay leaves, crumbled
1½ teaspoons salt
¼ teaspoon pepper
2 pounds grouper fillets or other firm-fleshed fish
4 large potatoes, peeled and cubed
2 large onions, chopped
2 cups milk or half-and-half
¼ teaspoon nutmeg

SHE-CRAB SOUP

Combine milk, lemon peel, and nutmeg in heavy saucepan or top part of double boiler. Heat over very low heat or boiling water until bubbles appear at edge. Remove lemon peel. Add salt, pepper sauce, and butter. Heat until butter is melted. Crumble in saltines and mix well to thicken soup. Add crab and heat well. Serve hot with more saltines. A splash of dry sherry may be poured into each bowl before ladling in soup if desired. MAKES 4–6 SERVINGS.

NOTE: Picking meat for She-Crab Soup is time-consuming but rewarding. Tear off legs. Lift apron on underside of shell and break off, then lift out body from front. Remove spongy fingers (called dead man), then pick out meat in corners of shell. With small fork, remove roe, the red nuggets near center of body, and white flakes of meat. Crack claws and remove meat.

1 quart milk
2 strips lemon peel, cut with vegetable peeler or lemon stripper
¼ teaspoon nutmeg or mace
1 teaspoon salt
⅛ teaspoon hot pepper sauce
¼ cup butter or margarine
4–6 saltines, finely crumbled
2 cups blue crab meat with roe (6–7 boiled crabs)
Dry sherry (optional)

SARASOTA GARLIC SOUP

Combine broth and water in saucepan and bring to a boil. Meanwhile, heat oil in skillet. Add garlic and cook until golden. Remove from heat at once to prevent scorching. Place a slice of bread in each soup bowl. Pour garlic and oil over bread, then fill bowls with hot broth. Sprinkle with cheese or place Swiss cheese over each serving to melt in hot soup. MAKES 4 SERVINGS.

2 10¾-ounce cans condensed chicken broth
1 broth can water
¼ cup olive oil or half vegetable oil
4–8 cloves garlic, crushed
4 thick slices dry Cuban or French bread
½ cup grated Parmesan or 4 thin slices Swiss cheese

BARRANCAS GAZPACHO

GARNISHES: ½ green pepper, ½ cucumber, 2 green onions, ½ cup garlic croutons

Place bread cubes in bowl, add tomato juice and garlic, and let stand until bread is soft. Turn into blender or food processor and blend at high speed until smooth. Add green pepper and blend until smooth, add cucumber and onion and blend again. Add salt, cumin, and pepper sauce, blend a few seconds, then add oil and vinegar and blend thoroughly. Turn into bowl, cover, and refrigerate several hours or overnight. Finely chop garnish vegetables and serve separately in small bowls. Serve soup in chilled bowls and let each guest add garnishes (including a bowl of croutons) as wished. If soup is too thick, add more tomato juice. MAKES 4–6 SERVINGS.

4 ounces dry French bread or hard rolls (about 2 cups cubes)
3 cups tomato juice
2 cloves garlic, minced
½ large green pepper, cut in strips
½ cucumber, peeled and cut in chunks
1 onion, peeled and sliced thick
1 teaspoon salt
2 teaspoons cumin seed
¼ teaspoon hot pepper sauce
2 tablespoons olive oil
2 tablespoons wine vinegar

OLD-TIME OKRA SOUP

Combine soup bone and water in large kettle. Peel small onions and stud with cloves. Add to soup along with salt, pepper, and bay leaf. Bring to a boil, skimming off any solids that rise to the surface. Cover and simmer 1–1½ hours. Remove soup bone. Cut off meat, scoop out any marrow, and return to soup. Add sliced onion and tomatoes and cut tomatoes with scissors or mash against side of pan to break up. Bring to a boil and add okra. Simmer 30–45 minutes. MAKES 4–6 SERVINGS.

1 soup bone (about 1½ pounds)
2 quarts water
2 small onions
4 whole cloves
1 tablespoon salt
½ teaspoon pepper
1 bay leaf, crumbled
1 medium onion, sliced
1 28-ounce can tomatoes
1 pound okra, sliced, or 1 10-ounce
  package frozen

SPINACH SUMMER SOUP

Cook spinach in water 3–4 minutes, breaking apart with fork. Drain well and reserve liquid. Combine spinach liquid with enough milk to make 3½ cups. Melt butter in large saucepan. Add onion and cook until tender but not browned. Stir in flour, salt, and nutmeg. Cook until bubbly, being careful not to let the mixture brown. Add milk mixture and cook, stirring constantly, until smooth and thickened. Add spinach and bring to a boil, stirring now and then. Turn into bowl, cover tightly, and chill several hours or overnight. Serve in chilled bowls, thinning with more milk or cream if thinner soup is wanted. MAKES 4 SERVINGS.

1 10-ounce package frozen chopped
  spinach
½ cup water
Milk
2 tablespoons butter or margarine
½ small onion, chopped fine
2 tablespoons flour
1 teaspoon salt
Dash nutmeg

TOMATO RICE SOUP

Melt butter in large saucepan. Add celery and onion and cook, stirring often, until onion is tender but not browned. Add tomatoes and mash to break up large pieces. Add undiluted beef broth. Bring to boil. Add rice, cover, and simmer 1 hour. Taste and add salt and pepper if needed. Serve in warm bowls. MAKES 4–6 SERVINGS.

2 tablespoons butter or margarine
¼ cup finely chopped celery
1 small onion, chopped
1 16-ounce can tomatoes, preferably plum
2 10½-ounce cans condensed beef broth
2 tablespoons rice
Salt and pepper to taste

SUMMER VEGETABLE SOUP

Combine soup bone and meat in large kettle with water, salt, pepper sauce, celery leaves, and 1 onion. Bring to a boil, skimming off any solids that rise to surface. Cover and simmer 1½ hours. Remove bone from soup, cut off any meat, scoop out any marrow, and return to soup. Add tomatoes, potatoes, carrots, beans or peas, chopped celery, squash, cabbage, okra, and remaining onions. Cover and simmer 15–20 minutes, until potatoes and carrots are tender. Cut up tomato with scissors or break up pieces by mashing against side of kettle. Add corn and simmer 5 minutes. Serve in large soup plates. Leftovers freeze well. MAKES 6–8 SERVINGS.

1 soup bone with marrow
1 pound beef stew meat
3 quarts water
1 tablespoon salt
⅛ teaspoon hot pepper sauce
1 bunch celery, leaves only (about 1 cup)
3 onions, chopped
1 16-ounce can tomatoes
2 large new potatoes, peeled and cubed
2 large carrots, peeled and sliced
1 cup snapped or shelled green beans, peas,
   butter beans, or combination
3 ribs celery, chopped
2 yellow summer squash, sliced
1 cup shredded cabbage
½ pound okra, sliced
1 7-ounce can whole kernel corn, drained,
   or 1 cup cut off cob

CREAM OF PEANUT SOUP

Melt butter in large saucepan. Add onion and celery and cook until onion is tender but not browned. Stir in flour. Add broth and milk. Cook, stirring frequently, until mixture comes to a boil and is smooth. Add peanut butter and beat until smooth, using rotary beater or wire whisk. Taste and add salt and pepper if needed. Ladle into warm bowls and sprinkle with peanuts or parsley. This soup can be served chilled. Thin with light cream if too thick. MAKES 4–6 SERVINGS.

2 tablespoons butter or margarine
½ small onion, chopped
1 rib celery with leaves, chopped (½–¾ cup)
2 tablespoons flour
1 10¾-ounce can condensed chicken broth
2 broth cans milk
½ cup smooth peanut butter
Salt and pepper to taste
Salted peanuts or parsley, finely chopped

SHORT-CUT PEANUT BUTTER SOUP

Melt butter in saucepan, add onion and celery, and cook until tender but not browned. Stir in soup and milk. Cook, stirring occasionally, until smooth and steaming. Add peanut butter and beat with wire whisk or rotary beater. Serve hot or chill well. When served chilled, add more milk or cream to thin to desired consistency. MAKES 4 SERVINGS.

1 tablespoon butter or margarine
2 tablespoons minced onion
¼ cup finely diced celery with leaves
1 10¾-ounce can cream of chicken soup
1 soup can milk
¼ cup smooth peanut butter

BAKED SHRIMP SOUP

Combine milk and, if used, cream, shrimp, celery, and butter in saucepan. Heat until bubbles form at edge of pan. Remove celery with slotted spoon. Stir in bread crumbs, salt, pepper, and mace. Preheat broiler. Transfer soup to a broiler-safe baking dish. Broil about 5 inches below heat until golden brown, stirring once or twice to break up and mix top skin. Ladle into warm soup bowls and garnish with parsley. MAKES 6 SERVINGS.

1½ quarts milk or 1 quart milk and 1 pint cream
1 pound shrimp, cooked and cleaned
1 rib celery, cut in chunks
3 tablespoons butter or margarine
½ cup dry bread crumbs
½ teaspoon salt
⅛ teaspoon pepper
Dash mace
Minced parsley (optional)

GULF SHRIMP BISQUE

Combine shrimp, milk, onion, celery, and salt in top of double boiler or in heavy saucepan. Heat over boiling water or very low heat 30 minutes. Purée in blender, ½ at a time making sure top is tightly closed to prevent splattering hot liquid. Add pimiento and chop fine. Melt butter in saucepan or double boiler top. Add flour and cook until bubbly. Add soup. Cook and stir until smooth and thickened. Serve hot, sprinkling each serving with paprika or parsley. Or soup may be chilled, thinned with cream or milk, and served cold. MAKES 4 SERVINGS.

¾ pound shrimp, cleaned and cooked (about 1½ cups)
2 cups milk
½ small onion, chopped fine
1 small rib celery, chopped fine
½ teaspoon salt
2 tablespoons chopped pimiento
2 tablespoons butter or margarine
2 tablespoons flour
Paprika or minced parsley

MEATS

Southerners became heavy meat eaters only after World War II, though grand occasions traditionally featured cured hams and great roasts of veal and pork. The thin, flavorful pork chops, cooked only as southern black and many white women know how, are part of the rich cultural heritage of the region. The artful ways of presenting meats, rather than the quantities consumed, represent the southern treatment.

New influences are evident everywhere in the South: spicy bolichi and picadillo of the Spanish and Cubans, the New Orleans adaptations of European dishes such as daube and grillades, and the incomparable southern barbecues, all full of flavor but distinctively different from the Carolinas to Texas.

Southerners broil steaks and roast beef, too, as do all Americans; for southern flavor try pork, ham, and the impressive spiced beef round, served at Christmastime in Virginia and Tennessee.

⌘⌘ STEAKS ⌘⌘

BUDGET BARBECUED STEAK

Combine catsup, vinegar, water, Worcestershire, garlic salt, and pepper sauce. Mix well. Place meat in shallow dish or plastic bag. Add sauce and turn to coat steak well. Cover or tie bag closed. Marinate in refrigerator several hours or overnight, turning once or twice. Remove meat from marinade and place on rack in broiling pan. Broil 4 inches from heat 15 minutes, basting once with marinade. Turn, baste once with marinade, and broil 10 minutes longer or until done as desired. Brush again with marinade, slice thinly across grain, and serve. MAKES 4 SERVINGS.

¼ cup catsup
2 tablespoons vinegar
2 tablespoons water
1 tablespoon Worcestershire sauce
1 teaspoon garlic salt
Dash hot pepper sauce or cayenne
1 chuck fillet steak 1½ inches thick (about 1½ pounds)

GRILLADES

This traditional New Orleans breakfast is served with grits and is good as a supper, brunch, or luncheon dish.

Pound steak with meat mallet or edge of heavy saucer to break up fibers and flatten to ¼ inch thick. Cut in 4-inch squares. Season well with salt and cayenne. Brown in oil in heavy skillet. Remove and keep warm. Add onions and garlic to pan drippings and cook until tender but not browned. Add flour and cook and stir until browned. Add green pepper, tomatoes, vinegar, water, bay leaf, and thyme. Stir until well mixed. Arrange grillades in sauce. Cover and simmer until tender. MAKES 4–5 SERVINGS.

1½ pounds round steak, ½ inch thick
Salt
Cayenne
1 tablespoon oil
2 onions, chopped
2 cloves garlic, minced
1 tablespoon flour
1 green pepper, chopped
2 tomatoes, sliced, or 1 cup canned
2 tablespoons vinegar
1 cup hot water
1 bay leaf, crumbled
¼ teaspoon thyme

SWISS STEAK

Pound meat with a meat mallet or edge of a heavy saucer to break up fibers. Rub in flour and pound again. If using round steak, coat surface of a heavy skillet well with oil. If using chuck steak, lightly grease skillet. Heat skillet, add meat, and brown slowly on both sides. Add onion and cook until tender but not browned. Pour off excess fat. Add bay leaf, salt, allspice, pepper, and tomato juice. Cover and simmer until meat is tender, about 1¼ hours. Add vegetable and heat. Serve with mashed or baked potato, rice, or noodles. MAKES 4 SERVINGS.

1½ pounds boneless round or chuck steak,
*   1–1½ inches thick*
Flour
Oil
1 onion, sliced thin
1 bay leaf, crumbled
1 teaspoon salt
⅛ teaspoon allspice
⅛ teaspoon pepper
1½ cups tomato juice
½ cup drained cooked or canned peas,
*   green beans, or carrots*

TAMALE-STUFFED FLANK STEAK

Bring ½ cup water to a boil. Stir in ½ the corn meal. Cook and stir until smooth (it should be the consistency of mush), about 5 minutes. Remove from heat. Chop ½ an onion and add to mush along with butter, baking powder, ½ teaspoon salt and chili powder. Score flank steak in a diamond pattern on both sides, making shallow cuts with knife. Spread corn meal mixture on one side of meat and roll from long side. Tie firmly with clean string. Coat meat with more corn meal and brown in hot oil in skillet. Slice remaining onion and brown lightly. Pour off excess oil. Add remaining water and ½ teaspoon salt. Cover tightly and simmer under tender, 1½–2 hours. A thick sauce will form. Place meat roll on warm platter and let stand 10 minutes before carving. If desired, thin sauce with red wine or bouillon. Slice across roll to serve. MAKES 4–6 SERVINGS.

1 cup water
¼ cup corn meal
2 onions
1 tablespoon butter, margarine, or bacon drippings
1 teaspoon baking powder
1 teaspoon salt
1 teaspoon chili powder or to taste
1 flank steak (about 1½ pounds)
Additional corn meal
2–3 tablespoons oil

❧❦ BEEF ROASTS AND STEWS ❧❦

ALABAMA POT ROAST

Place roast on a sheet of waxed paper. Mix the bay leaf, thyme, basil, salt, and pepper, and rub into roast. Heat oil in electric skillet, regular skillet, or Dutch oven with domed, vented cover. Add meat and brown slowly on all sides. When almost browned, add onion and garlic and brown lightly. Cover and open vent or prop lid open slightly. Turn heat low and simmer roast until fork-tender, about 2½ hours. Remove to warm platter. Skim excess fat from pan drippings. Stir in flour mixed to a paste with a little water and cook and stir until smooth. If too thick, add hot water or beef broth. Serve gravy with roast and rice or mashed potatoes. MAKES 4–6 SERVINGS WITH LEFTOVERS.

1 4-pound beef chuck or other pot roast
1 bay leaf, crumbled
1 teaspoon thyme
½ teaspoon basil
1 teaspoon salt
½ teaspoon pepper
1 tablespoon oil
1 onion, sliced
2 cloves garlic, minced
1 tablespoon flour

CHRISTMAS SPICED BEEF

This dish is served with hot biscuits, turkey, and other holiday foods in Virginia and Tennessee

Crack juniper berries by grinding with mortar and pestle or crushing with back of wooden spoon. Combine salt, brown sugar, pepper, juniper, allspice, cinnamon, nutmeg, and ginger. Mix well. Add gin if using instead of juniper berries. Cut salt pork in thin strips and roll in sugar mixture to coat well. Cut deep incisions down almost the entire length of the meat. Push salt pork into incisions, using handle of a wooden spoon to pack tightly. Place meat in large plastic bag or crock and rub remaining sugar mixture on the meat. Close bag or cover bowl and cure in refrigerator for 10–14 days. Turn meat daily. Preheat oven to 350°. When ready to cook, drain off liquid which has been drawn from meat. Place meat in roasting wrap, following manufacturer's instructions for sprinkling with flour and piercing bag. Add water and tie bag closed. Place in shallow pan and roast 3 hours. Cool, and remove meat from roasting wrap. Discard liquid. Wrap in fresh plastic wrap or foil, place in bowl, and weight with heavy objects such as cans wrapped in plastic bags. This makes beef firmer for carving in paper-thin slices. Refrigerate overnight and carve in thin slices. MAKES 12 SERVINGS.

2 teaspoons juniper berries or ¼ cup gin
1 cup salt
1 cup brown sugar, packed
2 teaspoons pepper
1½ teaspoons allspice
1½ teaspoons cinnamon
1 teaspoon nutmeg
1 teaspoon ginger
½ pound salt pork
1 6–8-pound eye round roast
½ cup water

OVEN-BARBECUED BRISKET

Combine soy sauce, vinegar, undiluted beef broth, garlic, and liquid smoke in plastic bag or bowl. Add meat, turn, and marinate 3–4 hours at room temperature or overnight in refrigerator. Turn occasionally to marinate evenly. Preheat oven to 300°. Remove meat from marinade. Place in deep pot, add 1 cup of the marinade and the water. Cover tightly and bake 3–4 hours, until meat is fork-tender. Remove to platter and let stand 20–30 minutes before carving. Carve across the grain and serve with pinto beans and rice. MAKES 5–6 SERVINGS.

1 5-ounce bottle soy sauce (⅔ cup)
⅔ cup vinegar (measure in soy sauce bottle)
1 10¾-ounce can condensed beef broth
2 cloves garlic, crushed, or ½ teaspoon garlic powder
3 teaspoons liquid smoke or more to taste
1 2½–3-pound point cut piece brisket
½ cup water

FLORIDA BOLICHI

Traditionally, bolichi is served with *Black Beans and Rice and *Fried Plantains.

Cut a pocket along one side of meat. Grind or chop fine chorizos, salt pork, olives, and garlic together, using coarse blade of meat grinder. Stuff mixture in meat pocket. Close opening using skewers, poultry lacing, or string. Heat oil in large heavy kettle, add meat, and brown slowly on all sides. Add onions, green pepper, tomato, celery, and bay leaf. Sauté vegetables around meat until tender. Add salt, pepper, and wine. Cover tightly and simmer until meat is tender, but not falling apart, about 2½ hours. Remove meat to carving board. Let cool while thickening gravy if thickened gravy is desired. Stir flour to a paste with a little water. Add to boiling pan juices and cook and stir until smooth and thickened. Turn heat low and simmer while carving meat. Remove skewers or string from meat. Slice thin with some stuffing in each slice. Return to gravy and keep warm or serve at once. Serve extra gravy separately. Leftovers can be frozen with gravy and reheated. MAKES 8–10 SERVINGS.

1 6–7-pound eye round roast
¼ pound chorizos (Spanish sausage) or smoked sausage
¼ pound salt pork or slab bacon
10–12 stuffed green olives
2 cloves garlic
⅓ cup oil
2 large onions, chopped
1 small green pepper, chopped
1 large tomato, peeled and chopped
1 rib celery, chopped
1 large bay leaf, crumbled
1½ teaspoons salt
½ teaspoon freshly ground pepper
1 cup dry red wine
¼ cup flour (optional)

FORGET-IT BEEF STEW

Preheat oven to 275°. Place meat in large kettle with ovenproof handles and add remaining ingredients. Do not stir. Cover tightly and bake 5 hours. If cover fits tightly and oven maintains low temperature, this stew needs no attention. If in doubt, check occasionally and add boiling water to prevent scorching. Serve with rice, hot cooked noodles, or crusty bread. MAKES 6 SERVINGS.

2 pounds beef stew meat, cut in 1-inch cubes
1 16-ounce can tiny green peas with liquid
2 large carrots, thinly sliced
2 onions, chopped
1 large potato, peeled and cubed
2 bay leaves, crumbled
1½ teaspoons salt
½–1 teaspoon pepper
1 10–10½-ounce can condensed tomato, mushroom, or celery soup

NEW ORLEANS DAUBE WITH SPAGHETTI

Preheat oven to 300°. Heat salt pork with oil in large kettle. Add beef and brown, turning to brown all sides. When about half done add onion and garlic and brown lightly. Add parsley, bay leaf, turnip, carrots, chile, and ½ cup beef broth. Cover and simmer over low heat or bake 1½ hours. Check and add more beef broth if needed and a sprinkle of salt. Cover and simmer 1½–2 hours more or until fork-tender. Check occasionally and add more beef broth if needed. Add sherry and simmer uncovered 5 minutes. Slice daube and serve with pan juices over hot cooked spaghetti. Use leftovers for sandwiches or cold plates. MAKES 6 SERVINGS.

2 ounces salt pork, diced
1 teaspoon oil
1 3–4-pound beef bottom round or rump roast
1 onion, chopped
1 clove garlic, minced
1 tablespoon minced parsley
1 bay leaf, crumbled
1 white turnip or parsnip, diced
3 carrots, peeled and diced
1 dried chile
1 cup (approximately) canned condensed beef broth
Salt to taste
2 tablespoons dry sherry
1–1½ pounds spaghetti, cooked

POT ROAST WITH BUTTERMILK GRAVY

Trim surface fat from meat and heat in Dutch oven or large kettle to render fat. Discard brown bits of fat. If roast has no surface fat, use a small amount of oil. Coat roast with flour, salt, and pepper. Brown slowly in fat, turning to brown all sides. Blend mustard with a little of the water until smooth, then add remaining water. Pour off drippings. Add mustard mixture, cover tightly, and simmer very slowly 2–2½ hours, until meat is fork-tender. Add buttermilk, onions, and carrots. Cover and simmer 45 minutes or until vegetables are tender. Remove meat and vegetables to warm platter. Bring pan liquid to a boil, stir in flour mixture, and cook and stir until smooth and thickened. Serve gravy with meat, vegetables, and mashed or boiled potatoes. MAKES 6–8 SERVINGS.

1 4–5-pound beef bottom round, chuck, or rump roast
Flour
Salt
Pepper
1 tablespoon dry mustard
¼ cup water
½ cup buttermilk
6–8 small onions
6–8 carrots, peeled and cut in chunks
3 tablespoons flour mixed to a paste with water

TEXAS BARBECUED BRISKET

Use grill with hood or smoke oven. Build fire at one end of grill and let burn down to hot coals. Place drip pan, wrapped in foil to facilitate cleaning, at other end of grill. Place brisket fat side up on grill over drip pan, close hood, and adjust dampers to maintain a slow steady fire. Add more charcoal as needed. Turn brisket as needed to prevent searing and to brown evenly. Cook brisket 4–5 hours, until meat thermometer registers 150°. Meanwhile, combine remaining ingredients, simmer 15 minutes, and let stand 1–2 hours to blend flavors. Remove meat to warm platter. Let stand about 10 minutes. Reheat sauce. Carve brisket in thin slices across the grain and serve with sauce. Leftovers make good sandwiches. MAKES 6–8 SERVINGS.

1 3–3¼-pound piece brisket
1 cup catsup
½ cup cider or wine vinegar
¼ cup butter or margarine
¼ cup Worcestershire sauce
3 ribs celery, chopped fine
1 small onion, chopped fine
1 clove garlic, minced
1–2 teaspoons chili powder
1 teaspoon sugar
1 teaspoon paprika
¼ teaspoon salt
⅛ teaspoon pepper
2 bay leaves, crumbled

CREOLE BOEUF À LA MODE

In large kettle or Dutch oven brown meat slowly in oil. Pour off as much fat as possible, add onions, carrots, and garlic and cook until onions are lightly browned. Add bay leaves, thyme, allspice, cayenne, and undiluted broth. Cover and simmer until meat is tender, 2–2½ hours. Remove meat from liquid, wrap in foil or plastic bag, and refrigerate several hours or overnight. Strain cooking liquid, discarding vegetables. Refrigerate broth several hours or overnight.

Slice beef thin and arrange in overlapping slices on deep platter. Soften gelatin in ½ cup of reserved broth. Place over low heat and stir until dissolved. Stir in wine and remaining broth. Chill until slightly thickened. Arrange peas around beef on platter. Carefully spoon broth over meat and peas, coating lightly. Chill until broth is jellied. If necessary, add another layer to coat well. Serve well jellied. MAKES 6–8 SERVINGS.

1 3½–4-pound boneless rump roast
1–2 tablespoons oil or other fat
2 onions, sliced
2 carrots, sliced
2 cloves garlic, minced
2 bay leaves
1 teaspoon thyme
1 teaspoon allspice
¼ teaspoon cayenne
2 10½-ounce cans condensed beef broth
1 envelope unflavored gelatin
¼ cup ruby port wine
1 10-ounce package green peas, cooked and drained

ROAST PEPPERED BEEF

Place roast in plastic bag. Sprinkle pepper and garlic powder on meat, turning to coat evenly. Place in bowl. Open end of bag, carefully add soy sauce, then close bag tightly. Turn bag and refrigerate several hours or overnight, turning occasionally.

About 4 hours before serving preheat oven to 250°. Carefully open bag and remove meat. Place in center of large piece of aluminum foil. Fold ends and sides up around roast. Pour marinade around meat. Fold ends and sides of foil closed. Roast 2½ hours. Unfold a small opening in foil package and insert meat thermometer in meat. Continue roasting at 250° until thermometer registers 130°. This will produce meat well done at the ends with medium done and rare meat in the interior. Turn off heat and let meat cool in oven up to 1 hour. Carve thin. If desired, juices can be thickened for gravy. Pour juices in skillet. Blend 2–3 tablespoons flour with water to make a smooth paste. Bring meat juices to a boil. Slowly stir in flour paste and cook and stir until smooth and thickened. Serve hot over roast beef. MAKES 6–8 SERVINGS WITH LEFTOVERS.

1 4–5-pound boneless rump, sirloin tip, or round roast
1 teaspoon pepper, preferably freshly ground
½ teaspoon garlic powder
½ cup soy sauce
Flour (optional)

RED WINE STEW

Mix carrots, diced onion, salt pork, and parsley flakes in Dutch oven. Add meat, mushrooms, whole onions, salt, herbs, pepper, and wine. Cover and simmer so liquid barely bubbles until meat and whole onions are tender, about 1½ hours. Check occasionally and add more wine if stew dries too rapidly. Taste and add more salt and pepper if needed. MAKES 4–6 SERVINGS.

2 large carrots, diced or thinly sliced
1 medium onion, diced
2 ounces salt pork or 3 strips bacon, diced
1 tablespoon parsley flakes
2 pounds beef stew meat, cut in 1-inch cubes
¼ cup dried sliced mushrooms
6 small onions
1½ teaspoons salt
2 teaspoons mixed herbs or 1 teaspoon thyme and 1 bay leaf, crumbled
¼ teaspoon pepper
½ cup dry red wine

CHATHAM STEAK

Shape beef in 1 large patty about 1 inch thick, pressing only enough to make meat cling together. Heat heavy skillet. Carefully add steak and cook over high heat until seared on one side. Turn and sear other side. Turn heat low and cook until done as desired, about 12 minutes total time for medium rare. Turn as needed to cook evenly. Place steak on warm platter. Sprinkle lightly with salt and pepper and slice crosswise. Pass small pitchers or cups of melted butter, lime juice, and cream mixed with mustard for each diner to add to his own serving according to taste. MAKES 4 SERVINGS.

1½ pounds lean ground beef
Salt
Freshly ground pepper
¼ cup butter or margarine, melted
2 tablespoons lime or lemon juice
2 tablespoons cream
1 teaspoon dry mustard

CHILI CORN CHIP BAKE

Preheat oven to 350°. Cook onion, green pepper, garlic, and beef in oil in large skillet or Dutch oven until meat loses its red color, breaking up with fork to keep meat crumbly. Add salt, chili powder, beans with their liquid, tomato sauce, and olives. Simmer uncovered 5 minutes to blend flavors. Stir in cheese. Spread ½ the corn chips in a greased 1½-quart baking dish. Pour in meat mixture. Top with remaining corn chips. Bake 30 minutes or until bubbly and corn chips are lightly browned. MAKES 4–6 SERVINGS.

1 onion, chopped
½ green pepper, chopped
1 clove garlic, minced
¾ pound lean ground beef
1 tablespoon oil
1 teaspoon salt
3 teaspoons chili powder or to taste
1 20-ounce can red, pink, or pinto beans
  with liquid
1 8-ounce can tomato sauce
½ cup ripe olives whole, pitted, or cut in
  wedges
1 cup shredded Cheddar cheese
2 cups corn chips

CAROLINA MEAT LOAF

Preheat oven to 350°. Combine all ingredients in bowl. Blend thoroughly, working with clean hands if necessary. Pack lightly into an 8×4-inch loaf pan. Bake 1 hour and 15 minutes or until done as desired. Cool in pan on rack 10 minutes and turn out on serving dish. Slice and serve with gravy (below), bottled meat sauce, or catsup. MAKES 4–6 SERVINGS.

1 pound lean ground beef
½ pound pork sausage meat
1 onion, chopped fine
1 cup cooked rice
1 egg
½ cup milk
1 teaspoon salt
½ teaspoon crushed dried red pepper
  (optional)

MEAT LOAF GRAVY

Heat fat in skillet. Stir in flour. Combine meat loaf drippings with enough water to make 1 cup. Stir into roux. Add salt and pepper. Cook and stir until smooth and thickened. Color with soy sauce if desired. MAKES 1 CUP.

2 tablespoons fat from meat loaf, butter, or
  bacon drippings
2 tablespoons flour
Lean meat loaf drippings
Water
½ teaspoon salt
⅛ teaspoon pepper
Soy sauce or brown cooking sauce
  (optional)

FAMILY MEAT LOAF

Preheat oven to 350°. Combine all ingredients in bowl and mix thoroughly. This is most easily done with the hands. Shape into a loaf and place in shallow baking dish such as a pie plate. Bake 1 hour or until done as desired, but not dry. Let stand 10 minutes at room temperature before slicing. Gravy can be made with pan drippings. MAKES 4–6 SERVINGS.

1 pound ground beef, preferably
  medium-lean
1 cup fine dry bread crumbs
1 large onion, finely chopped
1 tablespoon Worcestershire sauce
1 teaspoon salt
¼ teaspoon pepper
¼ cup catsup
¾ cup water
1 egg

CREAMED HAMBURGER

An old-fashioned name for this was Breakfast Hamburger. It is a simple, good-tasting emergency dish for any meal.

Heat oil in skillet, add beef, and cook, breaking up with fork to keep crumbly, until beef loses its red color. Add salt, milk, Worcestershire, and mushrooms. Simmer uncovered 15–20 minutes to blend flavors. If dry, add a tablespoon or two more milk. Serve on toast. MAKES 4 SERVINGS.

1 tablespoon oil
¾ pound lean ground beef
½ teaspoon salt
1 cup milk
1 tablespoon Worcestershire sauce
1 2½-ounce can mushrooms, drained (optional)
Toast

RALLY BEEF BARBECUE

Barbecue sauces similar to this one are popular with political candidates for rallies or gatherings of campaign workers.

Sauté beef, onion, and garlic in heavy kettle until meat loses its red color, breaking up with fork to keep crumbly. Pour off excess fat. Add tomato paste and juice, chili powder, salt, celery seed, sugar, Worcestershire, and vinegar. Cover and simmer 1 hour, stirring occasionally. Add 1 cup hot water after about 30 minutes and more if needed. Shred corned beef with fork and stir into barbecue. Serve at once over toasted buns or refrigerate until ready to serve and reheat. MAKES 4–6 SERVINGS.

1 pound lean ground beef
1 large onion, chopped
2 cloves garlic, minced
1 6-ounce can tomato paste
3 cups tomato juice
2 teaspoons chili powder or to taste
2 teaspoons salt
2 teaspoons celery seed
1 tablespoon sugar
1 tablespoon Worcestershire sauce
1 tablespoon vinegar
Hot water as needed
1 12-ounce can corned beef
4–6 hamburger buns, split and toasted

DIXIE CHOP SUEY

Cook meat in large skillet or Dutch oven until it loses its red color, breaking up with fork to keep crumbly. Drain off fat. Add onion, celery, mushrooms, and green pepper. Mix and cook 2–3 minutes. Add ¾ cup water and bring to a boil. Mix cornstarch, remaining ¼ cup water, sugar, and soy sauce. Stir in and cook until sauce is transparent and smooth. If using fresh bean sprouts, cover with boiling water and drain. Drain canned bean sprouts. Add to meat mixture. Simmer 5 minutes. Serve with rice and chow mein noodles on top if desired. Pass additional soy sauce. MAKES 4–6 SERVINGS.

1 pound lean ground beef
1 onion, cut in lengthwise strips
1 cup diagonally sliced celery
¼ pound mushrooms, sliced
1 small green pepper, sliced lengthwise
1 cup water
1 tablespoon cornstarch
1 tablespoon sugar
3 tablespoons mild soy sauce
¼ pound fresh bean sprouts or 1 16-ounce can
Hot cooked rice
Chow mein noodles (optional)

KEY WEST PICADILLO

Heat oil in large skillet. Add beef and break up with fork. Add onion and garlic and cook, stirring to keep meat crumbly, until it loses its red color. Add green pepper and cook, stirring once or twice, for 2 minutes. Add tomatoes, ½ teaspoon salt, and pepper. Mash tomatoes with fork or back of spoon to break up. Cook uncovered over moderately high heat about 25 minutes until most of liquid is evaporated. Add olives and simmer uncovered 5 minutes. Add capers and heat well. Serve on rice. MAKES 4 SERVINGS.

1 tablespoon oil
1 pound ground beef, preferably medium-lean
1 onion, chopped
2 cloves garlic, minced
1 green pepper, chopped
1 16-ounce can tomatoes
Salt to taste
¼ teaspoon pepper
¼ cup sliced stuffed green olives
2 tablespoons capers
Hot cooked rice

HAMBURGER PIZZA PIE

Preheat oven to 375°. Mix beef with bread crumbs and onion. Press into 9-inch pie pan to form a shell, making sides extra thick to allow for shrinkage. Bake 15 minutes. Meanwhile, heat oil in skillet, add green pepper, and cook until wilted. Add garlic and cook until lightly browned. Add tomatoes, salt, oregano, and pepper. Bring to a boil and simmer a few minutes. Remove meat shell from oven, pour off as much fat as possible, and fill with tomato mixture. Sprinkle with cheese. Bake 15 minutes longer. Cut in wedges. MAKES 4–6 SERVINGS.

1 pound lean ground beef
¼ cup seasoned fine dry bread crumbs
1 tablespoon instant minced onion
1 teaspoon oil
½ small green pepper, cut in thin wedges
1 clove garlic, minced
1 16-ounce can tomatoes
½ teaspoon salt
¼ teaspoon oregano
¼ teaspoon pepper
2–3 tablespoons grated Parmesan cheese

SKILLET MEAT BALLS AND NOODLES

Combine beef, egg, crumbs, parsley, 1 teaspoon salt, ¼ teaspoon pepper, and water. Mix lightly but thoroughly. Shape into balls about 1½ inches in diameter. Heat oil in large skillet. Add meat balls and cook over moderate heat until browned, turning carefully with tongs or 2 forks to brown all sides. Remove meat balls and keep warm. Drain off most of drippings, leaving brown bits and a thin layer of fat. Add tomatoes, water, remaining salt and pepper, garlic salt, basil, and oregano. Cut tomatoes with kitchen scissors to break up. Bring to a boil. Add noodles a few at a time. Cook 8 minutes or until noodles are tender, stirring often to prevent sticking. Add meat balls and cook 3 or 4 minutes longer to heat through. MAKES 6 SERVINGS.

1 pound ground beef
1 egg
½ cup fine dry bread crumbs
1 tablespoon parsley flakes
1½ teaspoons salt
½ teaspoon pepper
¼ cup water
2 tablespoons oil
1 28-ounce can tomatoes
1 cup water
½ teaspoon garlic salt
½ teaspoon basil
Pinch oregano (optional)
7 or 8 ounces egg noodles

TEXAS HASH

Cook onions and green peppers in oil in large saucepan until tender, stirring now and then. Add beef, garlic, chili powder, salt, cumin, and pepper. Cook, stirring to keep beef crumbly, until beef loses its red color. Add tomatoes and water. Bring to a boil, add rice, cover, and bring again to a boil. Stir once, turn heat low, cover, and simmer until most of liquid is absorbed and rice is tender, about 1 hour. MAKES 4–6 SERVINGS.

2 large onions, coarsely chopped
2 green peppers, coarsely chopped
3 tablespoons oil
1 pound ground lean beef
2 large cloves garlic, minced
1 tablespoon chili powder or more
1 teaspoon salt
½ teaspoon cumin
¼ teaspoon pepper
1 16-ounce can tomatoes
1 cup water
¾ cup rice

TEXAS CHILI CON CARNE

Cut beef in ½-inch cubes or have ground through chili plate, which produces coarse pieces. Cook onion in oil in large heavy saucepan until tender but not browned. Add garlic and meat and cook over moderate heat, stirring now and then, until meat is lightly browned. Add tomatoes, tomato paste, salt, and chili powder. Rub cumin seed with back of wooden spoon against board or small bowl to crack and add to chili. Bring to a boil. Cover and simmer 45 minutes. Add beans with liquid, heat, and serve. Or heat beans separately and serve on the side. This recipe can be doubled or tripled and extra portions frozen for serving later. MAKES 4 SERVINGS.

1 pound boneless beef chuck or round
1 large onion, chopped
1 tablespoon oil
1 clove garlic, minced
1 16-ounce can tomatoes
1 6-ounce can tomato paste
1 teaspoon salt
2 tablespoons chili powder or to taste
½ teaspoon ground cumin or seed
*1 20-ounce can kidney or pinto beans with
    liquid*

STUFFED PEPPERS

Cut tops off peppers and remove seeds and membranes. Boil pepper shells in lightly salted water in covered saucepan 10 minutes or until barely tender. Drain. Preheat oven to 350°. Mix beef, rice, onion, and ½ cup beef broth. Fill peppers with meat mixture. Any extra filling can be put in baking dish with peppers. Arrange peppers upright in baking dish. Pour remaining broth around peppers. Bake 35 minutes. Place a square of cheese on each pepper and bake 5 minutes longer. Serve with juices in baking dish or tomato sauce. MAKES 4 SERVINGS.

4 large green peppers
Salted water
*1–1½ cups finely chopped or ground
  cooked beef, pork, or chicken*
½ cup cooked rice
½ medium onion, chopped fine
1 10½-ounce can condensed beef broth
4 small squares Cheddar cheese

⊱✦VEAL AND LAMB✦⊰

VEAL MADEIRA

Heat butter and oil in Dutch oven or large kettle. Add veal and brown slowly, turning to brown all sides. Add carrots, onions, green pepper, and ham and cook, stirring 2 or 3 times, until tender but not browned. Sprinkle with salt and pepper and pour ¼ cup madeira over meat. Cover and simmer over low heat or in 300° oven until veal is tender, about 2 hours. Place meat on warm platter. Blend flour to a smooth paste with a tablespoon or two of madeira. Stir into boiling pan juices and cook and stir until smooth and thickened. Serve sauce with veal and noodles or rice. Vegetables such as carrots cut in chunks, mushrooms, or small potatoes can be cooked with veal if desired. MAKES 4–6 SERVINGS.

2 tablespoons butter or margarine
2 tablespoons oil
1 5–6-pound rump or leg of veal
2 carrots, diced
2 onions, diced
1 green pepper, chopped
¼ cup diced ham (2 ounces)
½ teaspoon salt
Freshly ground pepper
¼ cup madeira
2 tablespoons flour
Additional madeira

WHITE VEAL STEW

Place veal in large kettle. Peel 1 onion and stud with cloves. Add to veal along with carrots, celery, parsley, salt, cayenne, and bay leaf. Add boiling water, cover, and simmer 1 hour or until veal is tender. Meanwhile slice remaining onions and cook in oil in large skillet until lightly browned. Stir in flour, then mushrooms. Ladle most of liquid from stew into onion mixture and cook and stir until smooth. Stir onion sauce back into stew. Add wine to skillet and scrape up any brown bits, then stir into stew. Stir in lemon juice. Taste and add more salt and cayenne if desired. Serve on noodles or rice. MAKES 4 SERVINGS.

1 pound veal stew meat, cut in 1-inch cubes
3 medium onions
2 whole cloves
3 carrots, peeled and cut in chunks
2 ribs celery, cut in ½-inch slices
1 tablespoon minced parsley
1 teaspoon salt
⅛ teaspoon cayenne
½ bay leaf, crumbled
2 cups boiling water
2 tablespoons oil, butter, or margarine
2 tablespoons flour
¼ pound mushrooms, sliced
¼ cup dry white wine or chicken broth
Juice of ½ lemon

CREOLE ROAST LAMB

Make gashes in lamb and insert slivers of garlic. Place in plastic bag. Combine coffee, cream, brandy, and sugar. Pour around lamb. Tie bag closed. Place in shallow dish and refrigerate several hours or overnight. Turn bag now and then. About 3 hours before serving, preheat oven to 325°. Remove lamb from marinade and place fat side up on rack in shallow roasting pan. Roast, basting now and then with marinade, until meat thermometer inserted in meaty part registers 160° (medium). This will require 2½–3 hours. Let lamb stand 30 minutes before carving. Make gravy if desired, using remaining marinade as part of the liquid. MAKES 5–8 SERVINGS.

1 5–6-pound leg of lamb
1 large clove garlic, cut into slivers
1 cup strong coffee
½ cup cream
2 tablespoons brandy
1 teaspoon sugar

✺✛ PORK ✛✺

BAKED SPARERIBS WITH SAUERKRAUT

Preheat oven to 400°. Cut ribs in serving sections and place in 13×9-inch baking dish. Bake 45 minutes, turning ribs once or twice. Drain off as much fat as possible. Place onions among and around ribs. Bake 15 minutes longer. Rinse sauerkraut if very salty and drain well. Remove ribs from baking dish. Add sauerkraut and tomato sauce. Mix well. Arrange ribs over sauerkraut. Bake 30 minutes or until heated through and ribs are browned. MAKES 4–6 SERVINGS.

3–4 pounds ribs, conventional or
  country-style
2 onions, sliced
2 pounds sauerkraut, canned or fresh
1 8-ounce can tomato sauce

BARBECUED PORK ROAST

Combine orange concentrate, vinegar, mustard, and soy sauce in small saucepan. Stir over low heat until well blended. Let charcoal fire burn down to coals covered with gray ash. Before putting meat on grill close dampers, if any, in fire box and spread coals to a single layer under meat. Place meat about 6 inches above coals. Close hood if grill is equipped with one or place a sheet of foil loosely over roast to reflect heat onto meat. Do not wrap roast. Grill pork slowly, turning about every 15 minutes and extinguishing any flame by squirting with water from bottle or water gun. Roast 1¾ hours or until meat thermometer inserted in center registers 160°. Brush with glaze and roast 15 minutes longer or until internal temperature reaches 170°. Brush with any remaining glaze, remove to platter, and let stand 20 minutes before carving. MAKES 4 SERVINGS.

½ can frozen orange juice concentrate,
  thawed (6 tablespoons)
2 tablespoons vinegar
2 teaspoons prepared mustard
2 teaspoons soy sauce or 1 teaspoon salt
1 4-pound pork loin, rib end

BARBECUED PORK (leftover)

Mix onion, catsup, vinegar, brown sugar, Worcestershire, mustard, and garlic salt. Let stand about 30 minutes to blend flavors. Preheat oven to 350°. Arrange pork chops or slices in a single layer in greased baking dish. Spoon sauce over pork. Bake 30 minutes, turning once. If desired, broil a minute or two to brown lightly. MAKES ENOUGH SAUCE FOR 4 PIECES OF PORK.

½ small onion, finely chopped
¼ cup catsup
2 tablespoons vinegar
2 tablespoons brown sugar
1 teaspoon Worcestershire sauce
½ teaspoon dry mustard
¼ teaspoon garlic salt
Leftover cooked pork chops or sliced roast

BARBECUED SPARERIBS

Crack ribs. Mix water, vinegar, butter, catsup, relish, and pepper sauce in saucepan. Bring to a boil over low heat and mix well. Let charcoal fire burn down until coals are covered with gray ash. Spread coals to 1 or 2 layers deep and close any dampers in grill to prevent flames. Place ribs meaty side up over coals and sear well. Turn and sear other side. Brush with sauce and turn and baste until ribs are tender and cooked through, about 1 hour 10 minutes. Test by cutting a slit in a center section. Brush with any remaining sauce and serve. MAKES 4–6 SERVINGS.

3–4 pounds spareribs
⅓ cup hot water
⅔ cup vinegar
2 tablespoons butter or margarine
½ cup catsup
¼ cup sweet pickle relish
2 or 3 drops hot pepper sauce

DIXIE BOILED DINNER

Remove wrapping and casing, the thick translucent paper, from meat. Place meat in large saucepan or deep skillet with cloves, bay leaf, and water to almost cover meat. Cover tightly, bring to a boil, turn heat low, and simmer 45 minutes or until tender. Meanwhile, peel sweet potatoes and slice ¾ inch thick. Remove meat from broth. Bring broth to a boil and add sweet potatoes and onion. Cover and boil slowly until sweet potatoes are tender, about 20 minutes. Cut meat in thick slices. Drain beans if canned. Add beans to vegetables, add pork, cover, and heat thoroughly. Serve vegetables and meat hot with mustard if desired. MAKES 4–6 SERVINGS.

1 1–1½-pound smoked pork shoulder roll
6 whole cloves
1 bay leaf
Water
1–1½ pounds dark red sweet potatoes
1 onion, cut in quarters
1 16-ounce can cut green beans or 1
   10-ounce package frozen

48

COUNTRY PORK CHOPS

Every black cook and most whites prepare pork chops this way. Here at last is the deep dark secret, so simple that the recipe boggles the minds of most cookbook writers.

Trim most of fat from edges of chops. Heat heavy skillet or griddle over moderate heat. Rub hot skillet with pork fat. Coat chops generously with flour. Place as many in hot skillet as will fit without overlapping. Cook over moderate heat until browned. Sprinkle with salt and pepper. Turn and brown other side. This will take about 8 minutes on each side. Chops should be well cooked by this time. If not, turn heat low and cook a few minutes longer. Place chops on warm platter and continue cooking until all chops are done, pour water in hot skillet and boil about 1 minute, until colored and flavored with brown bits in pan and reduced to rich natural gravy. Pour over chops and serve at once. MAKES 4 SERVINGS.

8–12 thin pork chops, no thicker than
* ½ inch*
Flour
Salt
Pepper
½ cup hot water

PORK AND BEANS WITH TOMATOES

Combine beans and water in large saucepan. Cover, bring to a boil, and boil 2 minutes. Remove from heat and let stand 1–2 hours. Preheat oven to 325°. Drain beans, reserving the water. Cut ham or pork steaks in cubes, other meats in serving size or smaller pieces. Brown meat lightly in drippings if desired. Place in well-greased deep casserole. Add beans, onion, salt (using a smaller amount if ham is used), and chili powder to taste. Combine tomato sauce and 1½ cups of the liquid drained from beans in saucepan. Bring to a boil. Add to bean mixture and mix well. Cover and bake until beans are tender and most of liquid absorbed, about 2¼ hours. Check occasionally and add more hot bean liquid if needed. MAKES 4–5 SERVINGS.

1 cup dry pea beans
6 cups water
½–1 pound ham, pork steaks, neck bones,
* ribs, etc.*
Drippings or oil for browning (optional)
1 onion, sliced
1–2 teaspoons salt
1–2 teaspoons chili powder
1 8-ounce can tomato sauce

PORK CHOPS WITH LYE HOMINY

Trim fat off edges of chops and render in large heavy skillet. Coat chops with flour and brown slowly in hot fat. Turn, sprinkle with ½ teaspoon salt, and brown other side slowly. Pour off excess drippings and remove bits of fat. Push chops to edge of pan and add onion and garlic. Cook until onion is tender but not browned. Add hominy, mix well with pan drippings, and arrange chops over hominy. Heat 3 or 4 minutes. Sprinkle with pepper and remaining ½ teaspoon salt. MAKES 4 SERVINGS.

4 lean pork chops, ½–¾ inch thick
Flour
1 teaspoon salt
1 medium onion, sliced
1 clove garlic, crushed
1 15–16-ounce can lye hominy, drained
⅛ teaspoon pepper

PORK CHOP RICE SKILLET

Heat large skillet and rub with fat edges of chops. If chops are trimmed very lean, rub skillet with oil. Add chops and brown on both sides. Add onion, remove chops, and set aside. Add rice and cook over low heat, stirring often, until rice looks chalky and browns lightly. Add green pepper, water, tomatoes, 1 teaspoon salt, and pepper. Bring to a boil, stir lightly, and arrange chops on rice. Sprinkle remaining salt on chops. Cover tightly and simmer 30 minutes or until liquid is absorbed. Remove from heat and let steam 15 minutes longer. Arrange rice on platter with chops around it. MAKES 4 SERVINGS.

4 pork chops, ¾ inch thick
Oil (optional)
1 small onion, chopped
1 cup rice
1 green pepper, chopped
1½ cups water
1 16-ounce can tomatoes
1½ teaspoons salt
⅛ teaspoon pepper

ROAST PORK WITH CORN BREAD STUFFING

Have butcher cut roast almost through to backbone. Preheat oven to 325°. Place roast in shallow pan and roast 1 hour. Meanwhile mix corn bread and biscuit crumbs, sage, salt, pepper, and parsley. Heat oil in skillet. Add onion and celery and cook until tender but not browned. Add to crumb mixture along with broth. Mix lightly.

Remove roast from oven and drain off fat. Gently push chops apart with handle of a wooden spoon and fill with stuffing mixture. Spread remaining stuffing in pan. Place roast on stuffing and roast 1½–2 hours, until meat thermometer inserted in center chop registers 165°. Place meat on warm platter and stuffing in a serving bowl. Let roast stand 20–30 minutes before carving. MAKES 4–6 SERVINGS.

1 4–5-pound pork loin roast
4 cups corn bread crumbs
1 cup biscuit or stale bread crumbs
1 teaspoon sage
1 teaspoon salt
¼ teaspoon pepper
1 tablespoon parsley flakes
2 tablespoons oil or roast drippings
1 large onion, chopped
1 cup diced celery
1 10½-ounce can condensed beef broth or consommé

YBOR CITY ROAST PORK

Have butcher crack backbone and cut pockets between chops. Rub surfaces of meat and between chops with garlic. If desired, cut garlic into slivers and insert between chops. Cut limes and rub cut sides over meat, squeezing out juice to coat meat well. Sprinkle with oregano. Place pork and squeezed limes in bowl or plastic bag, cover, and refrigerate several hours or overnight. About 3 hours before serving, place pork fat side up on rack in shallow roasting pan. Sprinkle lightly with salt. Roast at 325° 2½–3 hours until meat thermometer inserted in center chop registers 165°. Remove to warm platter and let rest 20–30 minutes before carving. Serve with *Yellow Rice. MAKES 4–6 SERVINGS.

1 4–4½-pound pork loin roast
2 cloves garlic, split
2 limes, preferably Key limes
½ teaspoon oregano
Salt

BAKED HAM AND STUFFING

Preheat oven to 400°. Melt butter in skillet, add celery, and cook until tender. Stir in stuffing mix and water. Add pecans and mix well. Place 1 ham slice in greased 6×10-inch baking dish. Pat stuffing on ham and top with remaining ham slice. Cover with foil and bake 20 minutes. Uncover and bake 10 minutes longer. Serve with cranberry sauce if desired. MAKES 4–6 SERVINGS.

1 tablespoon butter or margarine
½ cup diced celery
1 cup herb stuffing mix
⅓ cup hot water
¼ cup chopped pecans
2 8-ounce ham slices

BUFFET HAM

Have butcher slice ham ¼ inch thick and tie in original shape. Preheat oven to 325°. Place ham in shallow baking dish. Bake 1 hour. Mix jelly with enough water or wine to make a thick syrup. Brush over ham. Continue to bake 20–30 minutes brushing with pan drippings 2 or 3 times to glaze. Cool 10–15 minutes or to room temperature. Place on platter. Carefully cut and remove string so ham holds its shape. Garnish with orange slices and parsley. MAKES 20 SERVINGS IF ACCOMPANIED BY OTHER MEAT, 16 OTHERWISE.

1 5- or 6-pound canned ham
3 or 4 tablespoons guava jelly or orange marmalade
Water or red wine
Orange slices
Parsley

COCA-COLA HAM

Preheat oven to 350°. Place ham in shallow pan without rack. Pour Coca-Cola over ham. Bake 2 hours, basting with Coca-Cola every 15 minutes or so. (For an alternate method, place ham in large kettle, add Coca-Cola to half cover ham, cover tightly, and simmer 2 hours or until bone loosens from meat and meat is very tender.) Remove ham from liquid and cut off skin. Score fat. Pour off liquid and return ham to roasting pan. Mix bread crumbs, sugar, and mustard. Spread over ham. Bake at 400° 30 minutes, basting with pan juices and another few tablespoons Coca-Cola every 10 minutes. Serve hot or cold. MAKES 10–12 SERVINGS WITH LEFTOVERS.

1 half ham (8–9 pounds)
1 quart Coca-Cola, or more
½ cup fine dry bread crumbs
½ cup brown sugar, packed
2 teaspoons dry mustard

GLAZED SMITHFIELD HAM

Scour ham vigorously with a brush and lukewarm water to remove excess seasonings and any mold. Place in large pot such as roaster or canning kettle. Cover with cold water and soak overnight. If less salty ham is preferred, change water after 3 or 4 hours.

Drain well, cover ham with fresh cold water, bring to a boil, cover, and simmer 4–6 hours, until meat is tender and shank bone pulls away from meat. Cool ham in broth or remove from broth and cool on board. Preheat oven to 350°. Cut off ham skin. Score fat and stud with cloves. Place ham in shallow pan. Mix equal parts of bread crumbs and brown sugar and press onto ham. Bake until glazed, about 30 minutes. Refrigerate overnight. Slice paper-thin, carving from shank toward butt end. A paper panty for holding shank bone is usually provided so carver can hold ham by bone to slice meat. Serve in hot biscuits if desired. Smithfield ham is rich, so provides 5–6 servings per pound as main meat for a meal, more servings with other meats for a buffet. Leftovers can be wrapped airtight and refrigerated for several weeks.

NOTE: Carolina, Kentucky, Tennessee, and other country hams are cooked by this method, but as they are less dry, they may be carved ¼ –½ inch thick.

1 12–15-pound Smithfield ham
Water
Whole cloves
Fine dry bread crumbs
Dark brown sugar

HAM SLICE WITH CRANBERRIES

Trim a few bits of fat off ham and heat in skillet until crisp. Remove fat bits, add ham, and cook slowly until browned. Turn and brown other side. Add cranberries, water, honey, and cloves. Bring to a boil and cook until berries pop open. If thicker sauce is wanted, cook rapidly uncovered 3 or 4 minutes. Remove ham to warm platter and pour sauce over it. MAKES 4 SERVINGS.

1 center slice ham (about 1 pound)
1 cup cranberries
½ cup water
3 tablespoons honey or ¼ cup brown sugar, packed
½ teaspoon cloves

53

CORN AND HAM SQUARES

Preheat oven to 350°. Beat eggs with milk until well mixed. Stir in corn, onion, salt, pepper sauce, rice, ham, and cheese. Turn into greased 10×6-inch baking dish. Sprinkle with paprika. Bake 45–50 minutes or until set. Let stand 10 minutes, then cut into squares to serve. MAKES 6 MAIN DISH OR 8–10 SIDE DISH SERVINGS.

3 eggs
¼ cup milk
1 17-ounce can cream-style corn
1 small onion, finely chopped
½ teaspoon salt
3 or 4 drops hot pepper sauce
1½ cups cooked rice (½ cup before cooking)
1½ cups diced cooked ham or canned pork ham luncheon meat (about 12 ounces)
½ cup diced or coarsely shredded sharp Cheddar cheese (about 2 ounces)
Paprika

HAM JAMBALAYA

Heat oil in a large Dutch oven, add onions, green pepper, and garlic, and cook until lightly browned, stirring now and then. Add ham and rice and cook and stir until rice is well coated with oil. Add bay leaf, thyme, salt, pepper sauce, tomatoes, and broth. Cover and simmer until rice is tender and liquid absorbed, 20–25 minutes. Taste and add more salt and pepper sauce if needed. MAKES 4–6 SERVINGS.

Chicken or Turkey Jambalaya: Substitute chopped cooked chicken or turkey for ham and use chicken or turkey broth.

Seafood Jambalaya: Omit oil and ham. Sauté ½ pound chorizo or hot pork sausage, sliced, until fat is rendered. Add onions, green pepper, and garlic and proceed as for Ham Jambalaya. Add 1 pound shrimp shelled, 1 pint oysters, 1 pound crab meat or rock lobster, cut in chunks, or a combination after adding water. Fish stock can be used instead of water.

2 tablespoons oil
2 large onions, chopped
1 green pepper, chopped
2 cloves garlic, minced
2 cups cubed cooked ham
1 cup rice
1 bay leaf, crumbled
½ teaspoon thyme
½ teaspoon salt
3–4 drops hot pepper sauce
1 16-ounce can tomatoes
½ cup ham broth, water, or chicken broth

54

FRIED HAM AND RED-EYE GRAVY

Red-eye gravy is a picturesque name for a simple sauce that is called meat gravy or grease gravy, to distinguish it from cream gravy, in some parts of the South. The gravy is served sparingly on grits or biscuits.

Slash fat around edges of ham to prevent curling. Heat skillet. Place 1 or 2 slices ham in hot skillet and fry until browned. Turn and brown other side. Remove to hot platter and brown remaining ham. Skim off excess fat in pan drippings, but reserve about 1 tablespoon fat and brown bits. Add water and stir or tilt pan over high heat until gravy is sizzling. Add coffee and heat. Pour over ham or serve in gravy boat with grits or *Fluffy Spoon Bread and hot biscuits. MAKES 4 SERVINGS.

4 thin slices Smithfield or other dry-cured ham
½ cup water
2 tablespoons hot coffee (optional)

❧SAUSAGES AND VARIETY MEATS❧

BACHELOR'S SAUSAGE SUPPER

If using bulk meat, shape in patties. Brown sausage in a heavy skillet over moderate heat. Place onion around sausage and cook until tender. Pour off as much fat as possible. Place potatoes over and around sausage. Sprinkle with salt and pepper, taking into consideration that the sausage is seasoned. Add water, cover, and simmer 25 minutes or until potatoes are tender. Place sausages on a serving plate, turn potatoes in drippings to coat with rich brown sauce, and mound in center of plate. MAKES 4 SERVINGS.

1 pound pork sausage links or meat
1 onion, sliced
4 or 5 potatoes, peeled and sliced
Salt
Pepper
1 cup water

SAUSAGE CORN BREAD

Preheat oven to 425°. Cook sausage in heavy skillet over moderate heat until it loses its red color and is crumbly. Break up with fork several times while cooking to keep crumbly. Drain sausage thoroughly, reserving drippings. Mix corn meal, flour, sugar, and baking powder in bowl. Add milk and egg and mix thoroughly. Add drained sausage and 2 tablespoons drippings. Mix well. Turn into well-greased 9-inch pie pan or skillet. Bake 25 minutes or until golden. Cut in wedges and serve hot with applesauce, scrambled or fried eggs, or fruit preserves. MAKES 4–6 SERVINGS.

NOTE: A 9-inch cast-iron skillet may be used for browning the sausage, then baking the corn bread.

¾–1 pound pork sausage meat, hot or mild
1½ cups corn meal, preferably white
½ cup flour
1 tablespoon sugar
4 teaspoons baking powder
1 cup milk
1 egg
2 tablespoons sausage drippings

SAUSAGE TAMALE BAKE

Preheat oven to 400°. Add ½ cup cheese to muffin mix, then prepare as directed on package. Spread in a 10×6-inch baking dish. Shape sausage into 6–8 patties. Fry in large skillet until browned. Arrange sausage patties on corn bread mixture. Pour off all but 1 tablespoon of the sausage drippings. Add onion and cook until tender but not browned. Add tomatoes, tomato paste, and salt. Bring to a boil, stirring 2 or 3 times. Pour tomato sauce over sausage and corn bread. Bake 15 minutes. Sprinkle with remaining cheese and bake 10 minutes longer or until cheese is melted and sauce bubbly. Cool 10 minutes. Cut into rectangles and serve. MAKES 4–6 SERVINGS.

1–1½ cups shredded Cheddar cheese
1 12-ounce package corn muffin mix
1 pound pork sausage meat, hot or mild
1 medium onion, chopped
1 16-ounce can tomatoes
1 6-ounce can tomato paste
½ teaspoon salt

BARBECUED FRANKS ON BUNS

Heat oil in skillet or saucepan. Add onion and garlic and cook until onion is tender but not browned. Add tomato sauce, molasses, vinegar, chili powder, salt, and cinnamon. Simmer uncovered 5 minutes to blend flavors and thicken slightly. Add franks and simmer 5 minutes longer. Serve franks with sauce on buns. MAKES 5 SERVINGS.

1 tablespoon oil
1 medium onion, thinly sliced
1 clove garlic, crushed
1 8-ounce can tomato sauce
¼ cup molasses or brown sugar, packed
¼ cup vinegar
2 teaspoons chili powder or to taste
1 teaspoon salt
¼ teaspoon cinnamon
1 pound frankfurters
10 frankfurter buns, split and toasted

BRAINS AND EGGS

This is a traditional quick supper, usually served with grits, a cooked vegetable, and corn bread or toast.

Rinse and drain brains. Bring water to a boil, add vinegar, salt, and brains. Cover, bring again to a boil, and simmer 10 minutes. Drain brains and cover with cold water. Beat eggs to mix well. Melt butter in skillet. Remove brains from cold water and break into pieces roughly the size of a walnut. Add brains to hot butter. Cook a minute or two, then add eggs. Cook, stirring gently so as not to mash brains, until eggs are set but not dry. Serve at once with catsup or, unorthodox but good, capers and lemon juice. MAKES 3–4 SERVINGS.

1 set calf's or pig's brains (¾–1 pound)
1 quart water
1 tablespoon vinegar
1 teaspoon salt
4 eggs
2 tablespoons butter or margarine
Catsup or capers and lemon wedges

SPANISH LIVER

Place liver in large shallow dish and sprinkle with garlic and vinegar. Cover and let stand 30–45 minutes. Heat oil in large skillet, add liver, and brown lightly on both sides. Add onion and green peppers, pushing under liver as it browns. Cook, turning and stirring occasionally, until onion and green peppers are tender. Add leftover marinade, salt, and pepper. Cook a minute or two longer. Place liver on warm platter and surround with vegetables. Serve with rice. MAKES 4–6 SERVINGS.

1 pound beef, pork, lamb, or calf's liver,
 ½ inch thick
1 large clove garlic, minced
2 tablespoons vinegar
2–3 tablespoons oil
1 medium onion, coarsely chopped
3 green peppers, coarsely chopped
1 teaspoon salt
⅛ teaspoon pepper

POULTRY

CHABLIS

Chicken every Sunday underestimates the southern taste for barnyard birds. Chicken flourished here because of mild winters and long summers, when "spring" chicken was always available only for the trouble. Broiler-fryers have become big business in the South—again due to a climate that makes climate-controlled chicken barns less expensive to maintain. Southern fried chicken is famous, but real fried chicken is rarely enjoyed except in homes where it is cooked reverently. Roadside Southern fried chickens are often short-order imitations, some of them greasy horrors. A generous amount of fat hot enough so it won't saturate the chicken crust assures nongreasy chicken. Chicken, too, inspires the Spanish, French, and cosmopolitan cooks of the South. Chicken salad commands top billing for luncheon, but with the passing of barnyard flocks, roosters so old they were crochety are no longer available, and it was this tough, long-flavored meat that made the tastiest salad. Turkey calls for corn bread stuffing, goose for fruit or rice, and Cornish hens for more sophisticated treatment.

REAL SOUTHERN FRIED CHICKEN

This misunderstood food requires plenty of shortening (the fat is reusable) and moderately high heat to prevent greasiness.

Place enough oil or shortening in a heavy deep skillet to a depth of ½ inch melted. Heat over moderately high heat. Salt and pepper chicken generously on both sides. If using milk, dip in milk, then coat with flour. Fat should sizzle as a piece of chicken is added. Add a few pieces of chicken, so they almost fill the pan, but don't overlap. Cook over moderately high heat until lightly browned on bottom. Turn and brown other side. Meaty pieces such as breasts and thighs take about 20 minutes if fat is hot and skillet not too crowded. When chicken is done, remove and drain on paper towel. Add remaining pieces to skillet until all the chicken is cooked. Serve immediately or cover with foil and keep warm in very low oven or chill and serve cold. Serve with hot cooked rice and Chicken Cream Gravy (see following page). ALLOW 2 MEATY PIECES OR 3 BONY PIECES PER SERVING.

Oil, shortening, or lard for frying
Salt
Pepper
Chicken parts (any preferred) or cut-up broiler-fryer
Buttermilk or fresh whole milk (optional)
Flour

CHICKEN CREAM GRAVY

Pour off all fat except 4 tablespoons and retain brown bits in pan after frying chicken. Heat drippings. Stir in flour, salt, and pepper. Cook, stirring frequently, until flour is browned. Add water. Cook and stir over moderate heat until smooth, thick, and boiling. Just before serving, float butter on top and stir to swirl lightly. Serve hot with rice and fried chicken. MAKES 2 CUPS. 4–6 SERVINGS.

Fried chicken drippings
4 tablespoons flour
1 teaspoon salt
¼ teaspoon pepper
2 cups water or half milk, half water
1 pat (about 1 teaspoon) butter or margarine

ARROZ CON POLLO

Fry chicken in oil in paella pan, large skillet, or kettle until browned, turning as necessary. Remove chicken from pan. Add onion, green pepper, tomato, and garlic. Cook, stirring often, until onion is tender but not browned. Add broth, salt, and bay leaf. Bring to a boil. Add saffron to a large spoonful of boiling broth and steam over remaining broth about 30 seconds. Stir dissolved saffron and turmeric into broth. Arrange chicken in boiling broth and sprinkle rice around it. Cover and simmer 10 minutes. Turn chicken. Cover and simmer 15 minutes longer or until rice is tender and liquid absorbed. Distribute peas over mixture and garnish with asparagus and pimiento. Heat and serve from paella pan or transfer to platter, reserving peas, asparagus, and pimiento to decorate top. MAKES 4 SERVINGS.

8 meaty pieces chicken (breasts or thighs)
½ cup oil, preferably half vegetable, half olive
1 onion, chopped
1 green pepper, chopped
1 small tomato, peeled and chopped, or ½ cup drained canned tomatoes
2 cloves garlic, crushed
3 cups chicken broth
2 teaspoons salt
1 bay leaf, crumbled
3 or 4 threads saffron or ½ teaspoon turmeric
1 cup rice
1 8-ounce can green peas, drained
4 cooked asparagus spears (optional)
1 2-ounce jar pimiento, cut in strips

BRUNSWICK STEW

Prepare broth and meat as for *Stewed Chicken or turkey soup. Bring 1 quart broth to a boil in large kettle. Add onion, green pepper, potato, tomatoes, chile, salt, and pepper. Cover and simmer until potato is almost tender. If using fresh okra, wash and slice off stem ends. Add okra, green beans and succotash or lima beans. Cover and simmer 20 minutes. Add cut corn and more broth, if needed to keep moist, though stew should not be soupy. Add meat, cover, and heat thoroughly. Serve in large deep bowls or soup plates. Crackers are usually served with Brunswick Stew, but squares of corn bread are good, too. MAKES 6 SERVINGS.

1–1½ quarts chicken or turkey broth
1 large onion, diced
1 large green pepper, diced
1 large potato, peeled and diced
1 16-ounce can tomatoes or 2 cups chopped peeled fresh
1 whole dried chile or hot pepper sauce to taste
Salt and pepper to taste
1 pound okra or 1 10-ounce package frozen
½ cup cut green beans
1 10-ounce package frozen succotash or 1 cup each shelled green lima beans and cut corn
3 cups cooked chicken or turkey in large chunks

CHICKEN AND OYSTERS

Skin chicken if desired. Mix flour, nutmeg, salt, and pepper. Coat chicken with flour mixture. Heat oil and butter in large heavy skillet. Add chicken a few pieces at a time and brown on both sides. Place in shallow baking dish. Bake at 400° 35 minutes or until tender. Baste with drippings once or twice. Chicken can be set aside an hour or two at this point or completed. Distribute oysters and their liquor around chicken. Pour cream over chicken and oysters. Bake 10–15 minutes longer, until edges of oysters curl. MAKES 4 GENEROUS OR 8 MEDIUM SERVINGS.

8 meaty chicken pieces (breasts, thighs, or drumsticks)
¾ cup flour
½ teaspoon nutmeg
1 teaspoon salt
¼ teaspoon pepper
½ cup oil
2 tablespoons butter or margarine
½ pint oysters
½ cup cream

CHICKEN BREASTS WITH CELERY PECAN STUFFING

Preheat oven to 400°. Cook onion and celery in 4 tablespoons butter in skillet until tender but not browned. Add pecans to stuffing mix, then add onion mixture. Rinse skillet with the hot water and pour over the stuffing. Mix well. Shape stuffing into oval patties and place on foil-lined rack of shallow pan. Place a chicken piece over each mound of stuffing and tuck in edges to form neat bundles. Melt remaining butter and brush over chicken. Bake 30–35 minutes or until juices run clear when chicken is pierced with a fork. MAKES 6 SERVINGS.

1 medium onion, chopped
1 cup diced celery
6 tablespoons butter or margarine
½ cup chopped pecans
2 cups herb stuffing mix
¾ cup hot water
6 small chicken breasts, boned, or 3 large, boned and split

CHICKEN HASHED IN CREAM

In skillet cook onion in butter until tender but not browned. Add chicken, salt, pepper, and sage. Stir well from bottom of pan. Pour cream over hash and cook uncovered until liquid is thickened, about 10 minutes, over moderate heat. Stir now and then while cooking to prevent sticking. Turn into serving dish and sprinkle with parsley. If desired, serve on rice, toast, or waffles. MAKES 4–5 SERVINGS.

1 small onion, finely chopped
2 tablespoons butter or margarine
2 cups finely chopped cooked chicken (or turkey)
1 teaspoon salt
¼ teaspoon pepper
¼ teaspoon sage
1 cup cream or undiluted evaporated milk
Minced parsley (optional)

CHICKEN LIVERS WITH MUSHROOMS

Drain chicken livers on paper towel and, if large, cut in halves. Coat with flour. Cook in butter in large skillet until lightly browned, turning once or twice. Add mushrooms and green onions. Turn heat low and cook, stirring gently now and then, until mushrooms and onions are lightly browned and livers no longer show red juices. Season with salt and pepper. Serve with rice. MAKES 4 SERVINGS.

1 pound chicken livers
Flour
2 tablespoons butter or margarine
¼ pound mushrooms, sliced
2 green onions with tops, sliced
½ teaspoon salt
¼ teaspoon pepper
Hot cooked rice

CHICKEN TOKAY

Preheat oven to 400°. Combine sugar, vinegar, and catsup in small saucepan. Bring to a boil and add butter and Worcestershire sauce. Simmer uncovered about 5 minutes, stirring once or twice. Add grapes and heat. Arrange chicken or Cornish hen pieces skin side up in a single layer in a shallow baking dish. Pour sauce over birds. Bake 45–60 minutes or until tender. Baste birds with sauce 2 or 3 times. Serve chicken and sauce with hot cooked rice. MAKES 4 SERVINGS.

¼ cup brown sugar, packed
¼ cup vinegar
¼ cup catsup
2 tablespoons butter or margarine
1 teaspoon Worcestershire sauce
1½ cups Tokay or other red grapes, split and seeded (about ¾ pound)
1 broiler-fryer, quartered, or 2 Cornish hens, halved

COUNTRY CAPTAIN

Preheat oven to 350°. Cook onion, green pepper, and garlic in butter in saucepan until tender but not browned. Add tomatoes and simmer uncovered 10 minutes. Add 2 teaspoons salt, white pepper, curry powder, parsley, and thyme. Mix well and simmer uncovered 5 minutes. Set aside.

Remove skin from chicken. Roll chicken in flour. Beat together eggs, remaining salt, and milk. Dip floured chicken in egg mixture, then roll in flour again. Heat about ½ inch oil in large skillet. Add chicken, being careful not to crowd, and brown lightly on all sides. Remove chicken and place in 2-quart baking dish. Pour sauce over it. Cover and bake 45 minutes or until chicken is fork-tender. Sprinkle with almonds and currants. Serve with fluffy hot rice. MAKES 4 SERVINGS.

1 medium onion, sliced thin
1 large green pepper, chopped
1 or 2 cloves garlic, minced
1 tablespoon butter or margarine
2 16-ounce cans tomatoes
3 teaspoons salt
1 teaspoon white pepper
1 teaspoon curry powder
1 teaspoon minced parsley
1 teaspoon powdered thyme
8 meaty pieces chicken or 1 broiler-fryer, cut up
½ cup flour
2 eggs
¼ cup milk
Oil for frying
¼ cup sliced blanched almonds
½ cup currants or chopped raisins

CHICKEN WITH BLACK CHERRIES

Remove skin from chicken if desired. Heat oil in large skillet. Add chicken a few pieces at a time and brown lightly on all sides. Remove chicken. Add onion and sauté lightly. Stir in flour. Drain cherries and set aside. Add syrup from cherries and chicken broth to skillet. Cook and stir until smooth. Add salt, allspice, lemon juice, and browned chicken. Cover and simmer until chicken is tender, about 40 minutes. Add cherries, heat, and serve with rice. MAKES 4–6 SERVINGS.

8–12 meaty pieces chicken
2 tablespoons (approximately) oil
1 onion, sliced
2 tablespoons flour
1 16-ounce can dark sweet cherries
1 10¾-ounce can condensed chicken broth
½ teaspoon salt
½ teaspoon allspice
Juice of ½ lemon

CHICKEN WITH SWEET POTATOES

Preheat oven to 400°. Heat butter in 13×9-inch baking dish in oven while preheating. Cut off stem and root ends of onions. Place in saucepan with sweet potatoes. Cover with water, bring to a boil, remove from heat, and let stand in hot water. Sprinkle chicken generously with salt and pepper. Beat egg lightly with water. Dip chicken in egg mixture, then coat thoroughly with bread crumbs. Coat chicken with melted butter and arrange in single layer in baking dish. Peel sweet potatoes and onions. Cut sweet potatoes in thick slices. Tuck sweet potato slices and onions around and under chicken pieces. Bake uncovered 1 hour or until chicken is tender and browned. Baste with pan juices several times. MAKES 4–6 SERVINGS.

½ cup butter or margarine
6 or 8 small boiling onions (about ½ pound)
2 large sweet potatoes (about 1 pound)
Water
6 or 8 meaty pieces chicken or 1 broiler-fryer, cut up
Salt
Pepper
1 egg
2 tablespoons water
1 cup fine dry bread crumbs

CHICKEN PIE DE LUXE

Preheat oven to 450°. Distribute chicken in shallow 11×7-inch baking dish. Slice mushrooms and cook in 1 tablespoon chicken fat in large saucepan until lightly browned. Scatter mushrooms and green peas over chicken. Bring broth to a boil in saucepan. Blend remaining chicken fat with flour. Stir into boiling broth and cook and stir until smooth and thick, about 2 minutes. Taste and add salt and pepper if needed. Pour sauce over chicken. Roll out pastry and place over chicken. Crimp to rim of baking dish and trim edges. Make several slits in pastry. Bake 30 minutes or until crust is browned. Let stand 10 minutes and serve with spoon or cut into squares. MAKES 6 SERVINGS.

4 cups coarsely chopped stewed chicken
½ pound mushrooms, sliced
3 tablespoons chicken fat, butter, or margarine
1 cup drained cooked green peas, carrots, or butter beans
2 cups well-seasoned chicken broth
3 tablespoons flour
Salt and pepper to taste
*Southern Short Pastry (double recipe)

MINORCAN PILAU

Chicken and rice in one form or another is almost universal to the South. The Minorcan pilau (pronounced *per-loo*) is a typical dish of St. Augustine, Florida. Some old-fashioned "mulls" (tomato sauce which is base for the pilau) were simmered for hours. This one gives authentic flavor but less arduously.

Sauté salt pork in 1 tablespoon oil until browned. Add onions, green pepper, and garlic and cook, stirring occasionally, until onions are golden. Add tomatoes, tomato paste, datil, marjoram, thyme, bay leaf, and salt and simmer uncovered 30 minutes. Chop tomato pieces occasionally. Meanwhile, brown chicken in more oil. Add to the mull (tomato mixture). Turn chicken to coat well with mixture. Add rice and boiling water. Bring to a boil. Cover and simmer 30 minutes or until rice is tender. Remove from heat, cover tightly, and let stand 20 minutes or until rice is fluffed. Pile rice on large platter and arrange chicken over rice. MAKES 4–6 SERVINGS.

¼ pound salt pork, diced
Oil
2 large onions, chopped
1 green pepper, chopped
3 cloves garlic, minced
1 16-ounce can tomatoes
1 6-ounce can tomato paste
1 datil or bird pepper or pickled jalapeño, minced
½ teaspoon marjoram
½ teaspoon thyme
1 bay leaf, crumbled
2 teaspoons salt
8–10 meaty pieces chicken or 2 broiler-fryers, cut up
2 cups rice
2 cups boiling water

MELT-IN-YOUR-MOUTH CHICKEN

Preheat broiler. Place chicken skin side up and in a single layer in shallow pan lined with foil. Broil 6 inches from source of heat until skin blisters and is browned, about 10 minutes. Turn chicken and broil 10 minutes longer or until browned. Turn and sprinkle water over chicken. Continue to broil, basting often with pan juices, 20 minutes. Sprinkle lightly with salt and pepper or seasoning of choice. Turn and broil 10 minutes longer or until juices run golden when chicken is pierced with a fork. MAKES 4 SERVINGS.

NOTE: Chicken cooked this way can be seasoned with hickory smoke salt; garlic, onion, or celery salt; seasoned salt; and chicken stock seasoning base.

8 meaty pieces chicken or 1 broiler-fryer, cut up
½ cup water
Salt, pepper, or other seasoning (see Note)

PORT WINE CHICKEN

Preheat oven to 350°. Brown chicken lightly in butter in skillet. Arrange 1 layer deep in 15×10-inch roasting pan without rack. Add undiluted soup and wine to butter remaining in skillet and stir over low heat to blend well. Pour over chicken. Bake uncovered 1 hour or until chicken is tender. Serve with rice if desired. MAKES 6 SERVINGS.

12 meaty pieces chicken (breasts and thighs)
½ cup butter or margarine
1 10¾-ounce can cream of chicken, mushroom, or celery soup
¼ cup ruby port wine

HERBED OVEN-FRIED CHICKEN

Rub chicken with broth seasoning and basil. Place in bowl with lemon juice and water. Turn to coat chicken well, cover, and refrigerate several hours or overnight. Turn chicken in juices 2 or 3 times. Preheat oven to 375°. Combine flour, salt, and pepper. Drain chicken well, reserving marinade. Coat chicken with flour mixture. Brown in about ½ inch hot oil in heavy skillet. As chicken browns, transfer to shallow baking dish, arranging in a single layer. Pour reserved marinade over chicken. Bake 45 minutes or until tender. MAKES 4 SERVINGS.

8 meaty pieces chicken (breasts, thighs, or drumsticks)
2 envelopes chicken broth seasoning
1 teaspoon dry basil leaves
⅓ cup lemon juice
½ cup water
¾ cup flour
1 teaspoon salt
¼ teaspoon pepper
Oil for frying

CLASSIC CHICKEN BARBECUE

Combine vinegar, 1 cup margarine, and salt. Heat slowly until margarine is melted. Add lemon juice and crushed pepper. Dip chicken in sauce. Grill over coals that have burned down so they are covered with gray ash. Turn on grill for even cooking and baste with sauce each time chicken is turned. Cook until chicken is tender and browned, about 1 hour for medium-sized broilers. Most of the sauce should be used by the time chicken is done. Add remaining ¼ cup margarine to remaining sauce and beat until blended. Toast buns and spread with buttery sauce. Serve with chicken. MAKES 4 SERVINGS.

2 cups cider vinegar
1¼ cups margarine or butter
1 tablespoon salt
1 tablespoon lemon juice
¼ teaspoon crushed dried red pepper (optional)
2 broiler-fryers, split
4 hard rolls or buns, split

STEWED CHICKEN

Have chicken cut in pieces. Place in large kettle with onion which has been studded with cloves, carrot, celery, salt, pepper, and water. Don't cover chicken completely with water or broth will be thin-flavored. Cover pan, bring to a boil, turn heat low, and simmer chicken 2–2½ hours or until tender. Cool chicken in broth and remove meat from bones and skin. To serve as stewed chicken and dumplings, skim as much fat as possible off broth. Return chicken pieces to broth, add dumplings and simmer 15 minutes or until tender. MAKES 6 SERVINGS.

NOTE: For use in salads and other dishes, refrigerate broth and meat separately. Before using, skim fat which has hardened on top off broth. Then proceed with recipe.

Pressure-Cooker Stewed Chicken: Follow recipe for Stewed Chicken, but reduce water to 2 cups. Cook at 15 pounds pressure 25 minutes. Let return to normal pressure gradually, remove cover, and proceed as in Stewed Chicken.

1 5½–6-pound stewing chicken
1 small onion
3 whole cloves
1 large carrot, peeled and cut in chunks
1 rib celery with leaves, cut coarsely
2 teaspoons salt
½ teaspoon pepper
4 cups water
*Chicken Dumplings

ROAST CHICKEN WITH VEGETABLES

Preheat oven to 400°. Melt butter in shallow roasting pan or ovenproof skillet large enough to accommodate chicken. Add onions and carrots and cook until lightly browned. Rub cavity of chicken with ½ teaspoon poultry seasoning, salt, and pepper. Place chicken on bed of onions and carrots and brush with pan drippings. Sprinkle with remaining poultry seasoning. Roast 1–1¼ hours, until chicken is browned and leg moves easily. Baste 2 or 3 times with pan drippings. Let stand 10–15 minutes before carving. Serve some of the vegetables and pan juices with each portion. MAKES 4 SERVINGS.

¼ cup butter or margarine
2 onions, chopped
2 large carrots, chopped
1 2½–3-pound broiler-fryer
¾ teaspoon poultry seasoning
½ teaspoon salt
¼ teaspoon pepper

SOUTHERN CREAMED CHICKEN

Cook mushrooms in fat in large saucepan until lightly browned. Add onion and cook until tender. Add salt and stir in flour. Cook until bubbly. Add broth, milk, and pepper sauce. Cook and stir until smooth and thickened, bring to a boil, and boil about 1 minute. Add chicken, eggs, and pimiento. Heat thoroughly. Serve on split hot biscuits, toast, or in patty shells. MAKES 4–6 SERVINGS.

1 cup sliced mushrooms (about ¼ pound)
¼ cup chicken fat, butter, or margarine
¼ cup chopped fresh onion or
*   1 tablespoon instant*
1 teaspoon salt
3 tablespoons flour
1 cup chicken broth
1 cup milk or cream
Dash hot pepper sauce
2 cups chopped cooked chicken
2 hard-cooked eggs, chopped
1 2-ounce jar pimiento, well drained and
*   chopped*

DIXIE SHORTCAKE

Place bottom pieces of corn bread on platter. Sauté ham quickly to brown lightly, adding a little fat if needed. Place a slice of ham on each piece corn bread. Ladle about ⅔ of the creamed chicken over ham, cover with top halves of corn bread, then remaining chicken mixture. MAKES 4 SERVINGS.

4 corn bread rectangles, split
4 1-ounce slices ham (optional)
*1 recipe *Southern Creamed Chicken*

STEAMED CHICKEN

Place chicken on steamer rack in large kettle or in steamer pan. Stud onions with cloves and arrange around chicken with carrot and celery. Add boiling water almost to level of rack. Add bay leaf, salt, and pepper. Cover and bring to a boil. Turn heat to moderate and steam until chicken is tender, 2–3 hours. Cool, then refrigerate chicken and broth separately. Discard vegetables or reserve for soup. Cut chicken as desired, discarding bones and most of skin. MAKES 4–4½ CUPS CHICKEN AND ABOUT 2 CUPS BROTH.

1 3½–4-pound stewing chicken, cut up
2 onions
4 whole cloves
1 large carrot, peeled and cut in chunks
2 ribs celery, cut in chunks
Boiling water
1 large bay leaf, crumbled
1½ teaspoons salt
¼ teaspoon pepper

ROAST TURKEY BREAST WITH RICE AND VEGETABLES

Thaw turkey completely if frozen. Preheat oven to 325°. Combine onion, carrots, celery, ½ teaspoon salt, and bay leaf in shallow baking dish. Place turkey skin side up on vegetables. Spread turkey with butter. Roast 3–3½ hours or until thermometer inserted in meaty portion reaches 180°. Baste with pan drippings several times while roasting. If skin browns too rapidly, cover with a loose cap of foil. Remove dish from oven. Place turkey in center of large square of foil and wrap to keep warm. Skim as much fat as possible off vegetables, but retain juices. Add rice, stir lightly, add remaining salt and boiling water. Cover tightly with foil and bake at 350° 25 minutes or until rice is tender and liquid absorbed. Place turkey on platter and surround with rice or serve rice in a separate bowl. MAKES 6–8 SERVINGS WITH LEFTOVERS.

1 whole or half turkey breast (5–6 pounds)
1 onion, chopped fine
2 large carrots, diced or sliced thin
2 large ribs celery, diced
2 teaspoons salt
1 bay leaf, crumbled
1 tablespoon butter or margarine
1½ cups rice
2 cups boiling water

71

BAKED TURKEY WINGS

Preheat oven to 400°. With poultry shears, cut wings at joints. Reserve tips for soup or broth. Arrange remaining wing sections in single layer in 13×9-inch baking pan. Melt butter in skillet or saucepan. Add garlic, sage, lemon juice, salt, pepper, and chicken broth. Bring to a boil. Pour over turkey. Bake uncovered 2 hours or until juices run golden or clear when meaty piece is pierced with fork. Baste several times with pan juices while baking. MAKES 4 LARGE SERVINGS.

4 small turkey wings
¼ cup butter or margarine
1 clove garlic, minced
½ teaspoon sage or poultry seasoning
1½ teaspoons lemon juice
1½ teaspoons salt
½ teaspoon white pepper
1 cup chicken broth or dry white wine

CORNISH HENS VERONIQUE

Thaw game hens thoroughly. Remove giblets and reserve for other uses. With scissors or sharp knife cut hens in halves along breastbones and backbones. Snap out breastbones and cut out backbones. Heat butter and oil in large heavy skillet. Add hen halves a few at a time and brown lightly. Remove browned birds and continue until all hens are browned. Add onion and brown lightly. Return hens to skillet. Sprinkle with salt and pepper. Add ¾ cup wine. Cover and simmer 20–25 minutes or until hens are tender. Remove hens to warm platter. Add grapes to pan drippings. Stir flour into remaining wine and stir into pan drippings and bring to a boil. Taste and add more salt and pepper if needed. Pour some sauce over hens and serve remainder separately. Serve with rice. MAKES 4 SERVINGS.

NOTE: If preferred, chicken parts such as breasts or thighs may be substituted for game hens.

4 Cornish game hens (about 1½ pounds each)
¼ cup butter or margarine
¼ cup oil
1 small onion, sliced
1 teaspoon salt
¼ teaspoon pepper
1 cup dry white wine
1 8¼-ounce can seedless grapes, drained, or 1 cup fresh
2 tablespoons flour

CRISPY TANGERINE DUCKLING

Preheat oven to 400°. Thaw duckling if frozen, and remove giblets and neck. Place duckling breast side up on rack in shallow roasting pan. Roast 1 hour, until golden. Meat will still be quite rare. Cool thoroughly, 2–3 hours, at room temperature.

Meanwhile, cut thin outer peel off tangerine and lemon with a vegetable peeler or very sharp knife. Cut peel into thin slivers. Remove remaining peel from tangerine. Slice tangerine over a small saucepan in order to retain juice. Discard any seeds and set the slices aside. Add the juice of 1 lemon, the cut peel, and water to saucepan. Stir in sugar, ¼ teaspoon salt, and dash pepper. Simmer uncovered 5 or 6 minutes. Sauce should be syrupy.

Preheat broiler. Cut duckling in half and cut out backbone and breastbone, using poultry shears. Remove rib bones, running a thin sharp knife under them and lifting with your fingers. Cut duck in quarters. Rinse roasting pan and rack and place duck pieces on rack meaty side up. Sprinkle lightly with salt and pepper. Broil 7–8 inches from heat, with heat at a moderate setting, until meat is lightly browned. Turn, puncture skin liberally with a fork, and brush lightly with tangerine sauce. Broil until skin is crispy and duck juice runs pale golden when meat is pierced, about 30 minutes. Adjust heat so skin sizzles but does not burn or blister. Arrange duck on warm platter and pour remaining sauce and peel over it. Arrange sliced tangerine around duck. MAKES 2 OR 4 SERVINGS.

1 4–5-pound duckling
1 large tangerine or tangelo
1 lemon
¼ cup water
2 tablespoons sugar
Salt
Pepper

ROAST CHRISTMAS GOOSE

Thaw goose thoroughly in its wrapper in refrigerator if frozen. Cook giblets (see recipe on following page for Giblet Gravy) promptly. Rinse bird, pat dry with paper towel, and refrigerate until just before roasting. Pull piece of fat out of body near tail and render for use in stuffing or other purposes. Pack stuffing loosely into neck and body cavities. Skewer neck skin to back of goose. Skewer tail cavity closed and tuck legs under band of skin or tie legs close to body. Skewer wings to carcass.

Preheat oven to 325°. Thoroughly grease inside of a large bag with goose or other fat. (Roasting goose in this fashion prevents excessive spattering.) Carefully place bird in bag, fold open end of bag closed, and fasten with 2 or 3 paper clips. Place bag with goose breast down on rack in shallow roasting pan. Roast 2 hours. Punch 8 or 10 holes with a pencil or knife tip in bag over goose back. Using pot holders and avoiding any juices that spurt, carefully turn so goose rests on its back. Continue roasting until thermometer inserted in thickest part inside thigh registers 185°, about 2 hours longer. From time to time remove drippings from pan with bulb baster to prevent excessive spattering. Remove goose from bag, place on platter, and let stand 20–30 minutes before carving. Serve goose and stuffing with gravy. MAKES 6–8 GENEROUS SERVINGS.

NOTE: Goose grease is excellent for cooking, so save in a jar as it is removed.

1 8–10-pound goose
*Apricot or other stuffing
*Giblet Gravy
Melted goose fat, margarine, or oil

APRICOT STUFFING FOR GOOSE

Cut apricots in small pieces with kitchen shears. Place in bowl with orange juice, cover, and let stand until softened, at least 2 hours. Cook onion in hot fat until tender but not browned. Stir in celery, poultry seasoning, and apricot mixture. Combine corn bread, bread cubes, and onion mixture. Add broth to form a stuffing that clings together when pressed into a ball on spoon. Taste and add salt and pepper if needed. Use to stuff goose. MAKES ENOUGH FOR 6–8-POUND GOOSE.

½ cup dried apricots
½ cup orange juice
1 small onion, finely chopped
2 tablespoons goose fat or oil
1 cup chopped celery
1 teaspoon poultry seasoning
2 cups crumbled corn bread
2 cups toasted bread cubes
¾–1 cup giblet broth or chicken broth
Salt and pepper to taste

GIBLET GRAVY

Place neck, gizzard, heart in medium-size saucepan. Cover with water. Cut celery in chunks and add along with onion, 1 teaspoon salt, and ¼ teaspoon pepper. Cover and simmer until gizzard is tender, from 45 minutes for a roasting chicken to 2 hours for goose or large turkey. Add liver and simmer 10 minutes longer or until liver is fork-tender. Promptly remove giblets and strain broth. Refrigerate cooked giblets and broth separately until ready to use. Cut meat off neck and chop neck meat and giblets fine, using sharp knife or coarse blade of food grinder.

Pour roast poultry drippings, including brown bits and ¼ cup fat, in a heavy skillet. Heat until sizzling. Stir in flour and cook and stir until flour is lightly browned. Add 2 cups broth or broth and water. Cook and stir until thickened and smooth. Stir in ½ teaspoon salt and ⅛ teaspoon pepper, then add giblets. Bring to a boil. Taste and add more salt and pepper if needed. Serve hot with poultry and stuffing. MAKES 4–6 SERVINGS.

Giblets from roasting chicken, turkey, goose, or other bird
Water
1 rib celery
1 ½-inch-thick slice onion
Salt
Pepper
¼ cup (approximately) roast poultry drippings
4 tablespoons flour

The long coastline and the rivers and lakes of the South supply a connoisseur's choice of fish—miniature fresh-water cat, fat pompano, delicate-flavored red snapper, red fish, grouper, mullet, flounder, and the incomparable Florida yellowtail, a relative of the snapper, not the tuna (whose relation is the Pacific yellowtail). Full-flavored blue crabs scramble along the coastal shelf as far north as Long Island, but are at their best from the Chesapeake, south to Savannah and Jacksonville, then in the Gulf from Pensacola around the snowy-sanded beach to New Orleans and Texas. This crab is used in *Crab Imperial and *Crab Norfolk. In the spring when the crab sheds its shell, it is sautéed as soft-shelled crab. Shrimp are in high repute on any table in the South. Oysters cling to mangrove roots, rocks, and anything else along the southern Atlantic and Gulf coasts. They are harvested commercially near Mobile (Bon Secour), at Fernandina in northeast Florida, and Apalachicola in northwest Florida. Oysters dug at Pine Island near Naples, Florida, are so tiny one barely covers a thumbnail.

Railroad lines once sped seafood inland from Mobile, New Orleans, or Fernandina. In my hometown, barrels of oysters came on Fridays from Mobile. Mr. Jeter, the hardware store operator and undertaker, sold the oysters. My mother took her own pot to buy a pint or quart of oysters.

⋙⊹ FISH ⊹⋘

BROILED FISH FILLETS

Preheat broiler. Melt butter in broilerproof platter or shallow pan (no rack is needed for fish). Turn fish in melted butter to coat well, then arrange in a single layer with skin side down. Sprinkle with salt and a generous amount of paprika. Broil 4 inches from source of heat until fish flakes with a fork, about 12 minutes. It is not necessary to turn fish fillets. Serve from broiling platter or carefully lift onto warm platter. Garnish with lime or lemon wedges. Serve with tartar sauce if desired. MAKES 4–6 SERVINGS.

¼ cup butter or margarine
2–2½ pounds fish fillets (Florida yellowtail, red snapper, mackerel, or pompano)
Salt
Paprika
Lime or lemon wedges
*Florida Tartar Sauce (optional)

DIXIE FRIED FISH

Sprinkle fish generously with salt and pepper. Coat with corn meal. Heat oil about 1 inch deep in heavy skillet. Fry fish a few at a time in fat. Turn when lightly browned and brown other side. Cook just until fish flakes easily with a fork, 4–5 minutes on each side. Overcooking makes it dry and tasteless. Drain on absorbent paper and keep warm while frying hush puppies. Serve with lemon wedges, tartar sauce, and catsup. MAKES 1 SERVING.

2 or 3 dressed pan fish (baby catfish, sunfish, fresh-water perch) or ⅓–½ pound fish fillets per person
Salt
Pepper
White corn meal
Oil or bacon drippings for frying
*Tallahassee Hush Puppies (optional)
Lemon Wedges
*Florida Tartar Sauce
Catsup

DAUPHIN STREET FLOUNDER

Preheat broiler. Combine bacon, onion, salt, and pepper. Line a broiler pan with foil. Place flounder skin side down on foil. Cut 3 diagonal slashes in belly side of flounder. Fill slashes with bacon mixture. Sprinkle remaining mixture over fish. Sprinkle with paprika and lemon juice. Broil 6 inches from source of heat until fish flakes, 15–18 minutes. Brush with pan drippings 2 or 3 times. Place on hot platter and garnish with parsley and lemon wedges. MAKES 4 SERVINGS.

1 strip bacon, finely chopped
½ small onion, finely chopped
¼ teaspoon salt
⅛ teaspoon pepper
1 flounder, cleaned (about 3 pounds)
Paprika
2 tablespoons lemon juice
Parsley sprigs
Lemon wedges

BAKED MULLET WITH SAUSAGE

Have fish man split mullet almost through and clean it. Fish will be juicier if baked with head on. Preheat oven to 375°. Place fish in shallow baking pan or broiler pan lined with foil. Fill body cavity with sausage and onion. Push fish back into shape and, if necessary, close with wood picks. Bake 45 minutes or until fish flakes easily with fork. Spread with butter and sprinkle with paprika. Broil 3–4 minutes or until glazed. Carefully lift fish from pan to warm platter. Remove head if desired. Garnish with lemon. To serve, cut thick crosswise slices through fish. MAKES 4 SERVINGS.

1 mullet or other mild-flavored fish (about 3 pounds)
¼ pound smoked sausage, thinly sliced
1 medium onion, sliced
2 tablespoons butter or margarine
Paprika
Lemon wedges

NEW ORLEANS COURT BOUILLON

Fillet fish, reserving head and trimmings. (Market man may do this.) Place head and trimmings in saucepan with water. Salt lightly. Cover and simmer 20 minutes to make stock. Combine bacon drippings and oil in heavy kettle. Heat and stir in flour. Cook, stirring often, until deep golden brown. Add onions, green pepper, bay leaves, and garlic. Cook slowly, stirring often, until onions are lightly browned. Add stock, tomatoes, tomato paste, allspice, and cayenne. Bring to a boil, cover, and simmer 1 hour, stirring now and then. Cut fish in chunks. Add to sauce and spoon a little sauce over each. Cover and simmer 20 minutes or until fish flakes easily with a fork. Add wine, stirring carefully from bottom to mix but taking care not to break fish. Serve fish and sauce on rice in soup plates. MAKES 4–6 SERVINGS.

1 3–4-pound red fish or red snapper
3 cups water
Salt
¼ cup bacon drippings, butter, or margarine
¼ cup olive oil
½ cup flour
2 large onions, chopped
1 green pepper, chopped
3 bay leaves, crumbled
3 cloves garlic, minced
2 16-ounce cans tomatoes
2 6-ounce cans tomato paste
1 teaspoon allspice
¼ teaspoon cayenne
1 cup dry red wine

CRAB IMPERIAL

Preheat oven to 400°. Pick over crab meat and remove bits of shell or cartilage. Melt butter in large saucepan. Stir in flour. Add milk and cook and stir until smooth and thickened. Stir in salt, pepper, celery salt, garlic salt, and cayenne. Stir a spoonful of sauce into egg yolk, then stir egg yolk into remaining sauce. Cook and stir over low heat until smooth and thickened, about 2 minutes. Remove from heat. Add 1 cup bread crumbs, onion, crab, and sherry. Turn into greased shallow baking dish or crab shells. Sprinkle with remaining bread crumbs and paprika. Bake until lightly browned and bubbly, about 15 minutes. MAKES 4–6 SERVINGS.

1 pound crab meat, preferably fine flakes
4 tablespoons butter or margarine
4 tablespoons flour
2 cups milk
1 teaspoon salt
⅛ teaspoon pepper
½ teaspoon celery salt
⅛ teaspoon garlic salt
Dash cayenne or hot pepper sauce
1 egg yolk, beaten
1½ cups fresh bread crumbs
2 tablespoons minced onion
2 tablespoons dry sherry
Paprika

CRAB NORFOLK

Carefully pick over crab to remove any cartilage or shell, but leave meat in as large lumps as possible. Divide among 4 individual shallow baking dishes or spread in small pie plate. Melt butter in small skillet. Stir in lemon juice, salt, and pepper sauce. Pour evenly over crab. Broil until sizzling (or bake in a 450° oven), about 5 minutes. Serve from baking dishes with sprig of parsley in each and lemon wedges on the side. MAKES 4 SERVINGS.

1 pound lump crab meat
½ cup butter or margarine
2 tablespoons lemon juice
½ teaspoon salt
Dash hot pepper sauce or cayenne
Parsley sprigs
Lemon wedges

CHESAPEAKE CRAB CAKES

Pick over crab meat, removing any shell or cartilage. Flake crab with fingers into small shreds. Combine with ½ cup bread crumbs, salt, pepper, mustard, Worcestershire, onion, and egg. Mix well, then mix in enough mayonnaise so mixture clings together. With hands, shape into 8 patties. Coat with remaining crumbs. Spread on plate or tray lined with waxed paper, cover with more waxed paper, and chill 1 hour or longer. Fry in about ½ inch hot oil in skillet until browned. Turn and brown other side. Serve with lemon wedges and tartar sauce if desired. MAKES 4 GENEROUS SERVINGS.

1 pound crab meat, preferably fine flakes
1 cup seasoned fine dry bread crumbs
½ teaspoon salt
¼ teaspoon pepper
1 teaspoon dry mustard
1 teaspoon Worcestershire sauce
¼ cup minced green onion with tops (about 2 onions)
1 egg
2–3 tablespoons mayonnaise
Oil for frying
Lemon wedges
*Florida Tartar Sauce (optional)

FRIED SOFT-SHELLED CRABS

Have market man clean crabs or lift up pointed apron on underside of shell and pull out "dead man," the fuzzy portions surrounding meat and shell. Wash and dry crabs. Mix eggs and water in shallow dish. Coat crabs with flour, then with egg mixture. Finally roll in cracker meal to coat well. Spread on cookie sheet lined with waxed paper, cover with another sheet of waxed paper, and refrigerate 1 hour or longer. Heat ½ inch oil or 3 or 4 tablespoons butter in heavy skillet. Sauté crabs in oil or butter a few at a time until golden, turning to brown evenly. Drain on paper towels and sprinkle lightly with salt and pepper. Serve with lemon wedges, tartar sauce, and if desired, french fried potatoes. MAKES 6 SERVINGS.

12 soft-shelled crabs
2 eggs
¼ cup water
Flour
Fine cracker meal, about ½ cup
Oil, butter, or margarine
Salt
Pepper
Lemon wedges
*Florida Tartar Sauce (optional)

FLORIDA LOBSTER CHILAU

Fry bacon in large pot until fat is rendered. Add onions and garlic and cook until tender but not browned. Add potatoes, 1½ cups water, salt, pepper sauce, and thyme. Bring to a boil, cover, and boil 15 minutes. With scissors, cut membrane from undersides of lobster tails and pull meat from shells. Cut meat in chunks. Add to stew along with tomatoes. Bring to a boil and simmer 10 minutes or until lobster and potatoes are done. If desired, stir in milk or half-and-half and, if needed, more water. Heat and ladle into warm soup plates. Serve with garlic bread to mop up the juice. MAKES 4–6 SERVINGS.

4 slices bacon or 3 ounces salt pork, diced
2 medium onions, chopped
2 cloves garlic, minced
2 potatoes, peeled and cubed (about 1 pound)
1½–2 cups hot water
1½ teaspoons salt
¼ teaspoon hot pepper sauce
¼ teaspoon thyme
4 lobster tails (about 8 ounces each), thawed if frozen
2 16-ounce cans tomatoes
1 cup milk or half-and-half (optional)

FERNANDINA FRIED OYSTERS

Line a baking sheet or platter with waxed paper. Beat together eggs, water, and salt. Make fine crumbs of saltines, using blender or rolling pin. Put cracker crumbs on one plate and flour on another. One by one, roll oysters in flour, coat with egg mixture, then roll in cracker crumbs. Place on lined baking sheet. When all oysters are breaded, cover with another sheet of waxed paper, and refrigerate at least 1 hour.

Fifteen minutes before serving heat 1 inch oil in skillet until an oyster sizzles immediately when dropped in oil. Fry oysters a few at a time until golden brown on both sides, about 3 or 4 minutes. Remove with slotted spoon, drain on absorbent paper, and keep warm until all oysters are fried. Turn onto platter and garnish with watercress or parsley. Serve with lemon wedges, catsup, and tartar sauce. MAKES 4 SERVINGS.

2 eggs
2 tablespoons water
½ teaspoon salt
¼ pound (approximately) saltines
½ cup (approximately) flour
1 pint select (large) oysters
Oil for frying
Watercress or parsley sprigs
Lemon wedges
Catsup
*Florida Tartar Sauce

OYSTERS POULETTE

Poach oysters with liquor in saucepan over low heat until edges curl, 2 or 3 minutes. Drain liquor from oysters into 2-cup measure. Set oysters aside. Melt butter in saucepan. Stir in flour. Add half-and-half or cream to oyster liquor to make 2 cups. Stir into flour mixture. Add salt and nutmeg. Cook and stir until smooth and sauce comes to a boil. Stir a spoonful of hot sauce into egg yolks. Pour yolks into hot sauce and cook and stir until slightly thickened. Do not boil. Add oysters and heat but do not boil. Serve at once on split biscuits, toast, or in patty shells. MAKES 4–6 SERVINGS.

1 pint oysters
2 tablespoons butter or margarine
3 tablespoons flour
Half-and-half or cream
½ teaspoon salt
⅛ teaspoon nutmeg
2 egg yolks, beaten
Hot biscuits, toast, or patty shells

OYSTER STEW

Melt ¼ cup butter in large saucepan over moderate heat. Add oysters with their liquor, celery salt, and Worcestershire. Cook over low heat until edges curl, 2–3 minutes. Add half-and-half and/or milk. Heat until bubbles form at edge. Do not boil. Add salt and pepper sauce. Ladle into soup bowls, float a small pat of butter on each serving, and sprinkle with parsley. MAKES 4–6 SERVINGS.

Butter or margarine
1 pint oysters
½ teaspoon celery salt
1 teaspoon Worcestershire sauce
1 quart half-and-half or part milk
1 teaspoon salt
⅛ teaspoon hot pepper sauce or cayenne
Minced parsley (optional)

RICH SCALLOPED OYSTERS

Preheat oven to 400°. Melt butter, add crumbs, and mix well. Spoon 2 or 3 tablespoons crumb mixture into greased deep 5-cup casserole. Add ½ the oysters with liquor and sprinkle with ½ the nutmeg and salt. Add a layer of crumbs, remaining oysters, nutmeg, and salt. Cover with remaining crumb mixture. Carefully pour milk at edge of casserole so it runs into lower layers. Milk should not cover top layer. Bake 30 minutes or until set. Serve hot. MAKES 4 SERVINGS.

½ cup butter or margarine
1 cup coarse cracker crumbs (about 2 ounces)
1 pint oysters
¼ teaspoon nutmeg
¼ teaspoon salt
½ cup milk

COCONUT CRUSTED SHRIMP

Shell and clean shrimp, leaving tails intact. Dry thoroughly. Beat eggs with flour and salt. Dip shrimp in egg batter, then in coconut. Coating will cling better if shrimp are spread on plate and refrigerated 1 hour or longer. Heat about 1 inch oil in heavy skillet until sizzling hot. Fry shrimp a few at a time until golden brown on both sides, turning once. Drain on paper towel. Serve with lemon or lime wedges and tartar sauce if desired. MAKES 4 SERVINGS.

1½ pounds large shrimp
2 eggs
2 tablespoons flour
½ teaspoon salt
½ cup shredded coconut or as needed
Oil for frying
Lemon or lime wedges (optional)
*Florida Tartar Sauce (optional)

BOILED SHRIMP

Combine water, celery, and seasonings in large kettle. Cover and bring to a boil. Add shrimp, cover, and bring again to a boil. When shrimp turn red and opaque, they are done. Cool a few minutes in liquid, then drain. Chill and use in salads, cocktails, or other dishes. Reserve shrimp broth for *Shrimp Creole. MAKES 4–6 SERVINGS.

NOTE: Crab boil is a mixture of spices and herbs available in many southern markets and seafood markets everywhere. Pickling spice is an acceptable substitute.

Water to cover shrimp generously (3–4 quarts)
1 rib celery, cut in pieces
1 tablespoon crab boil (see Note)
2 pounds shrimp, shelled and cleaned

KEY WEST SHRIMP SAUTÉ

Shell and clean shrimp. Heat butter and oil in large skillet. Add garlic, cook about 1 minute, and discard. Add shrimp, parsley, and Worcestershire. Cook, stirring occasionally, until shrimp turn pink and look opaque, about 10 minutes. Salt to taste. Serve at once with French bread to mop up sauce or rice. MAKES 4 SERVINGS.

1½ pounds shrimp, preferably large
3 tablespoons butter or margarine
1 tablespoon oil
2 cloves garlic, minced
1½ teaspoons parsley flakes
1 tablespoon Worcestershire sauce
Salt to taste

86

OKRA GUMBO

Prepare broth before starting gumbo.

Heat 2 tablespoons oil in large heavy kettle, add beef, ham, gizzards, and salt pork and cook until lightly browned, stirring often. Add onion, green pepper, celery, bay leaves, and garlic and cook until onion is tender but not browned. Add tomatoes, ½ cup broth, and salt. Simmer 1 hour, stirring now and then. Meanwhile, prepare okra. Cook slowly in remaining oil in large skillet, stirring often, until viscous juice is absorbed and okra is lightly browned. Add parsley and shrimp and cook until shrimp turns pink. Add to gumbo along with 1 cup more broth. Bring to a boil. Clean crabs, discarding "dead man," the spongy substance in the body. Break off claws and crack. Break body portions in half. Add crab to gumbo and simmer 10 minutes. Add pepper sauce to taste. Serve immediately or cool and reheat. Thin with more broth if desired. Serve over rice in deep soup plates with crackers and more pepper sauce if desired. MAKES 4 LARGE SERVINGS.

Shrimp Shell Broth (see below)
6 tablespoons oil
½ pound beef stew meat, cut in ½-inch cubes
½ pound ham or sausage links, sliced ½ inch thick
4–6 ounces chicken gizzards, thinly sliced
2 ounces salt pork, diced
1 large onion, finely chopped
1 green pepper, finely chopped
½ cup diced celery (1 rib)
2 bay leaves, crumbled
2 cloves garlic, crushed
1 16-ounce can tomatoes
1 teaspoon salt or to taste
1 10-ounce package frozen okra or 1 pound fresh, cut in 1-inch pieces
½ cup minced parsley
1 pound shrimp, shelled and cleaned
2 blue crabs
Hot pepper sauce or cayenne to taste

SHRIMP SHELL BROTH

Shell shrimp and reserve for gumbo. Place shells in large saucepan with water, celery, carrot, onion, and salt. Cover, bring to a boil, and simmer 30 minutes or longer. Drain and use broth for Okra Gumbo (above). MAKES 3½ CUPS.

1 pound shrimp
3 quarts water
1 rib celery, sliced
1 small carrot, sliced
1 onion, quartered
1 teaspoon salt

SHRIMP CREOLE

Heat oil in large skillet or Dutch oven. Stir in flour and cook and stir until golden brown. Add onion, green pepper, and garlic. Cook, stirring occasionally, until onion is tender but not browned. Add tomato paste and 3 paste cans shrimp broth (2¼ cups). Bring to a boil, stir well, and simmer uncovered until thickened, stirring occasionally. Add shrimp, salt, and pepper. Heat thoroughly. Taste and add more salt and pepper if needed. Serve on hot cooked rice. MAKES 4–6 SERVINGS.

¼ cup oil or bacon drippings
3 tablespoons flour
1 large onion, chopped
1 green pepper, chopped
1 or 2 cloves garlic, crushed
1 6-ounce can tomato paste
Shrimp broth or water
1 pound shrimp, cleaned and cooked
   (about 12 ounces after cleaning and
   cooking)
1 teaspoon salt
¼ teaspoon pepper

SHRIMP CURRY IN PINEAPPLE SHELLS

Cut pineapple in half lengthwise, keeping crowns intact. Cut out meat with grapefruit knife, leaving sturdy shells. Dice ½ the pineapple for use in curry, discarding core and reserving remaining pineapple for other uses. Invert shells and drain on absorbent paper.

Heat oil in large saucepan. Add onion, celery, and garlic. Cook until tender but not browned. Add diced pineapple. Stir in flour, curry powder, salt, and pepper sauce. Add broth and cook and stir until smooth and thickened. Add shrimp and heat.

Meanwhile, heat pineapple shells in 350° oven 15 minutes. Fill 1 large shell with curry and other with rice or mound rice in small shells and spoon curry over rice. Serve with chutney, chopped almonds or peanuts, shredded coconut, sliced green onion, and other condiments. MAKES 4 SERVINGS.

1 large or 2 small pineapples
⅓ cup oil
1 medium onion, chopped
1 cup diced celery
2 cloves garlic, crushed
¼ cup flour
3 tablespoons curry powder or to taste
½ teaspoon salt
Dash hot pepper sauce
2½ cups shrimp or chicken broth
1½ pounds cleaned cooked shrimp

PAELLA PAN-AMERICAN

Preheat oven to 350°. Heat oil in paella pan or large skillet. Add onion and green pepper and cook until tender but not browned. Meanwhile cut pork and chicken in chunks with scissors. Add and cook until lightly browned. Add garlic and cook until golden. Add bay leaves, salt, pepper sauce, and rice. Cook and stir until rice is coated with oil. Add chicken broth and bring to a boil. Crumble saffron into spoon and let steam over boiling broth a minute or two. Dip up broth into spoon, then stir saffron into rice. Cover and bake or simmer over low heat until liquid is absorbed and rice tender, about 30 minutes. Add boiling chicken broth to keep moist, if needed. Sprinkle white wine over paella. Stir in turmeric if deeper color is wanted. Arrange clams around edge of pan, cover, and bake 10 minutes. Distribute crab and shrimp over mixture. Arrange asparagus spears around edge. Garnish with green peas and pimiento. Cover and bake until shrimp is pink and clams are opened. MAKES 6 SERVINGS.

½ cup olive oil
1 onion, chopped
1 green pepper, chopped
½ pound (approximately) boneless pork
*   steaks or chops*
1 pound boneless chicken breasts or 1½
*   pounds thighs*
2 cloves garlic, minced
2 bay leaves, crumbled
1½ teaspoons salt
¼ teaspoon hot pepper sauce
2¼ cups rice (1 pound)
5 cups chicken broth
8 or 10 saffron threads
½ cup dry wine
Turmeric (optional)
1 dozen clams or mussels in the shell
½ pound crab meat
1 pound shrimp, shelled
1 10-ounce package frozen asparagus
*   spears*
1 8-ounce can green peas, drained
1 6-ounce can pimiento, drained

SHRIMP FONDUE

Shell shrimp, leaving tails intact, or shrimp can be cooked with shells on. Combine oil and butter in fondue pot to fill about ½ full or follow manufacturer's instructions. Heat. Each guest spears a shrimp on a fondue fork or bamboo skewer and cooks in hot fat. Shrimp cooks more evenly if only 3 are put in hot fat at a time. Cook until shrimp turn pink. Allow shrimp to cool, remove shell, and dip in sauce. MAKES 4 SUPPER SERVINGS.

1½ pounds shrimp
Half oil, half butter or margarine
*Spicy Red Cocktail Sauce
*Florida Tartar Sauce
*Instant Russian Dressing or *Garlic
*   Mayonnaise*

EGGS
AND
CHEESE

Eggs are big business in the South, but before the commercial era farm women and many city folk maintained flocks of laying hens, primarily to supply their families. Deviled eggs are on the table at every family reunion, picnic, and potluck in the South. Eggs are served for supper and for breakfast in the ordinary ways—scrambled, poached, soft-boiled, or fried. The sauce for hot cooked grits is often the semirunny yolk of a fried or poached egg.

Say "cheese" in the South and it means sharp Cheddar—the well-aged American-made cheese once referred to as "rat-trap cheese" for its fabled efficiency as a rat bait. In recent years, a few country stores in the South have specialized in buying commercial Cheddars in bulk and aging them in humidity-and-temperature-controlled rooms to approximate the old-time flavor and texture of the cheese. Cheddar goes into anything calling for cheese—macaroni and cheese primarily, with spaghetti and tomato sauce, cheese omelet or soufflé, for a golden glow atop casseroles, and in rich pimiento and cheese sandwich spread.

ASPARAGUS EGG CASSEROLE

Preheat oven to 350°. Drain asparagus, reserving liquid, and set aside. Melt butter in saucepan. Stir in flour, salt, and pepper sauce. Add milk to asparagus liquid to make 1½ cups. Add milk mixture to flour mixture and cook and stir until smooth and thickened. Add cheese and heat and stir until melted. Spread spoonful or two of sauce in greased 10×6-inch baking dish. Arrange 2 eggs in the sauce, then arrange asparagus over layer of eggs. Arrange remaining eggs over asparagus, then top with sauce. Sprinkle with bread crumbs. Bake 20 minutes or until bubbly. Serve on rice or toast.
MAKES 4 SERVINGS.

1 19-ounce can asparagus spears
2 tablespoons butter or margarine
3 tablespoons flour
½ teaspoon salt
Dash hot pepper sauce
Milk
1 cup shredded Cheddar cheese (4 ounces)
4–6 hard-cooked eggs, sliced
Fine dry bread crumbs

BAKED EGGS WITH CHEESE

Preheat oven to 350°. Place butter in 4 individual baking dishes or a 9-inch square pan or pie plate. Heat in oven until melted. Place tomatoes in hot butter, arranging 1 layer deep. Sprinkle generously with salt and pepper. Break eggs, 1 or 2 for each serving, over tomatoes. Sprinkle with salt and pepper. Place a slice of cheese on each egg or pair of eggs. Bake until eggs are done as desired, about 15 minutes for firm whites and soft yolks. MAKES 4 SERVINGS.

¼ cup butter or margarine
1 large or 2 small tomatoes, sliced
Salt
Pepper
4–8 eggs
4 1-ounce slices Muenster or Swiss cheese

BAKED EGGS WITH TOMATO

Preheat oven to 375°. Slice sausage links or smoked sausage. Grease heavy skillet lightly with oil. Heat, add sausage, and cook, stirring or turning now and then, until lightly browned. Divide sausage among 6 shallow individual baking dishes. Break an egg in each dish. Sprinkle lightly with salt and pepper, cover with tomato sauce, and sprinkle with cheese. Bake 12 minutes or until eggs are done to taste. MAKES 6 SERVINGS.

3 or 4 pork sausage links, ¼ pound hot sausage meat, or ¼ pound smoked sausage
Oil
6 eggs
Salt
Pepper
1 8-ounce can tomato sauce
½ cup shredded sharp Cheddar cheese

BAKED EGGS WITH PEPPERS

Preheat oven to 350°. Melt butter in 8- or 9-inch ovenproof skillet. Add green pepper and onion and cook over moderate heat until tender but not browned. Beat eggs, add flour, salt, baking powder, and pepper and beat hard until flour is blended in well. Pour over green pepper mixture. Bake 15 minutes or until top is puffed and lightly browned. Serve from skillet or lift out with wide spatula onto warm serving plate. Cut in wedges. MAKES 4 SERVINGS.

2 tablespoons butter or margarine
1 green pepper, coarsely chopped
1 small onion, chopped
6 eggs
¼ cup flour
1 teaspoon salt
½ teaspoon baking powder
⅛ teaspoon pepper

PLANTATION SHIRRED EGGS

Preheat oven to 350°. Cook sausage in large skillet until lightly browned, breaking up with fork to keep crumbly. Divide sausage among 6 individual baking dishes, leaving fat in skillet. Carefully break 1 or 2 eggs into each baking dish. Spoon a little of the sausage fat over the yolk of each egg. Bake until eggs are done as desired, about 12 minutes for firm whites and soft yolks. Place baking dishes on plates to serve. MAKES 6 SERVINGS.

1 pound pork sausage meat, preferably hot
6–12 eggs

COUNTRY SUPPER OMELET

Cook bacon in heavy 10-inch skillet until crisp. Pour off fat. Add onion and potatoes. Cook, stirring occasionally, until potatoes and onion are tender, about 10 minutes. Sprinkle generously with salt and pepper. Beat eggs just to blend. Pour over potato mixture. As edges cook, scrape toward center and allow uncooked portions to run underneath. When bottom is firm, cover skillet and let omelet cook a few minutes longer, until firm but not dry. Turn out on hot plate and cut in wedges to serve. MAKES 4 SERVINGS.

4 strips bacon, cut up
1 medium onion, chopped
2 small potatoes, peeled and sliced thin
Salt
Pepper
8 eggs

CREOLE EGGS

Cook onion, green pepper, and tomato in butter until onion is tender and mixture forms a thick sauce. Beat eggs lightly with salt and pepper sauce. Add to vegetable mixture. Cook over low heat, stirring from bottom of pan as eggs cook. When eggs are set but still moist, spoon onto toast or serve from platter with toast as accompaniment. MAKES 4 SERVINGS.

NOTE: To seed tomatoes, cut out core and squeeze tomato over sink until most of the seeds are removed.

1 onion, chopped
1 green pepper, chopped
1 tomato, peeled, seeded, and chopped
1 tablespoon butter or margarine
6–8 eggs
½ teaspoon salt
Dash hot pepper sauce
4 slices buttered toast

CURRIED EGGS DE LUXE

Mix soup, milk, and curry powder in saucepan. Add raisins. Heat, stirring once or twice, until steaming. Add eggs. Serve on muffins, rice, grits, or split biscuits with chutney or bacon curls on the side. MAKES 4 SERVINGS.

1 10¾-ounce can cream of chicken or celery soup
½ cup milk
1–2 teaspoons curry powder
¼ cup raisins, preferably golden
4 hard-cooked eggs, sliced
Toasted English muffins, rice, grits, or hot biscuits
Chutney
Bacon curls

FARMHOUSE MACARONI AND CHEESE

Preheat oven to 325°. Cook macaroni until barely tender and drain. Meanwhile, grease a 5- or 6-cup baking dish. Turn macaroni into baking dish and toss with butter until butter is melted. Add 3–3½ cups of the cheese and toss with macaroni. Mix milk, eggs, salt, and pepper. Pour over macaroni. Sprinkle remaining cheese over macaroni. Bake 30 minutes or until set and cheese on top is melted into a golden mass. MAKES 4 SERVINGS.

2 cups elbow macaroni (8 ounces)
1 tablespoon butter or margarine
4 cups coarsely shredded sharp Cheddar cheese (1 pound)
1 cup milk
2 eggs
1 teaspoon salt
⅛ teaspoon pepper

DEVILED EGGS

Shell eggs, cut in half lengthwise, and flick out yolks with tip of knife into bowl. Mash yolks and blend in vinegar, mustard, mayonnaise, and salt. Pile yolk mixture into whites. Cover and refrigerate until ready to serve. MAKES 4 SERVINGS.

4 hard-cooked eggs
1 teaspoon cider vinegar
1 teaspoon prepared mustard
1 teaspoon mayonnaise
½ teaspoon salt

CEREALS AND
PASTA

With a few exceptions, this chapter could be called Rice and Grits. Travelers from other parts laughingly refer to the cereal served with eggs and ham as "Georgia ice cream," and Southerners are horrified when Yankees ask to have grits or rice doused with cream and sugar.

Grits, sometimes called grist, goes with ham or bacon and eggs, red-eye gravy, or butter. Rice is served with fried chicken and cream gravy (one young southern woman called it a sin that mashed potatoes were served with chicken and gravy at a university in the North), black-eyed peas, Louisiana red beans, Creole-style seafood on the Gulf Coast and in jambalaya and *Hopping John. Rice recipes go from snowy white, the basic perfectly cooked rice, to red, beige, green, and yellow. Spanish Americans in Tampa, Miami, and Key West draw a fine distinction between yellow and white rice. Chicken and seafood are cooked with yellow rice, meats may be served with yellow rice, but Cuban-style black beans and picadillo go with white rice.

CHICKEN DUMPLINGS

Mix flour, salt, and baking powder in small bowl. Mix in fat, egg, and enough milk to make a stiff dough. Turn out on floured surface, knead a few strokes, then roll out ⅛ inch thick. Cut into squares or 1×3-inch strips. Drop into boiling broth, along with chicken. Cover and simmer 15 minutes. Add milk and let stand uncovered 2 or 3 minutes. Serve as side dish with fried or baked chicken or, if prepared with chicken, as main dish. MAKES 3 OR 4 SERVINGS.

1 cup flour
½ teaspoon salt
⅛ teaspoon baking powder
2 tablespoons chicken fat, butter, or margarine, melted
1 egg
2–3 tablespoons milk
3–4 cups boiling chicken broth
1 cup diced chicken, if main dish
½ cup milk

CORN MEAL DUMPLINGS (for greens or meat stews)

Mix flour, corn meal, baking powder, and salt in bowl. Beat in milk, egg, and drippings. For cooking, there should be a generous amount of liquid and enough vegetables or meat to support dumplings in a large kettle. Drop dumplings by tablespoonfuls onto boiling greens or meat. Cover tightly and steam 15 minutes. Serve dumplings with greens or meat and some of the pan liquid. MAKES 6 SERVINGS.

¾ cup flour
¼ cup corn meal
1½ teaspoons baking powder
½ teaspoon salt
⅓ cup milk
1 egg
2 tablespoons bacon drippings, melted butter, or margarine

GRITS SOUFFLÉ

Preheat oven to 400°. Slowly stir grits into boiling water, add salt, cover, and cook until grits are done, about 3 minutes for quick grits or 15 minutes for regular grits. Stir once or twice while cooking. Remove from heat and beat in egg yolks and butter. Cool slightly. Beat egg whites until foamy, add cream of tartar, and continue to beat until stiff peaks form. Fold into grits. Turn into well-greased 1½-quart soufflé or deep baking dish. Bake 30 minutes or until puffed and browned. Serve immediately with butter. MAKES 4–6 SERVINGS.

½ cup grits
2½ cups boiling water
1 teaspoon salt
3 eggs, separated
2 tablespoons butter or margarine
⅛ teaspoon cream of tartar

PIMIENTO CHEESE HOMINY

Preheat oven to 350°. Drain hominy, reserving liquid. Add water to hominy liquid to make 2 cups. Bring to a boil. Stir in salt, garlic salt, and grits. Cover and simmer until grits are tender and liquid absorbed, about 5 minutes for quick grits, 10 minutes for regular grits. Stir in hominy, ¾ cup cheese, and pimiento. Turn into greased 1-quart baking dish. Top with remaining cheese. Bake 25–30 minutes, until heated through and cheese is melted. MAKES 4–6 SERVINGS.

1 16-ounce can hominy, white or golden
Water
1 teaspoon salt
¼ teaspoon garlic salt
½ cup grits
1 cup shredded sharp Cheddar cheese (4 ounces)
1 4-ounce can pimiento, drained and slivered

PERFECT WHITE RICE

Use heavy saucepan with tight-fitting lid. If top-stove heat cannot be turned very low, use asbestos pad. Bring water to a boil in saucepan, stir in salt, and sprinkle in rice. Stir lightly with fork. Cover tightly, bring to a boil, turn heat as low as possible, and simmer 15–18 minutes, until rice is tender and liquid absorbed. Gently stir from bottom of pan to test for excess liquid. If any liquid remains, cook 2–3 minutes longer. Remove from heat and keep covered for 5 minutes. Fluff lightly with fork and serve at once. Long-grain rice provides fluffier texture, short-grain, stickier. MAKES 4 SERVINGS.

2 cups water
1 teaspoon salt
1 cup rice, long-grain or short-grain

BAKED RICE

Preheat oven to 350°. Heat butter in deep 1-quart dish in oven. Swirl butter in dish to grease sides. Add rice, stir well, and return to oven for 5 minutes. Add salt and boiling water. Cover tightly and bake 30 minutes or until rice is tender and liquid absorbed. MAKES 4 SERVINGS.

1 tablespoon butter, margarine, or oil
1 cup rice, preferably long-grain
1 teaspoon salt
2 cups boiling water

GREEN RICE

This hearty dish is customarily served as an accompaniment to meats and salads on a buffet table.

Bring water to a boil in large heavy saucepan. Add rice and salt. Stir once, cover, bring to a boil again, turn heat very low, and simmer 12 minutes or until most of liquid is absorbed and rice is almost tender. Stir in cheese until melted. Add onions, pepper, parsley, thyme, basil, and Worcestershire. Beat together eggs and milk. Stir into rice mixture. Turn into greased 1½-quart casserole. Bake at 325° 30–40 minutes, until bubbly. Casserole can be assembled several hours before baking and refrigerated. If refrigerated before baking, allow 1 hour in the oven. MAKES 8 SERVINGS.

3 cups water
1½ cups rice
2 teaspoons salt
¾–1 pound medium-sharp Cheddar cheese, diced
5 green onions with tops, thinly sliced
1 green pepper, chopped
1 cup chopped parsley
½ teaspoon thyme
2 teaspoons basil
2 tablespoons Worcestershire sauce
2 eggs
½ cup milk or half-and-half

BEIGE RICE

Melt butter in heavy saucepan with tight-fitting lid. Add rice and stir over moderate heat until rice looks opaque and is lightly browned. Add mushrooms with liquid, salt, and water. Bring to a boil, cover tightly, turn heat very low, and simmer until rice is tender and liquid absorbed, about 15 minutes. MAKES 6 SERVINGS.

2 tablespoons butter or margarine
1 cup rice
1 2½-ounce jar sliced mushrooms with liquid
1 teaspoon salt
2 cups water

YELLOW RICE

Heat oil in heavy saucepan, add onion and green pepper, and cook until onion is tender but not browned. Add rice and stir until coated with oil. Add broth and salt (smaller amount if using broth). Bring to a boil. Add saffron to a large spoonful of boiling broth and steam over boiling mixture for 30 seconds, then stir dissolved saffron back into saucepan. Bijol does not require steaming, but is stirred directly in. Cover tightly and simmer 20 minutes or until rice is tender and liquid absorbed. Remove from heat and let steam 5 minutes longer. Fluff with fork and, if desired, garnish with pimiento. MAKES 4 SERVINGS.

NOTE: Bijol is a coloring and flavoring blend for yellow rice which comes in packets measured for 1 cup uncooked rice. It is available in Cuban and Puerto Rican markets.

2 tablespoons oil, preferably olive
1 onion, chopped
½ green pepper, chopped (optional)
1 cup rice
2 cups chicken broth or water
½–1 teaspoon salt
6 or 8 threads saffron or 1 packet bijol (see Note)
1 pimiento, cut in strips (optional)

RED RICE

Cook bacon in heavy saucepan until crisp. Remove bacon and drain on paper towels. Cook onion in drippings until tender but not browned. Add rice and stir until well coated with drippings and opaque in appearance. Add tomatoes, water, salt, and pepper sauce. Cover tightly and simmer until rice is tender and liquid absorbed. Crumble bacon and sprinkle on rice. MAKES 4–5 SERVINGS.

2 or 3 strips bacon
1 medium onion, chopped
1 cup rice
1 16-ounce can tomatoes
½ cup water
1 teaspoon salt
2 or 3 dashes hot pepper sauce

SUPER WILD RICE

Melt butter in large saucepan. Add wild rice and celery and stir over moderate heat until celery is tender and rice well coated with butter. Add mushrooms with liquid, chicken broth, tomato juice, salt, and pepper. Cover and simmer, stirring occasionally, until rice is tender and most of liquid absorbed, about 1 hour 10 minutes. Serve with meat or poultry. MAKES 6 SERVINGS.

½ cup butter or margarine
1 cup wild rice
1 cup diced celery
1 4½-ounce jar mushroom caps with liquid
1 10¾-ounce can condensed chicken broth
1 broth can tomato juice
1 teaspoon salt
⅛ teaspoon pepper

SOUTHERN SPAGHETTI WITH MEAT SAUCE

Heat oil in large pot, add onion, garlic, beef, green pepper, celery, mushrooms, and parsley. Cook, stirring often to keep meat crumbly, until meat loses its red color. Add tomatoes and break up with a spoon or cut large pieces with kitchen shears. Add carrot, salt, and pepper sauce. Cover, bring to a boil, turn heat low, and simmer 45 minutes, stirring now and then. Meanwhile, cook spaghetti, drain, and place on large warm platter. Toss ½ the cheese with spaghetti. Pour sauce over spaghetti and top with remaining cheese. Pass crushed pepper at table to sprinkle on spaghetti. MAKES 6 SERVINGS.

2 tablespoons oil
1 onion, chopped
2 cloves garlic, minced (optional)
1 pound lean ground beef
1 green pepper, chopped
1 cup diced celery
¼ pound mushrooms, sliced (optional)
½ cup parsley sprigs, chopped, or 2 tablespoons parsley flakes
1 28-ounce can tomatoes
1 cup shredded carrot
2 teaspoons salt or to taste
⅛ teaspoon hot pepper sauce
1 pound thin spaghetti, cooked and drained
1 cup shredded sharp Cheddar cheese (4 ounces)
Crushed red pepper (optional)

CHICKEN SPAGHETTI

Heat fat in large kettle, add onion, garlic, and green pepper, and cook until tender but not browned. Add celery and sauté a minute or two. Add tomatoes, broth, bay leaf, salt, and pepper. Cover and simmer 1 hour. Uncover and boil rapidly until thick as cream soup, about 30 minutes. Stir occasionally while boiling to prevent sticking. Add chicken to sauce. This dish is easier to serve if spaghetti is broken or cut in short lengths. Layer spaghetti, sauce, and cheese in 2 greased 2-quart baking dishes, ending with cheese. Cover and refrigerate several hours before baking. Bake at 350° 45 minutes or until bubbly. MAKES 12 SERVINGS.

NOTE: The casseroles can be wrapped airtight and frozen before baking. Thaw and allow longer cooking time.

2 tablespoons chicken fat, butter, or margarine
1 large onion, chopped
2 cloves garlic, minced
1 green pepper, chopped
2 cups celery, chopped (about 3 ribs)
1 16-ounce can tomatoes
2½ cups well-seasoned chicken broth
1 bay leaf, crumbled
2 teaspoons salt
½ teaspoon pepper
2–3 cups cubed cooked chicken
1 pound spaghetti, cooked
4 cups shredded sharp Cheddar cheese (1 pound)

VEGETABLES

In a TV show in the sixties comedian Bill Cosby almost weekly had a letter from his mother asking if he had eaten his greens. Greens are regarded as delicious, nutritious, and necessary to provide pot "likker" for moistening corn bread. The late Huey Long once enriched a long filibuster with detailed instructions on preparing turnip greens. He had them washed through several time-killing hours.

Southerners still take trouble with vegetables, though frozen vegetables are rapidly becoming commonplace. Old-fashioned vegetable dinners still exist in the South when fine fresh things are available, and a late July dinner on a southern farm usually consists of fresh field peas, fresh corn on the cob cooked almost the moment it is gathered, fresh butter beans, fresh okra, fresh summer squash and, for salad, a platter of red ripe tomatoes and aromatic cucumbers and green peppers.

That's real southern eatin'!

ASPARAGUS SAUTÉ

Wash asparagus and snap off butts, which will snap at point where tenderness begins. Thinly slice stalks diagonally, leaving tips in longer pieces. Heat skillet, add butter, and tilt to melt butter. Add asparagus and cook over moderate heat, stirring often, until glazed and crisp-tender. Sprinkle with salt, pepper, sugar, and lemon juice. Transfer to serving dish. MAKES 4 SERVINGS.

1 pound asparagus
2 tablespoons butter or margarine
Salt
Pepper
Pinch sugar
Few drops lemon juice

LONGBRANCH GREEN BEANS

Snap off tips but leave beans whole. Wash and place in saucepan. Add water to a depth of ½ inch. Add butter and salt. Cover and cook over moderate heat until beans are barely tender, 10–12 minutes. Shake pan 2 or 3 times while cooking to prevent scorching. Check about halfway through cooking time and add boiling water if needed, but most of the liquid should be evaporated when beans are tender. Serve hot. MAKES 4–6 SERVINGS.

1½ pounds tender small green beans
Water
2 tablespoons butter or margarine
½ teaspoon salt

KEY WEST BLACK BEANS AND RICE

Cover beans generously with water and soak overnight. Or bring to a boil, cover, and soak 2 hours. Place beans with soaking water in large kettle. Add ½ the salt pork, ½ the green pepper, ½ the onion, and ½ teaspoon salt. Cover, bring to a boil, turn heat low, and simmer until beans are tender and begin to burst, 1–2 hours, depending on age and moisture content of beans. Stir now and then while cooking and add water if needed to keep beans from sticking. Heat oil and remaining salt pork in skillet until pork bits begin to brown. Add remaining green pepper, onion, salt, and garlic. Cook until onion is tender but not browned. Add to beans with vinegar. Simmer 45 minutes. Mash some of beans against sides of kettle to thicken liquid. It should resemble gravy. Serve over rice and pass onion to sprinkle on as desired. MAKES 6–8 SERVINGS.

1 pound dried black beans
Water
½ pound salt pork, diced
2 large green peppers, coarsely chopped
2 medium onions, coarsely chopped
1½ teaspoons salt
¼ cup olive or other oil
2 cloves garlic, crushed
1 tablespoon vinegar
Hot cooked rice
Finely chopped onion

NEW ORLEANS RED BEANS AND RICE

Combine beans and 5 cups water in large kettle. Soak overnight or bring to a boil, cover and boil 2 minutes, and let stand 30 minutes. Add ham hock, cover, bring to a boil, turn heat low, and simmer 1½ hours or until beans are tender. Meanwhile, sauté salt pork, onion, and garlic in oil until onion is tender but not brown. Add parsley and cook, while stirring, a few seconds. Add to beans, season with salt, cover, and simmer 30 minutes longer. Serve over hot cooked rice. MAKES 4 SERVINGS.

2 cups red kidney beans (12 ounces)
5–6 cups water
1 ham hock or ham bone
¼ pound salt pork, diced
1 onion, chopped
2 cloves garlic, minced
2 tablespoons oil
2 tablespoons instant minced parsley or 4
*   tablespoons fresh*
1½ teaspoons salt or to taste

SWEET AND SOUR SNAP BEANS

Cook bacon slowly in an aluminum, stainless-steel, or porcelain-lined skillet until crisp. Remove bacon and drain. Add onion to drippings. Cook until tender but not browned. Drain 1 can beans, but use liquid in other can. Add the beans with liquid from 1 can to onion mixture. Add sugar and vinegar. Mix well, cover, and simmer 24–30 minutes. Transfer to serving bowl and crumble bacon over beans. Serve hot. MAKES 4–6 SERVINGS.

2 slices bacon
½ onion, sliced
2 16-ounce cans cut green beans
⅓ cup sugar
⅓ cup vinegar

BAKED BUTTERED BEETS

No salt is needed in this dish.

Preheat oven to 350°. Peel beets and slice thin. Arrange ½ the beets in greased 5-cup baking dish. Cut ½ the butter in small pieces and distribute over beets. Sprinkle with lemon juice, 1 teaspoon sugar, and pepper to taste. Arrange remaining beets over first layer, top with remaining butter, sugar, and pepper to taste. Cover tightly, using foil if baking dish has no cover, and bake 1 hour or until beets are tender. MAKES 4 SERVINGS.

4–5 medium beets (1 bunch)
2 tablespoons butter or margarine
1 teaspoon lemon juice
2 teaspoons sugar
Pepper

BROCCOLI GOLD COAST

Wash broccoli, cut off stems, and cut stems in chunks. Put stems and leaves in large skillet or saucepan. Arrange flowerets over stems. Sprinkle lightly with salt and add boiling water to a depth of ½ inch. Cover, bring to a boil, and cook until broccoli is barely tender, 15–18 minutes. Drain, reserving liquid for gravy or soup. Arrange broccoli in a shallow baking dish with stem portions underneath and flowerets on top. Spoon mayonnaise in a strip across broccoli. Sprinkle mayonnaise with cheese. Broil until cheese and mayonnaise are golden, about 4 minutes. MAKES 4–6 SERVINGS.

1½ pounds broccoli or 2 10-ounce
  packages frozen
Salt
Boiling water
½ cup mayonnaise
2 tablespoons grated Parmesan cheese

BROCCOLI PUDDING

Preheat oven to 350°. Place butter and onion in 1½-quart baking dish and place in heated oven. Beat eggs in bowl, then beat in milk, salt, and pepper sauce. Add crumbs and chopped broccoli and mix well. Remove baking dish from oven. Tilt dish to grease sides. Pour onion and butter into broccoli mixture, mix well, then turn mixture into prepared dish. If used, press a few broccoli flowerets into pudding. Bake 1 hour or until center remains firm when dish is shaken. A knife inserted in center will come out coated with liquid due to moistness of broccoli, but no uncooked egg mixture will cling to knife. Serve hot as a vegetable or with creamed eggs or cheese sauce as an entree. MAKES 4–6 SERVINGS.

2 tablespoons butter or margarine
1 small onion, finely chopped
2 eggs
1 cup milk
1 teaspoon salt
Dash hot pepper sauce
½ cup Italian-style fine bread crumbs
1½ cups coarsely chopped drained cooked broccoli
Broccoli flowerets (optional)

PAN-BRAISED CABBAGE

Shred or chop cabbage. Heat drippings or fat in large skillet or saucepan. Add cabbage, sprinkle with salt, cover, and braise over moderate heat 10 minutes or until cabbage is slightly wilted. Stir from bottom of pan, add water, cover, and braise 10 minutes longer, stirring once or twice. Serve hot with vinegar or Old Sour on the side. MAKES 4 SERVINGS.

1 small or ½ large head cabbage
2 tablespoons bacon drippings, oil, butter, or margarine
1 teaspoon salt
2 tablespoons water
Vinegar or *Key West Old Sour

SPRING CABBAGE

Combine cabbage in large saucepan or skillet with salt, pepper, and milk. Cover and simmer 10–12 minutes, until cabbage is crisp-tender. Beat eggs lightly and stir a spoonful or two of the hot cabbage liquid into eggs. Stir egg mixture into cabbage and cook and stir a minute or two, until eggs are mixed through cabbage and set. Serve hot with vinegar, Pepper Vinegar, or Old Sour on the side. MAKES 4 SERVINGS.

1 small or ½ large head cabbage, shredded
1 teaspoon salt
¼ teaspoon white pepper
½ cup milk
2 eggs
Vinegar, *Pepper Vinegar, or *Key West Old Sour

BAKED CARROTS

Preheat oven to 350° (or higher, up to 400°, if carrots are to be baked along with other dishes calling for higher temperatures). Melt butter in a 1½-quart baking dish in oven. Add carrots, green pepper, salt, and boiling water. Cover, using aluminum foil if baking dish has no cover. Bake 45 minutes or until carrots are tender. Sprinkle with parsley. MAKES 4 SERVINGS.

2 tablespoons butter or margarine
6–8 carrots, peeled and thinly sliced
½ small green pepper, diced
1 teaspoon salt
½ cup boiling water
Minced parsley

FRENCH CARROTS

Combine carrots and onions in saucepan. Add boiling water almost to level of combined vegetables and sprinkle with salt and pepper. Cover tightly and cook 1 hour or until most of liquid is absorbed and carrots are very tender. Add butter, mix, cover, and place over low heat about 1 minute. Transfer to a warm serving dish. MAKES 4–6 SERVINGS.

1 pound carrots, peeled and sliced
2 medium onions, chopped
Boiling water
1 teaspoon salt
⅛ teaspoon pepper
2 tablespoons butter, margarine, or bacon
  drippings

BUFFET CELERY WITH ALMONDS

Preheat oven to 350°. Combine celery, salt, and water in saucepan. Cover, bring to a boil, turn heat low, and cook 10 minutes or until celery is tender but not mushy. Drain well, reserving broth. Add milk or cream to broth to make 1 cup. Melt butter in saucepan. Stir in flour and broth seasoning. Add liquid and cook and stir until smooth and thickened. Add celery and almonds and mix well. Turn into greased 8- or 9-inch pie plate. Sprinkle with crumbs. Bake 25–30 minutes, until heated through. If desired, broil a minute or two to brown top. Serve hot. MAKES 4 SERVINGS.

4 cups coarsely sliced celery (about 1
  bunch)
½ teaspoon salt
½ cup water
Milk or cream
2 tablespoons butter or margarine
2 tablespoons flour
1 envelope or teaspoon chicken broth
  seasoning
¼ cup slivered blanched almonds
3–4 tablespoons fine dry bread crumbs

CORN ON THE COB

Cook corn as soon as possible after harvest and keep refrigerated until almost the moment of cooking. Avoid overcrowding pot when cooking by this method. Cook two potfuls if necessary.

In large skillet with tight-fitting lid or other large kettle bring 1 inch water to a boil. Shuck corn and remove silks, using small knife or stiff brush if helpful. Add corn 1 layer deep to boiling water and sprinkle lightly with sugar (about 1 teaspoon). Cover, bring again to a boil, and immediately remove from heat. Let stand covered 8–10 minutes. Corn cooked by this method can stand up to 30 minutes in hot water without overcooking. Serve hot with butter or margarine, salt, pepper, seasoned salt, onion or garlic salt, celery salt, or hickory smoke salt. ALLOW 2 EARS PER PERSON.

Water
6–8 ears fresh sweet corn
Sugar

GRANDMA'S CORN CUSTARD

Preheat oven to 350°. Heat butter in 1½-quart baking dish in oven. Beat eggs in bowl, then beat in flour, salt, pepper sauce, and milk. Add pimiento and corn and mix well. Remove baking dish from oven and tilt to fully grease sides. Pour butter into corn and mix well. Turn into prepared baking dish. Bake 1 hour or until knife inserted in center comes out clean. Serve hot as accompaniment to pork, ham, chicken, or meat loaf. MAKES 4 SERVINGS.

2 tablespoons butter or margarine
2 eggs
1 tablespoon flour
½ teaspoon salt
Dash hot pepper sauce
1 cup milk
1 2-ounce can pimiento, well drained and diced
1 16-ounce can cream-style corn, golden or white

GRILL-ROASTED CORN

Pull shucks down on corn, remove silks, then push shucks back in place. Tie with clean string if needed to hold shucks in place. Soak in large pail of ice water 30–60 minutes. Remove corn from ice water and place on grill over hot coals. Roast 30–45 minutes, turning frequently to cook evenly, until milk is set when a corn kernel is punctured with fingernail or tip of knife. Serve hot with salt, pepper, butter, and other desired condiments. ALLOW 2 EARS PER PERSON.

6–8 ears fresh sweet corn
Ice water

BROILED EGGPLANT AND CHEESE

Wash eggplant but do not peel. Cut into ¼-inch crosswise slices. Arrange on well-greased baking sheet. Brush generously with oil and sprinkle with garlic salt and pepper. Broil until tinged with brown, turn carefully, brush again with oil, and broil until lightly browned. Sprinkle cheese on eggplant and broil until melted. Sprinkle with parsley. MAKES 4–6 SERVINGS.

1 large eggplant
Oil
Garlic salt
Pepper
1–1½ cups shredded mozzarella or Cheddar cheese
Minced parsley

LOUISIANA STUFFED EGGPLANT

Preheat oven to 375°. Cut eggplants in halves lengthwise, place cut side down in greased baking pan, and add boiling water to a depth of ½ inch. Bake 30 minutes or until eggplant is tender when pierced with a fork. Turn eggplant cut side up and cool while preparing stuffing. Heat oil in large skillet. Add onion, green pepper, celery, and garlic. Cook, stirring now and then, until onion is tender. Add shrimp, cracker crumbs, salt, and pepper sauce. Mix well. Cut flesh from eggplant, leaving shells about ½ inch thick. Cut eggplant into small pieces. Add to shrimp mixture and mix well. Pile into eggplant shells. Return to baking pan. Add more boiling water if needed. Bake 15–20 minutes or until lightly browned. MAKES 4 SERVINGS.

2 medium eggplants
Boiling water
2 tablespoons oil
1 large onion, finely chopped
1 green pepper, finely chopped
1 cup finely chopped celery
2 cloves garlic, minced
½ pound cleaned cooked shrimp or 1½ cups chopped cooked ham
1 cup cracker crumbs
1 teaspoon salt or ½ teaspoon with ham
2 or 3 dashes hot pepper sauce

GREENS WITH CARROTS

Combine carrots, green pepper, and butter in large saucepan. Cover and cook over medium heat 5–10 minutes, until carrots are tender. Meanwhile, wash greens, snip leaves off stems, and shred coarsely. Add greens with the water that clings to them and salt to carrot mixture. Cover and cook until tender, about 10 minutes for kale or chard and 5 minutes for spinach. Mix lightly, transfer to serving bowl, and serve hot. MAKES 4 SERVINGS.

2 large carrots, peeled and thinly sliced
1 green pepper, thinly sliced
2 tablespoons butter or margarine
½ pound kale, spinach, or chard
1 teaspoon salt

GREENS AND POTATOES

Wash greens thoroughly, discard tough stems, and drain greens well. Heat oil in large kettle. Add turnip greens, kale, potatoes, boiling water, salt, and sugar. Cover and boil slowly 15 minutes. Add spinach and boil 5 minutes or until spinach is wilted. Add pepper and cayenne. Toss lightly, being careful not to mash potatoes. Transfer to warm serving dish. Serve hot. MAKES 4–6 SERVINGS.

1 bunch turnip greens
1 bunch kale
½ pound spinach
2 tablespoons oil, butter, or margarine
2 potatoes, peeled and cubed
¼ cup boiling water
1½ teaspoons salt
½ teaspoon sugar
¼ teaspoon pepper
Dash cayenne or hot pepper sauce

GREENS WITH CORN MEAL DUMPLINGS

Wash greens thoroughly by lifting up and down in large pan or sink of lukewarm water. Cut off tough stems and shred tops coarsely. Cut salt pork in thin slices from top almost to rind. Place in large pot with 1 inch water and the greens. Sprinkle with 1 teaspoon salt. Cover, bring to a boil, lower heat, and boil until greens are tender, about 1 hour for turnip greens, mustard greens, or kale and 1½ hours for collard greens. Taste and add more salt if needed. Drop dumplings by tablespoonfuls onto greens, cover tightly, and steam 15 minutes. Transfer greens, dumplings, and pot liquor to serving bowl. Serve with Pepper Vinegar to sprinkle on at the table. MAKES 6 SERVINGS.

2 or 3 bunches turnip greens, collard
  greens, mustard greens, or kale
¼ pound salt pork
Water
Salt
*Corn Meal Dumplings
*Pepper Vinegar

BAKED GREENS

Wash greens thoroughly, lifting in and out of large pan or sink of water. Snip off tough stems and discard discolored leaves. Shred if desired. Cut bacon in small pieces and place in large casserole. Place in 350° oven until bacon begins to sizzle. Add onion and mix well. Return to oven for 5 minutes. Add greens, salt, and boiling water. Mix well. Cover and bake at 350° 30 minutes or until greens are tender. Serve from baking dish with Pepper Vinegar. MAKES 4–6 SERVINGS.

2 pounds turnip greens, mustard greens, collard greens, kale, or chard
2 or 3 slices bacon
1 onion, sliced
1 teaspoon salt
1½ cups boiling water
*Pepper Vinegar

SOUTHERN GREENS (frozen)

Cut salt pork crosswise in thin slices almost to the rind. Place in saucepan with 1 inch water. Cover, bring to a boil, and boil 10 minutes. Add onion, cover, and cook 5 minutes. Add frozen greens and salt. Cover, bring again to a boil, and cook 15 minutes, breaking block of greens apart with a fork after about 5 minutes. Transfer to serving dish and place salt pork on top for those who like to slice off a bit to eat with the greens. Pass vinegar, Pepper Vinegar, or Old Sour to sprinkle on greens. MAKES 4–6 SERVINGS.

1 2×1×½-inch piece salt pork
Water
½ small onion, chopped
2 10-ounce packages frozen chopped mustard greens, turnip greens, collard greens, or kale
1 teaspoon salt
Vinegar, *Pepper Vinegar, or *Key West Old Sour

SOUTHERN-STYLE KALE

Place salt pork and boiling water in large kettle. Cover and simmer while preparing kale. Wash kale thoroughly, lifting up and down in large pan or sink of water. Shake off excess water and pinch leaves off stems. Add leaves to salt pork and water. Add onion, salt, sugar, and pepper. Cover and cook 20 minutes or until kale is tender. Transfer to warm serving dish. Serve with Pepper Vinegar or Pepper Relish if desired. MAKES 6 SERVINGS.

¼ pound salt pork, diced
½ cup boiling water
3–4 bunches kale
½ small onion, chopped
1 teaspoon salt
½ teaspoon sugar
⅛ teaspoon pepper
*Pepper Vinegar or *Classic Pepper Relish (optional)

BAKED MIRLITON (CHAYOTE)

The mirliton ("chayote" in Florida; "vegetable pear" in New Orleans) is a staple in the diets of Puerto Ricans, Cubans, and Mexicans, and is readily available in markets catering to Latin Americans. Mirlitons are shaped like a large knobby pear and have a pale green skin. When cooked, the flesh has a pastel green color and mildly nutty flavor.

Peel mirlitons, using a swivel blade peeler, then cut peel from crevices with sharp knife. Cut in halves and if seed is hard, cut out. (Undeveloped seeds are soft and can be cooked and eaten.) Cook mirliton halves in boiling salted water until tender when pierced with a fork, about 20 minutes. Meanwhile, fry bacon until crisp. Remove from skillet and crumble. Drain mirlitons and scoop out flesh, leaving thick shells. Cut flesh in small pieces and add to bacon drippings with onion and garlic. Cook until onion is tender. Stir in bread crumbs, water, salt, and pepper. Mix well. Place mirliton halves in shallow baking dish. Fill with crumb mixture. Bake at 350° 30 minutes. MAKES 4 SERVINGS.

2 mirlitons (chayotes)
2 slices bacon
1 onion, chopped
1 clove garlic, minced
½ cup seasoned bread crumbs
½ cup water
Salt and pepper to taste

CAROL'S OKRA

Heat butter in saucepan. Add onion and cook until tender. Add tomato and cook and stir over high heat until most liquid is evaporated, 2 or 3 minutes. If using fresh okra, wash and cut off stems. If using frozen okra, thaw until spears can be separated. Add okra to onion mixture and season with salt and pepper sauce. Cover and cook over moderate heat 10 minutes or until okra is tender, stirring 2 or 3 times. MAKES 4 SERVINGS.

2 tablespoons butter or margarine
1 onion, chopped
1 tomato, peeled and chopped
*1 10-ounce package frozen whole okra or
   1 pound fresh*
1 teaspoon salt
3 dashes hot pepper sauce

ONIONS BAKED IN BROTH

Preheat oven to 350°. Peel onions and cut into ½-inch slices. Arrange in a greased 10×6-inch baking dish. Pour undiluted broth over onions, cover, using foil crimped at edges of dish, and bake until onions are tender, about 45 minutes. Transfer to serving bowl and sprinkle with parsley or serve from baking dish. Any leftover broth can be used in gravies or soups. MAKES 4 SERVINGS.

5–6 medium yellow onions
1 10¾-ounce can condensed beef broth
Minced parsley

CREOLE PEAS

Preheat oven to 350°. Combine drained peas, tomatoes, and olives in saucepan. Simmer uncovered while preparing sauce. Melt butter in saucepan. Add onion and cook until tender but not browned. Stir in flour. Add milk, salt, and pepper sauce. Cook and stir until sauce comes to a boil. Spoon layer of green pea mixture into 1½-quart casserole. If desired, add a layer of hard-cooked eggs, then ½ the sauce. Continue with layers, ending with sauce. Bake uncovered 20 minutes or until bubbly. MAKES 6 SERVINGS.

1 16-ounce can green peas
1 16-ounce can tomatoes with liquid
½ cup sliced stuffed olives
2 tablespoons butter or margarine
½ small onion, chopped fine
2 tablespoons flour
1 cup milk
½ teaspoon salt
Dash hot pepper sauce
2 or 3 hard-cooked eggs, sliced (optional)

HOPPING JOHN

Place peas in large kettle, add water to cover generously, and soak overnight; or cover, bring to a boil, boil 2 minutes, and let stand 2 hours. Place ham hock, onion, red pepper, and water to cover in saucepan. Boil 30 minutes. Add ham hock mixture with liquid to peas. Add more water if needed to cover peas. Cover and boil 45 minutes or until peas are tender. Add more water as needed to keep peas juicy. Add rice and salt, stir lightly, cover, and simmer 20 minutes or until rice is tender. Add more boiling water if needed. Serve hot. Sliced sweet onion or Pepper Relish can be served with Hopping John. MAKES 6 SERVINGS.

½ pound dried black-eyed peas (1¼ cups)
Water
1 ham hock, split
1 onion, chopped
½ teaspoon crushed dried red pepper or more to taste
1 cup rice
1 teaspoon salt
*Classic Pepper Relish (optional)

FRIED PLANTAINS

This long green banana retains its firm texture when fully ripe, so is used exclusively for cooking.

Peel plantains or bananas and cut diagonally into ½-inch-thick slices. Fry cut side down in small amount of hot oil in skillet until browned and beginning to soften. Turn and brown other side lightly. Place between 2 sheets of waxed paper and flatten with palms of hands to chips about 2 inches in diameter. Drain on paper towels until 10 minutes before serving. Heat oil again in skillet, add plantain chips, and fry until crisp and golden. Drain on paper towels. Sprinkle with salt and sugar. Serve with *Florida Bolichi, other meats, or as a snack. MAKES 4 SIDE SERVINGS.

2 plantains or 3 firm bananas
Oil for frying
Salt
Sugar

CHEESE SCALLOPED POTATOES

Preheat oven to 350°. Layer potatoes and onion in well-greased 1½-quart baking dish. Sprinkle each layer with salt, pepper, and about 1½ tablespoons each flour and cheese. Repeat layers until all potatoes, onion, seasonings, and flour are used. Reserve about 2 tablespoons cheese. Pour warm milk over potatoes. It should not quite cover potatoes. Sprinkle cheese over top. Cover and bake 45 minutes. Uncover and bake 30–40 minutes longer, until potatoes are tender. Let stand 10 minutes before serving. MAKES 4–6 SERVINGS.

4 large potatoes, peeled and thinly sliced (about 2 pounds)
1 large onion, thinly sliced
1½ teaspoons salt
¼ teaspoon pepper
¼ cup flour
1 cup shredded sharp Cheddar cheese (4 ounces)
1½ cups (approximately) warm milk

GEORGIA RATATOUILLE

Heat oil in large heavy skillet. Add eggplant and cook, stirring now and then, until soft and lightly browned. Add onion and green pepper and cook until onion is tender but not browned, stirring now and then. Add tomatoes and mash to break up. Bring to a boil and add brown sugar, garlic salt, and Worcestershire. Cover and simmer 30 minutes, stirring 2 or 3 times. Sprinkle with cheese if desired. Serve hot or at room temperature. MAKES 4–6 SERVINGS.

¼ cup oil
1 medium or 3 finger eggplants, peeled and cubed
½ onion, chopped
1 green pepper, chopped
1 16-ounce can tomatoes or 2 cups chopped peeled fresh
¼ cup light brown sugar, packed
1 teaspoon garlic salt
1 teaspoon Worcestershire sauce
1 cup garlic or Italian croutons
2 tablespoons grated Parmesan cheese (optional)

COUNTRY RUTABAGA

Place salt pork in saucepan with ½ inch water. Cover, bring to a boil, and boil while preparing rutabaga. Cut off ends of rutabaga with sharp knife and cut crosswise into 1-inch slices. Peel slices and cut rutabaga into cubes. Add to boiling water along with salt and generous grinding of pepper (8 or 10 turns of pepper mill). Cover and boil slowly until rutabaga is tender, 20–25 minutes. Add boiling water if needed to prevent scorching. Transfer to serving bowl and serve hot. MAKES 4 SERVINGS.

¼ pound salt pork or slab bacon, diced
Water
1¼–1½ pounds rutabaga (yellow turnip)
1 teaspoon salt
Freshly ground pepper

BAKED SPINACH

Preheat oven to 350°. Cook spinach, using as little water as possible. If using fresh spinach, chop fine. Drain spinach in colander, pressing 2 or 3 times to extract as much liquid as possible. Melt butter in saucepan. Stir in nutmeg, salt, and spinach. Beat in eggs 1 at a time. Transfer to greased 1-quart baking dish. Bake until set, 15–20 minutes. Cut into wedges or rectangles to serve. MAKES 4 SERVINGS.

2 10-ounce packages frozen chopped spinach or 2 pounds fresh
2 tablespoons butter or margarine
Pinch nutmeg
½ teaspoon salt
2 eggs

SUMMER SQUASH MIX

Cut tips off and cut squash into thick slices. Cook onion in oil until tender but not browned. Add squash and tomatoes. Cook, stirring now and then, until squash is barely tender. If too much liquid remains, uncover and cook rapidly, stirring to prevent burning, until liquid is evaporated. Stir in corn, pepper sauce, and salt. Heat and serve. MAKES 4–6 SERVINGS.

1 pound yellow summer squash or zucchini
1 onion, thinly sliced
1 tablespoon oil or bacon drippings
2 medium tomatoes, peeled and chopped
1 8-ounce can whole kernel corn, drained, or ½ cup fresh
Dash hot pepper sauce
1 teaspoon salt or to taste

SUMMER SQUASH BAKE

Preheat oven to 350° (or higher, up to 400°, if squash is to be baked along with other dishes calling for higher temperatures). Melt butter in casserole in oven while preparing vegetables. Add vegetables, salt, and pepper. Mix with spoon. Cover tightly and bake until vegetables are tender, about 30 minutes. Stir once or twice while baking. MAKES 6 SERVINGS.

NOTE: This dish may be cooked over low heat on top of the range, but must be stirred several times, and 2 or 3 tablespoons hot water should be added if vegetables begin to scorch.

¼ cup butter or margarine
½ green pepper, slivered
½ cup sliced celery
1 small onion, chopped
1½ pounds yellow summer squash, sliced
1 teaspoon salt
¼ teaspoon pepper

STUFFED SUMMER SQUASH

Preheat oven to 350°. Wash squash, cut off stem tips, and cook whole squash in small amount of boiling salted water in covered saucepan until barely tender, about 15 minutes. Cool slightly and cut in halves lengthwise. Carefully scoop out centers, leaving thick shells. Place squash shells in well-greased shallow baking dish. In a skillet, heat butter, add onion, and cook until tender but not browned. Stir in squash pulp, stuffing mix, salt, and pepper. Spoon mixture into squash shells. Sprinkle with paprika. Bake until heated through, about 10 minutes if freshly made, 20 minutes if prepared in advance and cooled. MAKES 6 SERVINGS.

6 medium-size yellow squash (about 1⅓ pounds)
Boiling salted water
1 tablespoon butter or margarine
½ small onion, finely chopped
½ cup seasoned stuffing mix
¼ teaspoon salt or to taste
Pepper to taste
Paprika

BOURBON SWEET POTATOES

Cook sweet potatoes in about 1½ inches boiling water in covered saucepan until tender, about 30 minutes. Preheat oven to 400°. Cool sweet potatoes enough to handle, peel, and place in bowl with butter. Break up with potato masher or mixer. Add sugar, salt, cinnamon, and nutmeg. Mash or beat until smooth. Beat in milk and Bourbon. Add nuts if desired. Spoon into greased 1-quart baking dish. Bake uncovered 20 minutes. Serve hot. MAKES 4 SERVINGS.

1½ pounds sweet potatoes, preferably dark red
Water
2 tablespoons butter or margarine
2 tablespoons brown sugar
1 teaspoon salt
½ teaspoon cinnamon
¼ teaspoon nutmeg
½ cup milk
¼ cup Bourbon
½ cup chopped pecans (optional)

SWEET-POTATO CHIPS

Peel sweet potatoes, using a swivel blade peeler. Slice crosswise into chips about ⅛ inch thick and drop in water to which lemon juice has been added. Potatoes can be kept in this water for as long as 1 hour. Just before frying, remove potatoes from water and dry on paper towels. Deep-fry in oil heated to 375° or cook in 1½ inches hot oil in deep heavy skillet. Carefully drop in a few chips at a time and cook until lightly browned. Remove from hot fat in fry basket or with slotted spoon and drain on paper towels. Sprinkle with salt and sugar. Serve immediately. MAKES 4 SERVINGS.

2 large dark red sweet potatoes
1 quart water
1 tablespoon lemon juice
Oil for frying
Salt
Brown or granulated sugar

CANDIED SWEET POTATOES

Boil sweet potatoes until tender, peel, and cut lengthwise into thick slices or wedges. If using canned sweet potatoes, drain. Preheat oven to 400°. Layer sweet potatoes, sugar, and nutmeg in shallow baking dish. Dot with butter and add hot water. Cover with foil and bake until glazed, 20–30 minutes. Ladle syrup over potatoes several times. Remove foil, ladle syrup over potatoes again, and bake 10 minutes longer. MAKES 4–6 SERVINGS.

2½ pounds thin-skinned red sweet potatoes or 2 24-ounce cans
¾ cup sugar
2 teaspoons nutmeg
2 tablespoons butter or margarine
½ cup hot water

FRIED GREEN TOMATOES

Put corn meal on square of waxed paper or plate. Wash tomatoes and cut into ½-inch slices. Sprinkle liberally with salt and pepper. Coat thickly with corn meal. Fry in oil heated until almost sizzling in heavy skillet. Brown on one side, turn and brown the other. Drain on paper towels. Serve hot with bacon or sausage, eggs, and grits. MAKES 4 SERVINGS.

½ cup white corn meal, preferably water-ground
4 green but mature tomatoes
Salt
Pepper
Oil or bacon fat for frying

SCALLOPED TOMATOES

Preheat oven to 350°. Melt butter in large skillet, add bread cubes and 3 tablespoons parsley, and cook, stirring often, until bread is golden. Add green onions and continue cooking until lightly browned. Add bread cube mixture to tomatoes in greased 4–5-cup baking dish. Sprinkle with sugar, salt, and pepper and mix lightly. Bake 25–30 minutes. Sprinkle with remaining parsley and serve hot. MAKES 4–6 SERVINGS.

2 tablespoons butter or margarine
2 cups dry bread cubes
¼ cup minced parsley
4 large green onions, sliced
1 28-ounce can tomatoes
2 teaspoons sugar
1 teaspoon salt
½ teaspoon pepper

TOMATOES STUFFED WITH SUCCOTASH

Preheat oven to 375°. Drain corn and mix with beans, butter, ½ teaspoon salt, pepper, and cream. Cut off stem ends of tomatoes and scoop out pulp and juice, using a spoon. Reserve pulp for soups or other uses. Salt tomato cups lightly. Place in greased shallow baking dish. Fill with succotash. Top each with ⅓ slice bacon. Bake 25 minutes or until heated through and bacon is crisp. MAKES 6 SERVINGS.

1 1-pound can whole kernel corn, drained
1 cup drained cooked green lima beans
2 tablespoons melted butter or margarine
Salt
Pepper to taste
¼ cup heavy cream
6 large firm ripe tomatoes
2 slices bacon (optional)

SAUTÉED CHERRY TOMATOES

Wash tomatoes and remove stems. Heat butter and oil in skillet large enough to accommodate tomatoes in 1 layer. Add tomatoes and cook over moderate heat until tomato skins pucker and tomatoes are heated through, 4–5 minutes. Shake pan several times. Transfer to serving dish, sprinkle with salt and a few grinds of pepper. Serve hot. MAKES 4–5 SERVINGS.

1 basket cherry tomatoes (1 pint)
2 tablespoons butter or margarine
1 tablespoon oil
Salt, garlic salt, or seasoned salt
Freshly ground pepper

SALADS AND
DRESSINGS

Salads take many guises in Southern cuisine—from honest, crisp, and flavorful tossed greens to gooey sweet salads. Some of both kinds are here. Thanksgiving or Christmas dinner without the *Black Cherry Mold would be unthinkable in some homes. Sweet salads can serve as dessert. Fresh fruit salads can be lovely and beautifully presented, and avocados are daily fare on tables in Florida and Louisiana, buttery and dressed simply with lime juice and olive oil. Home-blended salad dressings are delicious, easy, and inexpensive. Try making your own mayonnaise and you'll taste the difference.

AVOCADO ON THE HALF SHELL

Old-timers still call the Florida avocado "alligator pear," and this is their preferred way of eating it. You need a perfectly ripened avocado, not too soft, not too hard.

1 avocado for each 2 servings
Lime or lemon wedges
Olive oil (optional)
Salt
Freshly ground pepper

Cut unpeeled avocado in half lengthwise. Rap seed sharply with side of knife blade and seed usually will fall out. If not, pry out seed carefully with tip of knife.

Put an avocado half on each salad plate. Garnish with 2 or more wedges of lime or lemon. Pass olive oil in cruet and salt and pepper. Each diner squeezes lime or lemon into the cavity, splashes in olive oil to taste, and sprinkles with salt and pepper.

NOTE: To test an avocado for ripeness, hold it between cupped hands and press gently. If the avocado yields slightly but does not feel mushy, it is ready to be eaten. Contrary to popular belief, a ripe avocado can be refrigerated overnight (better than letting it become too soft), but serve it as soon as possible.

VERA'S AVOCADO SALAD

Cut avocado in half, remove seed, and peel halves. Cut avocado into large cubes. Combine in bowl with onion, lime juice, and salt. Toss lightly. Add mayonnaise and pepper sauce. Toss lightly to coat avocado well with seasonings. Cover and let stand at least 30 minutes to blend flavors. Serve on greens. MAKES 4 SERVINGS.

1 large avocado
½ small onion, finely chopped
1 tablespoon lime or lemon juice
½ teaspoon salt
2 tablespoons mayonnaise
Dash hot pepper sauce
Crisp greens

AVOCADO GRAPEFRUIT SALAD

Cut avocados in half, whack seeds sharply with flat side of knife, and lift out. Peel halves and cut flesh in crescents into bowl. Cut thick slice of peel off each end of grapefruit and stand on board. Cut off peel in wide bands, cutting from top to board. Peel off remaining white pith. Holding grapefruit over avocado to catch juice, cut out each section by running knife along membrane to core, then turn knife to disengage section. Lightly toss grapefruit and avocado. Cover and refrigerate or serve at once. Line platter or individual salad plates with greens. Arrange avocado slices and grapefruit sections spoke-fashion or as desired. Pass dressing and serve on salad. MAKES 4 SERVINGS.

2 avocados
1 large grapefruit
Crisp greens
*Poppy Seed or *Chiffonade Dressing

CARROT AND APPLE SALAD

Combine carrots, apple, and lemon juice in bowl. Toss well. Add salt, pepper sauce, chives, and mayonnaise. Mix well. If a moister salad is desired, add more mayonnaise. Cover and refrigerate until ready to serve. MAKES 4 SERVINGS.

3 large carrots, peeled and shredded
1 unpeeled red apple, diced
Juice of ½ lemon
¼ teaspoon salt
Dash hot pepper sauce
2 teaspoons dried chives
3 tablespoons mayonnaise or to taste

WEST INDIES SALAD WITH AVOCADO

Pick over crab meat, removing any bits of shell or cartilage. Put ½ the onion in bowl. Add crab, then remaining onion. Sprinkle with salt and pepper sauce. Pour oil, then vinegar, then ice water over salad. Cover and refrigerate several hours. Just before serving halve and peel avocados. Cut large avocado into 4 wedges and small avocados in half. Lightly toss crab mixture, drain lightly, and spoon into avocado wedges or halves. Garnish with watercress and tomatoes. MAKES 4 SERVINGS.

½ pound lump crab meat
1 small onion, finely chopped
¼ teaspoon salt
Dash hot pepper sauce
¼ cup oil
3 tablespoons wine vinegar
¼ cup ice water
1 large or 2 small avocados
Watercress
Tomato wedges

ALABAMA COLESLAW

Combine cabbage, green onions, and green pepper in bowl. Mix well. Sprinkle lightly with salt and pepper. Combine pickle syrup and mayonnaise and beat together until blended. Pour over cabbage mixture and mix well but lightly. Taste and add more salt and pepper if needed. Cover and chill 2 or 3 hours. MAKES 4–6 SERVINGS.

4–5 cups shredded cabbage (about ½ head)
2 green onions with tops, finely sliced
½ green pepper, diced
Salt
Pepper
⅓ cup syrup drained from sweet pickles
⅓ cup well-seasoned mayonnaise

OVERNIGHT COLESLAW

Finely shred cabbage and place in bowl. Combine honey, oil, vinegar, and salt in saucepan. Bring to a boil. Pour over cabbage. Add celery seed and mix well. Cover tightly and refrigerate overnight or up to 3 days. Stir well before serving and, if desired, drain. Leftover dressing may be reheated and used for another batch of coleslaw. MAKES 4–6 SERVINGS.

1 head cabbage (about 1¼ pounds)
½ cup honey
½ cup oil
½ cup cider vinegar
1 tablespoon salt
1 teaspoon celery seed

HOT CABBAGE SALAD

Place cabbage in large bowl. Separate onion into rings and arrange over cabbage. Sprinkle with salt and pepper. Heat vinegar with butter until butter is melted. Pour over cabbage and toss lightly. Serve at once. MAKES 4 SERVINGS.

3 cups shredded cabbage
1 small onion, sliced
½ teaspoon salt
⅛ teaspoon pepper
¾ cup cider vinegar
2 tablespoons butter or margarine

FLORIDA SALAD BOWL

Combine lettuce, escarole, celery, and onion in large bowl. Toss lightly. Arrange lobster, tomatoes, grapefruit, avocado, and olives in groups on greens. Sprinkle with vinegar. Cover and refrigerate at least 1 hour. Beat cottage cheese in small bowl until almost smooth. Fold in sour cream, salt, and pepper. Serve over salad. MAKES 6 MAIN DISH SERVINGS.

2 cups torn Boston or Bibb lettuce
1 cup torn escarole
½ cup thinly sliced celery
¼ cup thinly sliced green onion
1 cup cubed shelled cooked lobster or split shrimp
¾ cup halved cherry tomatoes
1 grapefruit, peeled and sectioned
1 small avocado, peeled and sliced
5 pitted ripe olives, sliced
3–4 tablespoons wine vinegar
1½ cups cottage cheese
⅓ cup sour cream or plain yogurt
¼ teaspoon salt
Dash white pepper or hot pepper sauce

GREEN SALAD WITH WALNUTS

Wash and dry lettuce thoroughly. Wrap in a towel and refrigerate until ready to make salad. Blend mustard and salt in salad bowl. Add vinegar and oil and beat together with salad spoon until well blended. Break lettuce into bowl and toss gently to coat thoroughly with dressing. Add walnuts and toss. Serve at once. MAKES 4 SERVINGS.

1 head Boston or 2 heads Bibb lettuce
½ teaspoon Dijon-style mustard
¼ teaspoon salt
1 tablespoon vinegar
¼ cup oil
¼ cup walnut halves

HOST'S SALAD BOWL

Rub garlic on interior of large salad bowl, crushing slightly with back of spoon to extract aroma. Discard garlic pieces. Place about ⅓ of the greens in bowl and toss to coat well with garlic flavor. Add ⅓ of the eggs and cheese. Toss lightly, add a teaspoon or two of oil, a generous squeeze of lemon juice, salt, and pepper. Toss lightly. Repeat layers, seasoning, and tossing twice. Serve at once. MAKES 4–6 SERVINGS.

1 large clove garlic, split
2 quarts torn greens (lettuce, garden lettuce, chicory, watercress, or romaine)
2 hard-cooked eggs, finely chopped
½ cup shredded Cheddar cheese
2 tablespoons (approximately) olive oil
Juice of 1 lemon
Salt
Freshly ground pepper

OLIVE WALNUT CHICKEN SALAD

Combine chicken, celery, eggs, olives, walnuts, salt, and pepper. Mix lightly. Add enough mayonnaise to moisten and mix lightly but thoroughly. Cover and chill at least 1 hour to blend flavors. Serve on greens and, if wished, garnish with more olives. MAKES 4 SERVINGS.

2 cups chopped cooked chicken
1 cup diced celery
2 hard-cooked eggs, finely chopped
¼ cup sliced stuffed olives
¼ cup chopped walnuts
½ teaspoon salt
Dash pepper
½ cup (approximately) mayonnaise
Crisp greens
Additional sliced stuffed olives (optional)

TOMATO ASPARAGUS PLATTER

Thaw asparagus enough to separate spears. Place in steamer basket in large kettle over boiling water, salt lightly, cover, and steam until barely tender. Cool. Place in plastic bag, add dressing, seal, place in bowl, and refrigerate 3 hours or longer. Drain asparagus. (Dressing can be saved to use in other salads.) Arrange asparagus spears spoke-fashion around a large round plate. Place overlapping tomato slices in center and sprinkle with basil, sugar, and oil. Cover with plastic wrap and let stand at room temperature about 1 hour or in the refrigerator up to 3 or 4 hours. MAKES 8 SERVINGS.

3 10-ounce packages frozen asparagus spears
Salt
¼ cup oil-and-vinegar or Italian dressing
4 tomatoes (the reddest available), sliced
½ teaspoon dried basil or 1 tablespoon minced fresh
1 teaspoon sugar
1 tablespoon oil, preferably olive

CRISPED LETTUCE SALAD

Wash lettuce, drain thoroughly on paper towel, then dry well. Break lettuce into bite-size pieces and make a layer about 1 inch deep in salad bowl. Spread thinly with mayonnaise, then add a layer of onion. Sprinkle lightly with sugar. Add a layer of green peas. Repeat layers, using remaining lettuce and other ingredients and ending with peas. Cover tightly and refrigerate 2–3 hours. Sprinkle with bacon. Toss lightly, season with salt and pepper if desired, and serve. MAKES 4 SERVINGS.

1 small head iceberg lettuce
¼ cup mayonnaise
1 medium onion, thinly sliced
2 teaspoons sugar
1 8½-ounce can green peas, well drained
2 strips cooked bacon, crumbled
  (optional)
Salt
Pepper

SALAD MIMOSA

Wash lettuce and watercress and drain well. Tear into bite-size pieces into salad bowl. Press egg yolks through sieve with back of spoon. Sprinkle on lettuce. Cover and refrigerate until ready to serve. Meanwhile, mix salt, garlic salt, basil, and pepper. Add vinegar and water and stir until salts are dissolved. Beat in oil. Pour dressing over salad and toss well. MAKES 4 SERVINGS.

1 head lettuce
½ bunch watercress or arugula (roquette, rocket salad)
2 hard-cooked egg yolks
¼ teaspoon salt
¼ teaspoon garlic salt
½ teaspoon basil
⅛ teaspoon freshly ground pepper
1 tablespoon vinegar
1 tablespoon water
3 tablespoons oil

WILTED GREENS

To prepare greens, wash well and drain on paper towels. Cut out any stems or tough parts and shred greens into bowl. Sprinkle with salt and onion rings and let stand 30 minutes. Fry bacon until crisp. Remove from skillet, drain, crumble, and sprinkle over greens. Heat bacon fat. Add vinegar. When bubbling, pour over greens. Toss well and serve at once. MAKES 4 SERVINGS.

8 cups shredded garden or Boston lettuce or spinach
½ teaspoon salt
3 slices red onion, separated into rings
3 slices bacon
2 tablespoons cider or wine vinegar

MIRLITON (CHAYOTE) SALAD

Peel mirliton, using a swivel blade peeler and sharp knife, cut in half, and remove seed if hard. (Soft seed is edible, and adds a nutty flavor.) Place in saucepan, sprinkle with ½ teaspoon salt, and cover with boiling water. Cover and boil until tender but not mushy, 10–12 minutes. Meanwhile, mash garlic and remaining ½ teaspoon salt with back of spoon against bowl until garlic is almost a paste. Stir in vinegar, oil, and pepper sauce. Drain mirliton. Add to dressing, toss well, cover, and chill several hours. Remove mirliton from dressing, which can be saved for other salads. Arrange mirliton on crisp greens. Garnish with pimiento strips. MAKES 4 SERVINGS.

1 large or 2 medium mirlitons (chayotes)
1 teaspoon salt
Boiling water
1 clove garlic
2 tablespoons wine vinegar
½ cup olive or vegetable oil
Dash hot pepper sauce
Crisp greens
Pimiento strips

DECORATION DAY POTATO SALAD

Boil potatoes in their jackets in small amount of water until just tender. Drain and cool enough so potatoes can be handled. Slip off skins, cut potatoes into cubes, and place in bowl. Add French dressing to warm potatoes and toss well. Cover and chill 2–3 hours. Add onion, celery, green pepper, chopped eggs, salt, and pepper. Toss lightly. Add mayonnaise and toss until evenly moistened. Add more mayonnaise if a moister salad is wanted. Sprinkle with celery seed and garnish with green pepper rings and egg slices. Tuck greens around edge of bowl before serving. MAKES 6–8 SERVINGS.

6 medium to large potatoes, preferably
  waxy type
Water
¼ cup well-seasoned French dressing
2 tablespoons minced onion
½ cup diced celery
1 small green pepper or pimiento, diced
2 hard-cooked eggs, finely chopped
1 teaspoon salt
⅛ teaspoon pepper
½ cup (approximately) mayonnaise
½ teaspoon celery seed
Green pepper rings
Hard-cooked eggs, sliced
Crisp greens

ONION TOMATO SALAD

Combine onions, water, vinegar, sugar, and minced parsley in bowl. Cover and refrigerate 2 or 3 hours. Drain onions, add mayonnaise, celery seed, and salt. Mix well. Line plates or platter with lettuce. Arrange tomato slices in an oval or ring near edges. Pile onion mixture in center. Garnish with parsley sprigs if desired. MAKES 4 SERVINGS.

2 small onions, thinly sliced
¼ cup water
¼ cup cider vinegar
1½ teaspoons sugar
1 tablespoon minced fresh parsley or 1 teaspoon dried
2 tablespoons mayonnaise
1 teaspoon celery seed
½ teaspoon salt
Lettuce leaves
2 or 3 tomatoes, sliced
Parsley sprigs (optional)

GREEN BEAN SALAD

Drain beans thoroughly. Blend sugar, vinegar, salt, and pepper sauce in 1½-quart bowl. Beat in oil. Add beans, pimiento, onion, and celery. Mix well, cover, and refrigerate several hours or overnight. Drain, reserving dressing for other salads, and serve on greens. MAKES 4–6 SERVINGS.

1 16-ounce can cut green beans
½ cup sugar
½ cup cider or wine vinegar
1 teaspoon salt
Dash hot pepper sauce or cayenne
½ cup oil
1 4-ounce can pimiento, drained and chopped
1 medium onion, thinly sliced and separated into rings
1 cup diced celery
Crisp greens

❧ MOLDED SALADS ❧

ASHEVILLE SALAD

Soften gelatin in cold water in saucepan. Add soup and stir over low heat until gelatin is dissolved and well mixed. Beat cream cheese with mayonnaise until smooth. Beat into soup mixture along with lemon juice. Add green onions, green pepper, celery, and pimiento. Mix well. Turn into 1-quart mold which has been rinsed in cold water. Refrigerate until firm, at least 3 hours. Unmold onto serving plate. Garnish with crisp greens. Serve with mayonnaise if desired. MAKES 6–8 SERVINGS.

NOTE: Cooked and cleaned shrimp, crab, or canned tuna may be added to this salad along with vegetables to serve as a main dish. When fish or seafood is added, it is often chilled in a fish-shaped mold.

1 envelope unflavored gelatin
¼ cup cold water
1 10¾-ounce can condensed tomato soup
1 8-ounce package cream cheese, softened
½ cup mayonnaise
1 tablespoon lemon juice
2 green onions with tops, finely chopped
1 green pepper, chopped
½ cup chopped celery
1 canned pimiento, well drained and chopped
Crisp greens

EASY CRANBERRY SALAD

Dissolve gelatin in boiling water. Stir in cranberry sauce, breaking it up to blend well with gelatin. Chill until syrupy. Meanwhile, peel orange and remove sections. Cut sections in halves and remove any seeds. Fold orange and celery into gelatin mixture. Transfer to 1-quart mold which has been rinsed in cold water. Chill until firm. Unmold, garnish with greens, and pass mayonnaise. MAKES 6 SERVINGS.

1 3-ounce package strawberry gelatin
1 cup boiling water
1 16-ounce can whole cranberry sauce
1 large orange
1 cup diced celery
Crisp greens
Mayonnaise

CHICKEN SALAD LOAF

Combine chicken, chopped eggs, pimiento, and celery and mix well. Pack lightly in greased 8×4-inch loaf pan. Soften gelatin in cold water in saucepan. Stir over moderate heat until dissolved. Stir in chicken broth and lemon juice. Carefully pour over chicken. Chill overnight or until very firm. Unmold on platter. Garnish with greens, tomato, green pepper, and egg slices. Serve in slices. Pass mayonnaise if desired. MAKES 8 SERVINGS.

4 cups finely diced or coarsely ground stewed chicken
2 hard-cooked eggs, finely chopped
1 2-ounce can or jar pimiento, drained and cut in strips
1 cup diced celery
1 envelope unflavored gelatin
½ cup cold water
1 cup well-seasoned chicken broth
Juice of ½ lemon
Crisp greens
Tomato wedges
Green pepper strips
Hard-cooked-egg slices
Mayonnaise (optional)

CUCUMBER SALAD MOLD

Peel cucumbers and shred coarsely, using a salad maker or food processor. Drain in sieve over measuring cup while preparing gelatin. Press cucumber now and then to extract as much liquid as possible.

Meanwhile, soften gelatin in 1 cup cold water in saucepan. Stir over moderate heat until dissolved. Add cold water to cucumber liquid to make 1½ cups. Add to dissolved gelatin. Tint pale green with food color if desired. Chill until syrupy. Fold in cucumber, green onion, relish, and cottage cheese. Transfer to 8- or 9-inch square pan which has been rinsed in cold water. Chill until firm. Cut in squares, serve on greens, and garnish with cucumber slices and tomato wedges. Pass mayonnaise or dressing if desired. MAKES 6–9 SERVINGS.

2 cucumbers
2 envelopes unflavored gelatin
1 cup cold water
Additional water
Green food color (optional)
2 green onions with tops, finely chopped
¼ cup pickle relish
2 cups small curd cottage cheese
Crisp greens
Cucumber slices
Tomato wedges
*Mayonnaise or *Cream Dressing (optional)*

EASTER SUPPER SALAD

Soften gelatin in cold water in small saucepan. Stir over low heat until dissolved. Gradually blend dissolved gelatin, salt, mustard, cayenne, and lemon juice into mayonnaise. Chill until slightly thickened, stirring once or twice. Fold in eggs, olives, celery, and pecans. Transfer to 3- or 4-cup mold or 8-inch square pan which has been rinsed in cold water. Chill several hours or overnight. Unmold or cut into rectangles to serve. Garnish with greens. MAKES 4–6 SERVINGS.

1 envelope unflavored gelatin
¾ cup cold water
½ teaspoon salt
2 teaspoons dry mustard
⅛ teaspoon cayenne or hot pepper sauce
1 tablespoon lemon juice
1 cup mayonnaise
6 hard-cooked eggs, chopped
½ cup sliced stuffed green olives
½ cup diced celery
½ cup chopped pecans
Crisp greens

BLACK CHERRY MOLD

Whip cream cheese with spoon or electric mixer. Drain cherries well, reserving syrup. Add enough water to cherry syrup to make 1 cup. Put syrup in saucepan, bring to a boil, add gelatin, and stir until thoroughly dissolved. Add cola or wine. Gradually beat ¾ cup gelatin mixture into cream cheese. Beat thoroughly so no lumps of cheese remain. Mix ¼ cup of the pecans into cream cheese mixture. Pour into deep 3-cup mold which has been rinsed in cold water. Chill until set. Meanwhile, chill remaining gelatin until syrupy. Cut cherries in halves. Add cherries and remaining nuts to clear gelatin. Carefully pour over cream cheese layer. Chill until firm. Unmold and serve with whipped cream or whipped cream cheese as dessert dish or with mayonnaise as salad. MAKES 4–6 SERVINGS.

1 3-ounce package cream cheese, softened
1 8¾-ounce can dark sweet cherries
Water
1 3-ounce package black cherry gelatin
¾ cup cola beverage or ruby port wine
½ cup chopped pecans

JADE HORSERADISH RING

Dissolve gelatin in boiling water. Chill until set at edges of pan. Beat at high speed of electric mixer or rotary beater until fluffy and light-colored. Add cottage cheese and beat until almost smooth. Add onion, vinegar, horseradish, mayonnaise, salt, and pepper sauce. Beat until well blended. Turn into 5- or 6-cup ring or other mold which has been rinsed in cold water. Chill until set, 3–4 hours. Unmold on platter covered with greens. Fill center of ring with tuna or chicken and top with a little Russian Dressing. Garnish with cucumber and radishes and serve with more dressing. MAKES 6 SERVINGS.

1 3-ounce package lime gelatin
1½ cups boiling water
1½ cups cottage cheese
1 tablespoon minced onion
1 tablespoon vinegar
2–3 tablespoons prepared horseradish
1 tablespoon mayonnaise
½ teaspoon salt
Dash hot pepper sauce
Crisp greens
Cubed tuna or chicken or cooked cleaned shrimp (optional)
*Instant Russian Dressing
Sliced cucumber
Radish roses

GOLDEN PERFECTION SALAD

Mix sugar, gelatin, and salt in bowl. Add boiling water and stir until thoroughly dissolved. Add cold water and vinegar. Refrigerate until syrupy, about 1½ hours. Fold in cabbage, carrot, celery, and pimiento. Turn into 1-quart mold which has been rinsed in cold water. Refrigerate until set, 2–3 hours. Unmold and garnish with greens. Serve with mayonnaise. MAKES 4–6 SERVINGS.

3 tablespoons sugar
1 envelope unflavored gelatin
½ teaspoon salt
¾ cup boiling water
¾ cup cold water
¼ cup cider or white vinegar
1 cup coarsely shredded cabbage
½ cup shredded carrot
½ cup diced celery
1 2-ounce can pimiento, well drained and diced
Crisp greens
Mayonnaise or *Cream Dressing

GINGER ALE SALAD

Dissolve gelatin in boiling water. Add lemon juice and ginger ale. Chill until syrupy. Meanwhile, peel orange, cut into sections, and cut sections in halves, removing any seeds. Wash apple and cut into quarters, then slice crosswise very thinly. If using grapes, cut in half and flip out seeds. Fold in orange, apple, and celery. Transfer to mold which has been rinsed in cold water. Chill until firm. Unmold and garnish with greens. Pass mayonnaise. MAKES 4–6 SERVINGS.

1 3-ounce package lemon gelatin
¾ cup boiling water
1 tablespoon lemon juice
1 cup ginger ale
1 orange
1 red or golden apple or 1 cup red grapes
½ cup diced celery
Crisp greens
Mayonnaise

⋙⋅DRESSINGS⋅⋘

MAYONNAISE

Place egg yolks, sugar, salt, and paprika in blender and blend until mixed. Add lemon juice and blend a few seconds. Place top on blender and open pouring spout. Blend at low speed and add oil in a fine stream. If oil begins to puddle on top, turn off motor and stir with spatula, then continue until all oil is used. If mayonnaise should separate, pour into a measuring cup, start with a fresh egg or egg yolks and proceed as above. To make mayonnaise with mixer, beat egg yolks with seasonings and lemon juice in small deep bowl. Add oil a drop or two at a time, beating at medium-high speed. Put mayonnaise in bowl or jar, cover tightly, and store in refrigerator. MAKES ABOUT 2 CUPS.

2 egg yolks or 1 whole egg
1 teaspoon sugar
1 teaspoon salt
½ teaspoon paprika
Juice of 1 large juicy lemon
1½ cups oil

GARLIC MAYONNAISE

Peel garlic and put in press. Squeeze over mayonnaise in small bowl. Mix well and serve within an hour or two. The fragrance of fresh garlic is important to this sauce. Serve on seafood or hot cooked vegetables. MAKES ½ CUP.

1 large clove garlic
½ cup mayonnaise, homemade or high-quality commercial

INSTANT RUSSIAN DRESSING

Combine mayonnaise, chili sauce, and garlic salt in small bowl. Beat together until smooth. Serve on head lettuce, mixed vegetable, or seafood salads. This dressing can also be served as seafood cocktail sauce. MAKES ½ CUP.

½ cup mayonnaise, homemade or high-quality commercial
2 tablespoons bottled chili sauce or catsup
Dash garlic salt

POPPY SEED DRESSING

Mix poppy seeds, salt, mustard, onion, and sugar in small bowl. Add vinegar and mix well. Let stand 20 minutes. Mix again, then beat in oil. Serve at once, or store in covered jar and shake or beat just before serving. MAKES ABOUT 1 CUP.

1 tablespoon poppy seeds
1 teaspoon salt
¾ teaspoon dry mustard
1 tablespoon grated onion
½ cup sugar
¼ cup white or cider vinegar
¾ cup oil

LEMON OR LIME FRENCH DRESSING

Blend salt, paprika, sugar, cayenne, and pepper in small bowl or jar with tight-fitting lid. Add juice and stir until seasonings are dissolved. Add oil and beat or cover jar and shake until blended. Serve at once on greens or avocado halves or stir or shake again to mix just before serving. MAKES ⅔ CUP.

½ teaspoon salt
½ teaspoon paprika
½ teaspoon sugar
Dash cayenne
Dash black pepper
⅓ cup lemon or lime juice
⅓ cup oil

CLASSIC FRENCH DRESSING

Rub garlic inside of small bowl or jar with tight-fitting cover. If stronger garlic flavor is wanted, mash garlic with salt until garlic is almost a pulp. Add salt if not mashed with garlic, pepper, paprika, and sugar. Mix well, add vinegar, and beat or shake until sugar and salt are dissolved. Add oil and beat or shake until blended. Let stand at room temperature 1 hour or longer, then beat or shake to blend just before tossing with greens. MAKES 1¼ CUPS.

1 clove garlic, split (optional)
½ teaspoon salt
⅛ teaspoon pepper
¼ teaspoon paprika
1 teaspoon sugar
¼ cup wine or cider vinegar
1 cup oil, preferably olive oil

Mustard Dressing: Blend 1 teaspoon dry mustard with salt and garlic for Classic French Dressing.

Chiffonade Dressing: Add 2 tablespoons minced parsley, 2 tablespoons finely chopped sweet red pepper or pimiento, 1 tablespoon finely chopped green onion tops, and 1 hard-cooked egg, finely chopped, to Classic French Dressing, cover, and refrigerate 1 hour or longer before serving. Beat or shake just before serving.

Roquefort or Blue Cheese Dressing: Add 2–4 tablespoons crumbled Roquefort or blue cheese and 1 teaspoon minced chives or green onion tops. Beat or shake vigorously to blend.

COTTAGE CHEESE DRESSING

Pass cottage cheese through sieve or mix in blender until smooth and creamy. Stir in buttermilk, vinegar, parsley, garlic, salt, and pepper sauce. Cover and chill until ready to use. If too thick, thin with a little more buttermilk. Serve on green salads, sliced tomatoes, cucumbers, or avocado. MAKES 1½ CUPS.

1 cup skim milk cottage cheese
½ cup buttermilk
2 teaspoons cider vinegar
1 tablespoon minced parsley
1 clove garlic, minced (optional)
½ teaspoon salt
Dash hot pepper sauce

Blue Cheese Buttermilk Dressing: Crumble 1–2 ounces blue cheese into dressing before chilling.

Buttermilk Honey Dressing: Substitute 1 tablespoon lemon juice for vinegar in Cottage Cheese Dressing. Omit garlic and add 2 tablespoons honey. Serve on fruit salads.

CREAM DRESSING

Blend salt, mustard, and sugar in small bowl, breaking up mustard lumps. Add undiluted evaporated milk and beat until well blended. Slowly stir in vinegar. Cover and let stand at room temperature until thickened and creamy, about 1 hour. Serve at once or refrigerate until ready to serve. Serve with gelatin salads, fruit salads, or as dressing for coleslaw or potato salad. MAKES ABOUT 1 CUP.

½ teaspoon salt
½ teaspoon dry mustard
1 tablespoon sugar
1 5-ounce can evaporated milk (⅔ cup)
3 tablespoons cider or wine vinegar

CRYSTAL DRESSING

Blend sugar, salt, and cayenne. Beat in vinegar and water. Beat in oil a few drops at a time. Serve on tossed green salads. This is especially good with leaf lettuce. MAKES ⅓ CUP, ENOUGH FOR 1 BUNCH LEAF LETTUCE.

1 tablespoon sugar
¼ teaspoon salt
Dash of cayenne or hot pepper sauce
1 tablespoon cider vinegar
1 tablespoon water
3 tablespoons oil

HONEY LIME DRESSING

Blend sugar, salt, paprika, mustard, and pepper in small bowl or jar with tight-fitting lid. Add lime juice and stir until other ingredients are dissolved. Add oil and beat or shake until well blended. Add honey and beat or shake again. Refrigerate until ready to serve. Beat or shake to mix just before serving. MAKES 1¼ CUPS.

¼ cup sugar
1 teaspoon salt
1 teaspoon paprika
1 teaspoon dry mustard
¼ teaspoon white pepper or few drops hot
  pepper sauce
¼ cup lime juice
¾ cup oil
¼ cup honey

SAUCES, PICKLES, PRESERVES, AND JELLIES

An important dinner in the South traditionally called for an enormous array of pickles, relishes, and other trimmings put up laboriously as fruits and vegetables for pickling came in season. Such ostentatious accessories have gone the way of gargantuan appetites, but a few well-chosen relishes are still put up and served proudly. Some of the most delectable are here, many recipes trimmed down to the limited time and storage space available today.

FLORIDA TARTAR SAUCE

Melt butter in small heavy skillet. Stir in lemon juice and beat in as much mayonnaise as will blend smoothly into mixture. Stir in green onion. Cool to room temperature and serve with fish or seafood. MAKES ABOUT ½ CUP, 4 SERVINGS.

¼ cup butter or margarine
Juice of 1 lemon or lime
2–3 tablespoons mayonnaise
4 green onions with tops, finely chopped

SPICY RED COCKTAIL SAUCE

Oysters on the half shell are accompanied by lemon wedges, hot pepper sauce, and horseradish. This sauce is served with shelled chilled oysters, shrimp, or lump crab in stemmed glasses or icers.

Mix all ingredients, chill 2 or 3 hours, and serve with seafood cocktails or as dip for fried seafood and fish. MAKES 1¼ CUPS, 4–6 SERVINGS.

1 cup bottled chili sauce or catsup
2 tablespoons prepared horseradish
2 tablespoons lemon juice or cider vinegar
⅛ teaspoon hot pepper sauce

MUSTARD SAUCE

Blend mayonnaise with mustard, vinegar, sugar, salt, parsley, and garlic salt. Serve as a dip for shrimp or other seafood or with *Shrimp Fondue. MAKES 1¼ CUPS.

1 cup mayonnaise
2 tablespoons prepared mustard
2 teaspoons vinegar
2 teaspoons sugar
Dash salt
1 tablespoon minced parsley
Dash garlic salt

MOCK HOLLANDAISE

Combine all ingredients in small bowl. Mix well. Let stand 1–2 hours in warm place. Serve over hot cooked snap beans, asparagus, or broccoli. MAKES ½ CUP, ABOUT 4 SERVINGS.

NOTE: This sauce can be served at room temperature, but if desired warm, set bowl in small pan of hot water and let stand a few minutes.

½ cup mayonnaise
Juice of ½ lemon
Dash cayenne
Yellow food color (optional)

NEW ORLEANS ONION PICKLE

Cut off stem and root ends of onions and boil in salted water in covered saucepan until skins slip off easily, about 5 minutes. Onions should still be crisp. Slip off skins. Combine beet liquid, vinegar, pickling spice, and sugar. Bring to a boil and pour over onions in jar or bowl. Add red pepper. Cover and chill 2 or 3 days before serving. If pickles are kept for long periods, seal in jars and process in boiling water bath 5 minutes. Drain onions to serve. MAKES ABOUT 1 PINT.

1 pound small boiling onions
Salted water
¼ cup liquid drained from cooked or canned beets
¾ cup cider or white vinegar
1 teaspoon whole pickling spice
2 tablespoons sugar
¼ teaspoon crushed dried red pepper or 1 small dried red chile

SWEET GREEN TOMATO PICKLE

Combine tomatoes and onion in bowl. Sprinkle with salt, cover, and let stand overnight. Drain off liquid that accumulates. Combine vinegar, pickling spice, peppercorns, celery seed, and sugar in large kettle. Bring to a boil. Add tomatoes and boil 5 minutes. Stir gently 2 or 3 times, being careful not to break tomato slices. Ladle into hot sterilized pint or half-pint jars and seal. For insurance against spoilage, process 5 minutes in boiling water bath. MAKES 1½ PINTS.

2 quarts thinly sliced green tomatoes
1 small onion, thinly sliced
2 tablespoons salt
1 cup white vinegar
1 tablespoon mixed whole pickling spice
½ teaspoon black peppercorns
½ teaspoon celery seed
1 cup sugar

PICKLED OKRA

Wash okra and trim stem ends. For spicier flavor, slit each pod on side. Pack okra vertically and snugly so it stands erect in clean half-pint canning jars. Add 1 pepper pod or ⅛ teaspoon crushed pepper and garlic clove to each jar. Combine vinegar, water, and salt. Bring to a boil. Add celery or mustard seed. Pour over okra, leaving ½ inch head space. Seal and process in boiling water bath 5 minutes. MAKES ABOUT 10 HALF PINTS.

1½–2 pounds okra, 2½–3 inches long
Hot red or green pepper pods or crushed dried red pepper
Garlic cloves, peeled
3 cups cider vinegar
3 cups water
½ cup salt
1 tablespoon celery seed or mustard seed (optional)

EASY PICKLED BEETS

Drain beet liquid into saucepan. Add brown sugar and vinegar. Bring to a boil, stirring until sugar is dissolved. Add beets and simmer 2 or 3 minutes. Remove from heat, add onion rings, cover, and let stand until cooled. Pour into bowl and chill until ready to serve. MAKES 4–5 SERVINGS.

1 8½-ounce can small whole or sliced beets
2 tablespoons brown sugar
2 tablespoons vinegar
1 or 2 slices onion, separated into rings

CLASSIC PEPPER RELISH

Wash peppers, quarter, and remove seeds and ribs. Peel onions and quarter. Grind peppers and onions into bowl, using coarse blade of food grinder. Cover with boiling water, let stand 5 minutes, and drain. Combine vinegar, sugar, celery seed, mustard, and salt in large saucepan. Bring to a boil, stirring with wooden spoon until sugar is dissolved. Add pepper mixture. Boil uncovered 10 minutes. Ladle into sterilized half-pint jars and seal. For insurance against spoilage, process in a boiling water bath 5 minutes. Serve with meats, vegetables such as black-eyed peas or greens, or spread with cream cheese as sandwich filling. MAKES ABOUT 2 PINTS.

*6 bell peppers, preferably 2 or 3 red
   (about 1½ pounds)*
3 medium onions (about 1 pound)
Boiling water
1 cup cider vinegar
1 cup sugar
½ teaspoon celery seed
½ teaspoon dry mustard
1½ tablespoons salt

MOTHER'S WATERMELON SWEET PICKLES

Trim green and red parts off rind. Cut white rind in strips, squares, or other shapes. Place in bowl. Sprinkle with salt and add cold water to cover. Let stand 3 hours and drain. Dissolve alum in boiling water. Pour over rind and let stand 1 hour. Drain and chill promptly in ice water to crisp rind. Rind may be refrigerated overnight in ice water, if more convenient.

Drain rind. Stir 4 quarts cold water and 4 cups sugar over low heat until sugar is dissolved. Add rind and simmer 4–6 hours, until tender. Drain and discard syrup. Make a heavy syrup of vinegar, cinnamon, nutmeg, cloves, and remaining sugar. Bring to a boil. Add cherries and rind. Boil 5 minutes. Remove from heat, cover, and let stand 24 hours. Bring again to a boil and ladle pickles with cherries into hot sterilized jars. If syrup is not thick enough, boil rapidly until thick. Fill jars to within ½ inch of rims and seal. If utensils used, including tongs for lifting jars and handling lids and cloths for wiping rims of jars, are sterilized, pickles need no further processing. However, to ensure sterilization, process 10 minutes in a boiling water bath. MAKES 18–24 PINTS.

*Rind of 1 large watermelon, thick-rinded
   preferred*
¼ cup salt
Cold water
*1 tablespoon alum (available at
   pharmacies)*
4 quarts boiling water
Ice water
8 pounds sugar (16 cups)
1 quart cider vinegar
6 sticks cinnamon, broken
1 tablespoon nutmeg
2 tablespoons whole cloves
*1 12-ounce bottle maraschino cherries with
   syrup (optional)*

CANDIED CRANBERRIES

Combine sugar and water in saucepan. Bring to a boil, stirring until sugar is dissolved. Add orange peel and cook until syrup is thickened. Add cranberries and cook over low heat 10 minutes or until berries begin to pop. Carefully skim berries from syrup, using a slotted spoon. Boil syrup rapidly until very thick, stirring often. Pour over cranberries. Chill well. Sprinkle with additional orange peel. Serve as relish with poultry, ham, or roast pork. MAKES 8–10 SERVINGS.

1 cup sugar
1 cup water
Peel of 1 orange, slivered
1 pound cranberries
Additional slivered orange peel

SPICED MADEIRA JELLY

Thoroughly mix sugar, cloves, and cinnamon in large saucepan. Add wine. Cook and stir over medium heat to just below the boiling point. Continue stirring until sugar is dissolved, about 5 minutes. Do not boil. Remove from heat, immediately stir in pectin, and mix well. Skim off any foam and pour jelly quickly into sterilized glasses. Seal with paraffin. MAKES 6–8 SMALL GLASSES JELLY, ABOUT 3¼ CUPS.

3 cups sugar
½ teaspoon ground cloves
½ teaspoon cinnamon
2 cups madeira wine
½ bottle liquid fruit pectin

ORANGE ROSEMARY JELLY

Soak rosemary in water 3 or 4 hours. Strain if desired. Measure sugar into saucepan, add water in which the rosemary soaked, and mix well. Place over high heat, bring to a full rolling boil, and boil hard 1 minute, stirring constantly. Remove from heat and stir in orange concentrate and lemon juice. Add pectin and mix well. Quickly pour into sterilized glasses. Seal with paraffin or, for short-term storage, refrigerate. Serve as a relish with pork or lamb. MAKES 6–8 SMALL GLASSFULS, ABOUT 3¼ CUPS.

1 tablespoon dried rosemary
1 cup water
3¼ cups sugar
1 6-ounce can frozen orange juice
  concentrate, thawed
3 tablespoons lemon juice
½ bottle liquid fruit pectin

HOT PEPPER JELLY

To prepare peppers, wash, drain, cut out seeds and pulpy membranes. Cut into chunks and grind or process in blender until finely chopped. Add sugar and vinegar and bring to a boil. Remove from heat and let stand 20 minutes, stirring 3 or 4 times. Return to heat and bring to a full rolling boil. Boil hard 2 minutes. Remove from heat and immediately stir in pectin. Alternately skim off foam and stir for 3 minutes to prevent pepper bits from floating. Pour into sterilized jars and seal with paraffin. Spread pepper jelly with cream cheese on small bread rounds to serve with cocktails, or serve as relish with meats. MAKES 6–8 SMALL JARS, ABOUT 3¼ CUPS.

2 cups ground sweet green pepper (about 10 peppers), including juice
¼ cup ground red chiles (12 tiny chiles) or 1 tablespoon hot pepper sauce
6½ cups sugar
1½ cups cider vinegar
1 bottle liquid fruit pectin

RED PEPPER JAM

Wash and seed peppers, chop and process in blender or food processor until minced. Turn into bowl, sprinkle with salt, and let stand overnight. Combine in large saucepan with vinegar and sugar. Bring to a boil, stirring occasionally. Simmer uncovered in wide pan until thick and jamlike in consistency, about 20 minutes. Stir frequently while cooking. Taste and add red pepper. Ladle into hot jars, seal, and process in boiling water bath 5 minutes. Serve as relish with meats or spread with cream cheese on melba toast as canapé. MAKES ABOUT 2 PINTS.

6 large sweet red peppers
2 long hot red peppers or to taste
2 teaspoons salt
1 cup white vinegar
1½ cups sugar
Crushed dried red pepper to taste

ROSY TOMATO PRESERVES

Cover tomatoes with boiling water, let stand about 1 minute, then peel and cut out cores and stems. Layer tomatoes and sugar in bowl. Cover and let stand several hours or overnight. Stir to mix any undissolved sugar. Drain juice into large wide kettle. Bring to a boil and boil rapidly, stirring frequently, until liquid is syrupy and spins a thread. Add tomatoes, butter, and lemon. Boil rapidly until thick, 10–15 minutes. Ladle into hot sterilized jars and seal. MAKES ABOUT 1½ PINTS.

2 pounds tomatoes
Boiling water
3 cups sugar
½ teaspoon butter
1 unpeeled lemon, thinly sliced and seeded

KEY WEST OLD SOUR

A bottle of this pungent condiment sits on every table in Key West, just as salt and pepper are on tables everywhere. It is kept for months, sometimes years.

1 pint Key lime juice
1 tablespoon salt
1 bird or other small hot pepper (optional)

Strain lime juice into bottle or cruet. Add salt and pepper. Cap tightly and shake well to dissolve salt. Let stand in dark cupboard until juice has turned dark amber color. Use at table as seasoning for seafood, greens, soups, and seafood stews. MAKES 1 PINT.

PEPPER VINEGAR

The simplest version of this condiment is the vinegar poured off commercially pickled peppers, but making it is easy.

Bird or datil peppers, chiles piquin, or
*   other small hot pepper*
Cider or wine vinegar

Wash peppers and drain. For spicier flavor, slit each. Pack loosely in a narrow-necked bottle. Fill with vinegar. Plug bottle neck with twisted waxed paper to keep peppers submerged. Cap bottle and let stand at room temperature 3–4 weeks. Remove waxed paper plug and cork bottle. Serve at table to sprinkle on greens, seafoods, salads, and vegetable soup.

Pepper Sherry: Substitute dry or cream sherry for vinegar in Pepper Vinegar. Serve as a condiment for greens, seafoods, salads, vegetable soup, and, especially, turtle soup.

BREADS

Hot biscuits, corn bread, muffins, spoon bread, and other home-baked delicacies were once served three times a day in southern homes. The addiction to freshly baked hot breads has faded somewhat, but hot biscuits remain a gastronomic indulgence in the South, and one easily produced. Typical southern breads are mixed quickly, raised quickly with soda or baking powder, baked and served quickly—piping hot with plenty of butter to melt into the steaming interiors.

Corn bread is as controversial as politics and religion. Southern corn bread contains no sugar (though I remember that Aunt Lucy, a proud black lady who cooked in our house, added a teaspoonful of sugar to help corn bread brown). Traditionally, southern corn bread is baked of white water-ground corn meal, and local millers still sell corn meal the day it is ground, thus ensuring a flavor unmatched by corn meal kept longer on the shelf.

Yeast breads were baked in southern homes, since store bread, deprecatingly called light bread, was not always available. Hot rolls were and still are served for special feasts such as Thanksgiving or church suppers.

But hot biscuits remain the hallmark of fine southern baking. Split and filled with paper-thin country ham, they tell a tale of culinary artistry in two bites.

NOTE: Unless otherwise specified, the following recipes call for all-purpose flour.

BUTTERMILK ANGEL BISCUITS

Heat buttermilk until warm. It may separate into curds and whey, but this does no harm. Stir in yeast, sugar, salt, and soda until yeast is dissolved. Stir in 1½ cups flour, melted butter, then enough additional flour to make a soft dough. Turn out on floured surface. Cover with waxed paper and let rest 10 minutes. Knead 5 minutes or until smooth and elastic. Pat or roll out to ½-inch thickness. Cut with floured 1½-inch biscuit cutter. Place biscuits on greased baking sheet. Cover and let rise until doubled, about 45 minutes. Preheat oven to 400°. Bake 10–15 minutes, until lightly browned. Serve hot with butter or margarine. Angel Biscuits can be reheated. MAKES ABOUT 2½ DOZEN.

1 cup buttermilk
2 envelopes dry yeast
1 teaspoon sugar
1 teaspoon salt
¼ teaspoon soda
3–3½ cups flour
3 tablespoons butter or margarine, melted

155

MAYONNAISE BISCUITS

Preheat oven to 450°. Mix flour, baking powder, salt, and soda in bowl. Mix in mayonnaise with fork. Add buttermilk and stir quickly until dough forms a ball. Turn out on floured surface and knead a few strokes. Pat or roll out to ½-inch thickness. Cut with floured biscuit cutter. Bake on ungreased baking sheet 12 minutes or until lightly browned. Serve hot with butter. MAKES 14–16 2-INCH BISCUITS.

2 cups flour
2 teaspoons baking powder
1 teaspoon salt
½ teaspoon soda
⅓ cup mayonnaise
⅔ cup buttermilk

SOUTHERN SODA BISCUITS

Preheat oven to 450°. Mix flour, salt, and soda. Cut in shortening and butter with pastry blender or 2 knives. Stir in with fork enough buttermilk to make a soft dough that clings together. Turn out on floured surface and knead a few strokes. Pat or roll out to ½-inch thickness. Cut with floured cutter. Place on ungreased baking sheet. Bake 10–12 minutes, until lightly browned. Serve hot with butter. MAKES 2 DOZEN 1¾-INCH BISCUITS.

NOTE: Biscuit dough can be mixed in a food processor. Combine dry ingredients and fats. Process a few seconds until shortening particles are mealy. Add milk and process until dough forms a ball and leaves sides of processor.

2 cups flour
1 teaspoon salt
½ teaspoon soda
⅓ cup vegetable shortening
1 tablespoon soft butter or margarine
⅔ cup (approximately) buttermilk

SWEET-POTATO BISCUITS

Preheat oven to 450°. Place sweet potato, milk, sugar, and nutmeg in small bowl of electric mixer or blender. Beat rapidly or blend smooth. Add baking mix to sweet potatoes. Blend with fork until smooth. Turn out on floured surface, knead 8 or 10 times, then pat out to ½-inch thickness. Cut with floured round cutter. Bake on ungreased cookie sheet 12 minutes or until puffed and golden brown. MAKES 8–10 1¾-INCH BISCUITS.

1 9-ounce can sweet potatoes, well drained
2 tablespoons milk
1 teaspoon sugar
Dash nutmeg
¾ cup buttermilk baking mix

CREAM AND EGG BISCUITS

Preheat oven to 400°. Beat egg well, then beat in cream. Add flour, baking powder, and salt. Mix well. Drop by tablespoonfuls onto greased baking sheet. Bake 20–22 minutes, until golden. Serve hot with butter or margarine and, if desired, strawberry or blackberry jam. MAKES 8.

1 egg
⅓ cup heavy cream
1 cup flour
1 teaspoon baking powder
½ teaspoon salt

BUTTERMILK EGG BREAD

Preheat oven to 400°. Heat drippings or butter in 8-inch square or 10×6-inch baking pan in oven. Mix corn meal, flour, soda, and salt in bowl. Add buttermilk and eggs. Beat until smooth. Pour into hot pan. Bake 30 minutes or until bread pulls away from edges of pan. If not brown as desired, put under broiler for 1 or 2 minutes. Turn out onto plate, cut in squares, and serve hot with butter or margarine. MAKES 6 SERVINGS.

2 tablespoons bacon drippings, butter, or
  margarine
1 cup white corn meal
2 tablespoons flour
½ teaspoon soda
½ teaspoon salt
1 cup buttermilk
2 eggs

CRANBERRY NUT BREAD

Preheat oven to 350°. Mix flour, sugar, baking powder, soda, and salt in bowl. Add orange juice and peel, milk, and egg. Stir until dry ingredients are moistened. Add oil and mix. Stir in nuts and cranberries. Turn into greased and floured 9×5-inch loaf pan. Bake 1 hour and 10 minutes or until a wood pick inserted in center comes out clean. Cool in pan 10 minutes, turn out on rack, and cool thoroughly. Wrap in foil or plastic film and let stand overnight before slicing. Slice thin and serve with butter, margarine, or cream cheese. MAKES 1 LOAF.

2½ cups flour
1 cup sugar
2 teaspoons baking powder
½ teaspoon soda
½ teaspoon salt
Juice and grated peel of 1 orange
1 cup milk
1 egg
3 tablespoons oil
½–1 cup chopped nuts
1 cup sliced cranberries

APRICOT NUT BREAD

Soak apricots in brandy 1 hour or until softened. Drain, reserving liquid. Preheat oven to 375°. Snip apricots into small pieces, using kitchen scissors. Beat egg and beat in sugar and oil. Add orange juice to brandy to make ¾ cup. Add to egg mixture. Add flour, baking powder, soda, and salt and mix just until dry ingredients are moistened. Stir in nuts. Turn into greased 9×5-inch loaf pan. Bake 1 hour or until wood pick inserted in center comes out clean. Cool 10 minutes in pan. Turn out of pan and cool on wire rack. Thinly slice with a serrated knife, as crust is rather hard. MAKES 1 LOAF.

½ cup dried apricots (¼ pound)
½ cup apricot brandy or orange juice
1 egg
¾ cup sugar
2 tablespoons oil
Orange juice
3 cups flour
3 teaspoons baking powder
¼ teaspoon soda
½ teaspoon salt
1 cup chopped walnuts

DE LUXE BANANA BREAD

Preheat oven to 350°. Cream butter with sugar until fluffy. Add banana chunks and beat vigorously until smooth. Beat in eggs 1 at a time. Stir in flour, baking powder, soda, salt, and vanilla. Fold in nuts. Turn into greased 9×5-inch loaf pan. Bake 55–60 minutes, until browned and a wood pick inserted in center comes out clean. Turn out on rack to cool. Wrap in foil or plastic film and let stand overnight before slicing. MAKES 1 LOAF.

½ cup butter or margarine
1 cup sugar
3 small or 2 large soft bananas, peeled and cut in chunks
2 eggs
2 cups flour
1½ teaspoons baking powder
½ teaspoon soda
½ teaspoon salt
1 teaspoon vanilla extract
1 cup chopped walnuts or pecans

FLUFFY SPOON BREAD

Heat milk in saucepan until tiny bubbles appear at edges. Slowly stir in corn meal and cook and stir over medium heat until consistency of mush. Remove from heat and stir in butter until melted, salt, baking powder, and egg yolks. Cool 20–30 minutes. Preheat oven to 375°. Beat egg whites until stiff. Carefully fold into corn meal mixture. Transfer to well-greased 1½-quart baking dish. Bake 30–40 minutes, until puffed and golden brown. Serve immediately with butter, spooning onto plate with meat. MAKES 4 SERVINGS.

3 cups milk
¾ cup white corn meal, preferably water-ground
2 tablespoons butter or margarine
1½ teaspoons salt
1 teaspoon baking powder
3 eggs, separated

PEANUT BUTTER PRUNE BREAD

Preheat oven to 350°. Combine flour, baking powder, salt, and sugar in a bowl. Add peanut butter, milk, egg, and oil. Mix just until dry ingredients are moistened. Fold in prunes. Turn into greased 9×5-inch loaf pan. Bake 50 minutes or until wood pick inserted in center comes out clean. Cool 10 minutes in pan, then turn out on wire rack and cool. Slice thin and serve with cream cheese, butter, margarine, or jelly. MAKES 1 LOAF.

2 cups flour
3 teaspoons baking powder
1 teaspoon salt
½ cup sugar
¾ cup creamy peanut butter
1 cup milk
1 egg
¼ cup oil
1 cup chopped moisturized prunes

MRS. WARD'S WHOLE WHEAT BREAD

When I was a child, being sick was almost worth the confinement to have Mrs. Ward bring this fragrant bread. Her children and grandchildren's final admonition—"Do not cut until thoroughly cool!"—is still law.

Mix 1 cup white flour, sugar, and yeast well in large bowl. Stir in hot water, cover with cloth and lid, and let rise in warm place about 1 hour, until bubbly. Stir in bran flakes, whole-wheat flour, honey, salt, warm water, oil, and enough white flour, 2–2½ cups, to form dough that clings together. Knead on floured surface until smooth and elastic, 8–10 minutes, kneading in about 1 cup more flour. Shape into a ball. Place in greased bowl, turn to grease top, cover with waxed paper or plastic film, cloth, and lid. Let rise in warm place until doubled, about 12 hours. Punch down and let stand 20 minutes. Punch down again, divide in half, and shape each half into a loaf. Place in well-greased 8×4- or 9×5-inch loaf pans.

Cover with greased waxed paper or plastic film and a cloth and let rise in warm place until doubled, about 1½ hours. Preheat oven to 375°. Bake 30–35 minutes, until browned and bread sounds hollow when thumped. Turn out on wire racks, brush with butter, and cover with clean cloth. Cool thoroughly before slicing. MAKES 2 LOAVES.

4½ cups (approximately) white flour
2 tablespoons sugar
1 envelope yeast
1 cup hot tap water
⅔ cup 40% bran flakes
2 cups whole-wheat flour
⅔ cup honey
1 tablespoon salt
1 cup warm water
⅔ cup oil
Melted butter or margarine

NORA'S CORN BREAD

Preheat oven to 450°. Combine corn meal, flour, baking powder, sugar, and salt in bowl. Mix well. Add milk, buttermilk, and egg and beat until smooth. Stir in oil. Turn into well-greased 10×6-inch glass baking dish. Bake 20 minutes or until top springs back when lightly touched. If not sufficiently browned, put on highest rack in oven about 5 minutes longer to brown. Cut into squares and serve hot with butter. Leftovers can be split and toasted in the broiler. MAKES 6–8 SERVINGS.

1 cup white corn meal
½ cup flour
1½ teaspoons baking powder
1½ teaspoons sugar
½ teaspoon salt
1 cup milk
½ cup buttermilk
1 egg
¼ cup oil

MONKEY BREAD

Peel and dice potato. Place in small saucepan with water to cover. Cover and boil until potato is tender. Drain, reserving water. Add hot water to potato water to make ¾ cup. Pour into large bowl and cool to warm. Meanwhile, mash potato, cut ¼ cup butter into 4 pieces, add to potato, and beat until well mixed. Sprinkle yeast on warm water and stir until dissolved. Stir in sugar and salt. Add mashed potato mixture and 1½ cups flour. Beat at high speed until smooth. Add warm milk and 1½ cups more flour and mix well. Turn out on floured surface and knead in enough additional flour to make a manageable dough.

Shape into a ball and place in greased bowl. Turn to grease top. Cover and let rise in warm place until doubled, about 35 minutes. Punch down, cover, and let rise 20 minutes. Roll out on floured surface to a rectangle ½ inch thick. Cut into diamonds or shape into balls about 1 inch in diameter. Melt remaining butter. Dip dough pieces in butter and arrange in overlapping circles in a 10-inch tube pan. Cover and let rise until doubled, about 50 minutes. Preheat oven to 400°. Bake until browned, about 35 minutes. Let cool in pan 5 minutes and invert on plate. Break apart with 2 forks to serve. MAKES 1 LARGE RING, ABOUT 2 DOZEN PIECES.

1 medium potato
Water
¾ cup butter or margarine
2 envelopes dry yeast
¼ cup sugar
1 teaspoon salt
4–4½ cups flour
1 cup warm milk

OVERNIGHT FRENCH BREAD

Pour water into large bowl, stir in yeast and sugar. Let stand until bubbly, about 30 minutes. Stir in ½ cup flour. Cover and let stand at cool room temperature (65°–70°) overnight or until bubbly. Stir in the salt and enough additional flour to make a dough that clings together. Work with dough hook or mixer until smooth and elastic or knead 6–8 minutes. Shape into a ball, place in greased bowl, cover, and let rise at cool room temperature until doubled, about 1½ hours. Punch down and let stand 10 minutes. Turn out on floured surface and shape into long oval loaf, tapering ends by rolling on surface and pressing ends lightly. Place on well-greased baking sheet which has been sprinkled with corn meal. Cover and let rise until doubled, about 1 hour. Preheat oven to 375°. Bake, spraying with water from atomizer used for house plants or brush with cold water every 10 minutes. Bake until loaf sounds hollow when thumped and is golden, about 1 hour. Cool on wire rack.
MAKES 1 LOAF.

1¼ cups warm water
1 envelope dry yeast
1 tablespoon sugar
3¼–3¾ cups flour
1½ teaspoons salt
Corn meal

OLD-TIME MOLASSES BREAD

Traditionally, this bread is served with butter or margarine, but it is good with Cheddar cheese, too. It can also be served as dessert with whipped cream or *Lemon Sauce.

Preheat oven to 350°. Melt butter in 8-inch square baking pan in oven. Beat egg, then beat in sugar, molasses, and buttermilk. Add flour, baking powder, soda, salt, ginger, and cinnamon. Cool butter slightly, tilt pan to coat with butter, and pour remaining butter into batter. Mix, then turn batter into greased pan. Bake 55–60 minutes. Cool in pan 10 minutes, then turn out on rack.
MAKES 9 SERVINGS.

¼ cup butter or margarine
1 egg
¼ cup sugar
½ cup molasses
½ cup buttermilk
2 cups flour
2 teaspoons baking powder
1 teaspoon soda
½ teaspoon salt
1½ teaspoons ginger
½ teaspoon cinnamon

CALAS TOUS CHAUDS (HOT RICE FRITTERS)

Cook rice in 1¾ cups water until very soft. Mash or process in blender until nearly smooth. Cool. Meanwhile, dissolve yeast in ½ cup warm water. Stir in rice. Cover and let rise overnight at room temperature. Next morning, beat in eggs, granulated sugar, nutmeg, salt, vanilla, and ¾ cup flour. Cover and let rise 20 minutes. Stir in ½ cup more flour or enough to make a soft dough. Heat fat 1½ inches deep to 360° or until a fritter sizzles in fat. Fry a test cala. If batter separates, stir in a little more flour. Fry calas a few at a time until golden brown on both sides, turning once. Remove from fat with a slotted spoon and drain on paper towel. Keep warm in oven until all are fried. Sprinkle with confectioners' sugar and serve immediately or reheat in moderate oven. MAKES ABOUT 2 DOZEN.

½ cup rice
2¼ cups water
1 envelope dry yeast
3 eggs, well beaten
¼ cup granulated sugar
⅛ teaspoon nutmeg
½ teaspoon salt
½ teaspoon vanilla extract
1¼ cups (approximately) flour
Fat for frying
Confectioners' sugar (optional)

RICE HOT BREAD

Preheat oven to 400°. Melt butter in 9-inch pie plate in oven. In blender or with electric mixer, blend or beat together egg, milk, and rice until almost smooth. Add flour, baking powder, and salt and blend or beat until well mixed. Swirl butter in pie plate to coat well. Pour butter into batter. Turn batter into hot buttered pie plate. Bake 30–35 minutes, until golden brown. Cut into wedges and serve hot with butter or margarine and jelly or jam. MAKES 4–6 SERVINGS.

3 tablespoons butter or margarine
1 egg
½ cup milk
¾ cup cooked rice
½ cup flour
1 teaspoon baking powder
½ teaspoon salt

BALTIMORE RUM ROLLS

Mix 1 cup flour, yeast, and salt in large bowl of electric mixer. Combine water, butter, and sugar in small saucepan. Place over moderate heat until hot, about 130°. Butter does not have to melt. Gradually add to dry ingredients and beat at low speed of mixer, scraping bowl occasionally, 2 minutes. Add eggs and ½ cup flour and beat at medium speed, scraping bowl occasionally, 2 minutes. Gradually stir in enough additional flour to make a dough that forms a ball. Knead on floured surface until smooth and elastic, 8–10 minutes. Shape into a ball. Place in greased bowl and turn to grease top. Cover and let rise in warm place until doubled, about 1 hour. Punch down, turn out on lightly floured surface, and let rest 10 minutes.

Divide dough in half. Roll each to a rectangle 12×9 inches. Spread each with ¼ of the Rum Filling and Frosting. Roll from long side, pressing firmly to seal in filling. Cut each roll into 12 pieces. Place cut side down in well-greased muffin cups or shallow baking pan, spacing 2 inches apart for brown-sided rolls, 1 inch apart for soft-sided rolls. Let rise uncovered in warm place until doubled, about 1 hour.

Preheat oven to 350°. Bake 20 minutes or until golden brown. Cool slightly and frost with remaining Rum Filling and Frosting. Wrap leftover rolls airtight and freeze to store for longer than a day or two. Frozen rolls can be reheated and frosted before serving. MAKES 2 DOZEN.

Rum Filling and Frosting: Melt 2 tablespoons butter or margarine in small saucepan. Blend in 1½ cups confectioners' sugar, 1 1-ounce bottle (2 tablespoons) rum extract, and enough light rum or milk to achieve proper thick spreading consistency.

3½ cups (approximately) flour
2 envelopes yeast
1 teaspoon salt
¾ cup water
¼ cup butter or margarine
⅓ cup sugar
2 eggs
Rum Filling and Frosting (see below)

TEXAS CORN BREAD

Preheat oven to 425° if using metal pan, 400° if using glass baking dish. Mix corn meal, salt, and soda. Add buttermilk and egg and beat until smooth. Place butter in 8-inch square pan or baking dish. Melt in preheated oven. Split jalapeños and remove seeds and stems. Pour ½ the batter in hot pan. Spoon corn over batter, scatter jalapeños over corn, and sprinkle with cheese. Top with remaining batter. Bake until golden brown, 20–25 minutes. Serve hot. MAKES 6–9 SERVINGS.

1½ cups yellow corn meal
1 teaspoon salt
1 teaspoon soda
1½ cups buttermilk
1 egg
2 tablespoons butter, margarine, or bacon drippings
2 or 3 pickled jalapeño or drained canned chiles
1 8½-ounce can cream-style corn
1 cup shredded sharp Cheddar cheese (4 ounces)

MYRA MURRAY'S REFRIGERATOR ROLLS

Combine milk, lard, and sugar in large saucepan and bring to a boil. Remove from heat and allow to cool slightly. Meanwhile, soften yeast in warm water (lukewarm for cake) and stir until dissolved. Add to milk mixture with 3 cups flour or enough to make a cakelike batter. Cover and let rise in warm place until doubled and puffy, about 1¼ hours. Add salt, soda, and baking powder and enough additional flour to make a soft dough. Knead until smooth and elastic, adding flour to make a manageable dough. Place in greased bowl, cover, and refrigerate up to 1 week.

About 1¼ hours before serving, remove a portion of dough and roll out to a thickness of ½ inch on floured surface. For Parker House rolls, cut with a 1½-inch round cutter. Dip 1 side in melted butter, fold buttered side over, and pinch edges together. Place on greased baking sheet and brush tops with melted butter. Cover and let rise until doubled, about 1 hour. Preheat oven to 425°. Bake 12 minutes or until browned. Serve hot. MAKES ABOUT 2½ DOZEN.

2 cups milk
½ cup lard or shortening
½ cup sugar
1 envelope or cake yeast
¼ cup warm water (use lukewarm for cake yeast)
5½ cups (approximately) flour
½ teaspoon salt
½ teaspoon soda
1½ teaspoons baking powder
Melted butter or margarine

RICH BROWN 'N' SERVE ROLLS

Mix 1¼ cups flour, sugar, salt, and yeast in large bowl. Combine milk, water, and butter in saucepan. Heat until very warm (120°–130°). Butter does not need to melt. Gradually add milk mixture to dry ingredients and beat 2 minutes at medium speed of electric mixer, scraping bowl now and then. Add egg and ¼ cup flour. Beat at high speed 2 minutes. Stir in enough additional flour to make a stiff dough that clings together.

Turn out on floured surface and knead until smooth and elastic, about 10 minutes. Shape into ball, place in greased bowl, and turn to grease top. Cover and let rise in warm place until doubled, about 1 hour.

Turn out on floured surface and shape into rolls as desired. Place on greased baking sheets, cover with greased waxed paper, and let rise until doubled. Preheat oven to 275°. Bake 20–25 minutes, until rolls begin to color lightly. Cool and pack in plastic bags and refrigerate. Rolls keep up to 7 days in the refrigerator.

For final baking, preheat oven to 400°. Place as many rolls as wanted on baking sheet and bake 6–8 minutes or until lightly browned. MAKES 2 DOZEN.

4–5 cups flour
½ cup sugar
1½ teaspoons salt
2 envelopes dry yeast
½ cup milk
½ cup water
⅓ cup butter or margarine
1 egg

QUICK ORANGE COFFEE BREAD

Preheat oven to 400°. Choose a baking pan in which bread fits snugly. An 8×4-inch loaf pan fits a pull-apart loaf. Place butter in pan and melt in oven while preheating. Stir sugar, orange peel, and juice into butter. Holding bread or rolls with tongs or on fork, turn in syrup, then place top down in syrup. Bake 10 minutes. Turn top up and bake 10–15 minutes longer, until golden. Transfer to plate and pour any syrup in pan over bread or rolls. Tear loaf apart with 2 forks. Serve hot. MAKES 6–8 SERVINGS.

1 tablespoon butter or margarine
¼ cup sugar
1 tablespoon grated orange peel
(½ orange)
2 tablespoons orange juice (½ orange)
1 8-ounce loaf brown 'n' serve pull-apart
bread or rolls

CINNAMON NUT TWISTS

Preheat oven to 450°. Mix flour, salt, and baking powder in bowl. Pour oil into measuring cup and add milk to make ½ cup. Add all at once to dry ingredients and mix quickly with fork to form a soft dough. Turn out on floured surface and knead 5 or 6 strokes. Pat out to a rectangle 6×8 inches. Brush with butter, sprinkle with cinnamon sugar and nuts. Fold in half the long way, press firmly, and cut into 12 strips about ¾×3 inches. Turn each strip twice to form a twist and place on greased baking sheet. Bake 10–12 minutes, until lightly browned. Serve hot. MAKES 12.

1 cup flour
½ teaspoon salt
1½ teaspoons baking powder
2 tablespoons oil
Cold milk
2 tablespoons melted butter or margarine
2 tablespoons cinnamon sugar
¼ cup finely chopped walnuts or pecans

FRENCH MARKET DOUGHNUTS

Combine 1 cup flour, yeast, salt, and nutmeg in large bowl. Combine milk, granulated sugar, and butter in saucepan. Heat until very warm (120°–130°). Gradually add liquid to flour mixture and beat at medium speed of electric mixer 2 minutes. Stir in egg and enough additional flour to make a soft dough. Cover and let rise in warm place until doubled, 40–50 minutes. At this point, all or ½ the dough may be covered and refrigerated overnight. If refrigerated, allow to warm to room temperature.

Roll or pat out on floured surface to a thickness of ½ inch. Cut in 1½-inch squares. Cover loosely with waxed paper or plastic film and let rise until puffy, 20–30 minutes. Deep-fry a few at a time in fat heated to 375° or cook in 1 inch hot fat in heavy skillet until browned and puffed. Turn and brown other side. Drain and shake in bag of confectioners' sugar to coat well. Serve at once. *Café au lait* is traditional with doughnuts. MAKES ABOUT 2½ DOZEN.

2½–3 cups flour
1 envelope dry yeast
½ teaspoon salt
½ teaspoon nutmeg
1 cup milk
¼ cup granulated sugar
2 tablespoons butter or margarine
1 egg
Confectioners' sugar

MILK AND HONEY LOAVES

Mix 2½ cups flour and yeast in large bowl of electric mixer. Set aside. Combine evaporated and fresh milk, butter, honey, and salt in saucepan. Heat until very warm (120°–130°). Butter does not have to melt. Gradually add milk mixture to flour mixture and beat at medium speed of mixer 2 minutes, scraping side of bowl and beaters now and then. Add 1 cup flour or enough to make a thick batter and beat at high speed 2 minutes, scraping bowl often. Stir in enough additional flour to make a stiff dough. Turn out on floured surface and knead until smooth and elastic. Shape into a ball.

Place in large greased bowl and turn to grease top. Cover and let rise in warm place until doubled, about 1 hour. Punch down and turn dough in bowl. Cover and let rise again until doubled, about 25 minutes. Turn out on floured surface and divide dough in halves. Roll each to rectangle about 14×9 inches. Roll up from short end, pressing together firmly to form loaf. Seal edges and place sealed side down in well-greased 9×5-inch loaf pans. Cover and let rise in warm place until almost doubled, about 30 minutes. Bake at 400° until browned and bread has a hollow sound when thumped, 35–40 minutes. Turn out on wire racks and cool. MAKES 2 LARGE LOAVES.

Cinnamon Bread: Milk and Honey Loaves can be made one plain, one cinnamon. While dough is rising melt 2 tablespoons butter or margarine and mix ¼ cup sugar and 1 teaspoon cinnamon. Brush one of the dough rectangles with butter, then sprinkle with the cinnamon-sugar mixture. Shape by pressing together very firmly to prevent loaf separating while rising and baking. Bake and cool as for Milk and Honey Loaves.

6–6½ cups flour
2 envelopes dry yeast
1 tall can evaporated milk (1⅓ cups)
1 milk can fresh fluid milk (can use nonfat)
¼ cup butter or margarine
¼ cup honey
1 tablespoon salt

TALLAHASSEE HUSH PUPPIES

Hush puppies originated near Apalachicola, southwest of Tallahassee, Florida, where fishing is still prime sport. According to legend, fried corncakes were tossed to the dogs, which yapped around any piney woods activity, with the admonition "Hush, puppy!" The oniony corncakes now go with fried fish everywhere in the South—and many other parts of the country. There are dozens of ways to make hush puppies. Some recipes call for beer, catsup, or tomato juice instead of milk, while others call for a generous sprinkling of black pepper.

1 cup white corn meal
¼ cup flour
1 teaspoon baking powder
½ teaspoon soda
¼ teaspoon pepper
1 onion, finely chopped
1 egg
¾ cup (approximately) buttermilk
Fat for frying

Combine corn meal, flour, baking powder, soda, and pepper in bowl. Mix well. Add onion, egg, and enough buttermilk to make a thick batter. Fat should be about ½ inch deep. Heat fat, drop in batter by large spoonfuls, fry until browned, turn and brown on other side. Drain on paper towels and serve hot with fried fish. MAKES 6–8 HUSH PUPPIES.

NOTE: Hush puppies are usually fried in fat in which fish was fried, but you can also use oil or shortening.

If buttermilk is not available, substitute whole or skim milk, omit soda, and increase baking powder to 3 teaspoons.

CORN MEAL GRIDDLECAKES

Mix corn meal and salt in bowl. Stir in boiling water and let stand 5–10 minutes. Beat in flour, baking powder, and egg. Drop by large spoonfuls in small amount hot bacon fat in heavy skillet. Cook until bubbles form on tops, begin to burst, and dry out. Turn and brown other side. Serve hot with butter or margarine and ribbon cane or sorghum syrup. MAKES 14 4-INCH GRIDDLECAKES.

½ cup white corn meal
½ teaspoon salt
1 cup boiling water
½ cup flour
1 teaspoon baking powder
1 egg
Bacon fat

MUFFINS

Preheat oven to 425°. Mix flour, baking powder, sugar, and salt in bowl. In another bowl beat egg lightly, add milk and oil, and mix. Add liquids to dry ingredients and mix just until dry ingredients are moistened. Spoon into muffin pans which have been greased or sprayed with nonstick coating. Fill pans about ⅔ full. Bake 20–25 minutes, until browned. Serve hot with butter. MAKES 6–8 MEDIUM MUFFINS.

1 cup flour
2 teaspoons baking powder
2 tablespoon sugar
½ teaspoon salt
1 egg
½ cup milk
2 tablespoons oil

Surprise Muffins: Spoon ½ the dough into muffin cups. Add a dab of jelly, jam, or peanut butter, a cheese cube, a few raisins or nuts, and top with remaining dough. Bake as indicated above.

Corn Muffins: Drain 1 8¼-ounce can whole kernel corn well (or use ¾ cups corn cut off cooked corn on the cob). Add to dry ingredients with liquids and mix lightly. Bake as indicated above.

Whole-wheat Muffins: Use ½ whole-wheat flour and, if desired, mix ¼ cup raisins with liquids. Bake as indicated above.

BRAN APPLE MUFFINS

Preheat oven to 400°. Combine bran and milk and let stand 10–15 minutes. Stir in flour, sugar, baking powder, and salt. Add apple, egg, and butter and mix lightly but thoroughly. Spoon into well-greased or paper-lined muffin cups, filling ½ full. Bake 25 minutes or until wood pick inserted in center of a muffin comes out clean. MAKES 8–12 MEDIUM MUFFINS.

1 cup whole bran cereal
1 cup milk
1¼ cups flour
½ cup sugar
3 teaspoons baking powder
½ teaspoon salt
1 cup finely chopped peeled tart apple
1 egg
¼ cup butter or margarine, melted

NORTH TEXAS COFFEECAKE

Preheat oven to 350° if using glass baking pan, 400° if using metal pan. Combine 6 tablespoons sugar, 2 tablespoons flour, and cinnamon. Blend well. Set aside. Combine 2 cups flour, baking powder, salt, and 1 cup sugar in large bowl of electric mixer. Mix well. Add milk, egg, and oil. Beat at medium speed 3–4 minutes or by hand until smooth. Stir in vanilla. Turn into well-greased 8- or 9-inch square pan. Carefully drizzle butter over coffeecake, then sprinkle with the cinnamon topping. Bake about 35 minutes, until a wood pick inserted near center comes out clean. Cool 15 minutes in pan and cut in squares to serve. MAKES 6–9 SERVINGS.

6 tablespoons sugar
2 tablespoons flour
1½ teaspoons cinnamon
2 cups flour
4 teaspoons baking powder
½ teaspoon salt
1 cup sugar
1 cup milk
1 egg
6 tablespoons oil
1 teaspoon vanilla extract
¼ cup butter or margarine, melted

VIRGINIA SALLY LUNN

Thoroughly mix 1¼ cups flour, sugar, salt, and yeast in large bowl. Combine milk, water, and butter in saucepan. Heat over low heat until liquids are very warm (120°–130°). Butter does not have to melt. Gradually add warm liquid to dry ingredients, mixing slowly. Beat with mixer or heavy wooden spoon 2 minutes, scraping bowl occasionally. Beat in eggs 1 at a time, then beat in 1 cup flour. Beat at high speed 2 minutes. Stir in enough additional flour to make a stiff batter. Cover and let rise in warm place until doubled in bulk, about 1 hour. Stir batter down to its original volume, then beat vigorously with spoon about 30 seconds. Turn into well-greased and floured 9-inch tube pan. Cover and let rise in warm place until doubled, about 1 hour. Bake at 400° 30 minutes or until browned. Cool in pan 10 minutes. Turn out on rack and cool slightly or completely. Transfer to cake plate and serve. Sally Lunn is best when warm; it can also be sliced and toasted. MAKES 1 LARGE LOAF.

3½–3¾ cups flour
¼ cup sugar
1 teaspoon salt
1 envelope dry yeast
½ cup milk
½ cup water
½ cup butter or margarine
3 eggs at room temperature

MORAVIAN SUGAR CAKE

Preheat oven to 350°. Peel and cube potato. Cook in boiling water to cover until soft. Drain, reserving water, and mash potato until smooth. Set aside. Mix 1½ cups flour, granulated sugar, salt, and yeast in large bowl of electric mixer. Combine 1 cup of the potato water and ½ cup butter in small saucepan. Place over moderate heat until very warm (120°–130°). Butter does not have to melt. Gradually add to dry ingredients and beat 2 minutes at medium speed of electric mixer, scraping bowl now and then. Add mashed potato, eggs, and ½ cup flour or enough to make a thick batter. Beat at high speed 2 minutes, scraping bowl now and then. Stir in 2½ cups flour or enough to make a soft dough that leaves sides of bowl. Turn out on floured surface and knead in enough additional flour to make a dough that clings together and continue to knead until smooth and elastic.

Shape into a ball, put in greased bowl, turn to grease top, cover, and let rise in warm place until doubled, about 1¼ hours. Punch down and let rest 15 minutes. Turn dough into well-greased 13×9-inch baking pan, pushing into corners, to fill pan. Cut remaining butter into small slivers. Punch deep dents at 1-inch intervals with handle of wooden spoon over cake. Push a sliver of butter into each and fill with as much brown sugar as dent will hold. Sprinkle with cinnamon. Cover and let rise in warm place until raised slightly above edge of pan. Uncover and bake 45 minutes. Cut into rectangles or squares and serve warm or cold. MAKES ABOUT 24 SERVINGS.

1 large potato (10–12 ounces)
Water
5–6 cups flour
½ cup granulated sugar
1 teaspoon salt
2 envelopes dry yeast
¾ cup butter or margarine
2 eggs
½ cup brown sugar, packed
Cinnamon to taste

SOUTHERN WAFFLES

Beat egg whites until stiff and set aside. Beat egg yolks until well mixed, then beat in milk, oil, flour, baking powder, and salt. Gently fold in egg whites. Spoon batter into hot well-seasoned, lightly greased or nonstick coated waffle iron, spreading with spoon or scraper to the edges. Bake until steaming stops and waffle can be loosened easily from iron, 3–4 minutes. Serve hot with butter and syrup or honey. MAKES 4 4-SECTION WAFFLES.

3 eggs, separated
1¼ cups milk
½ cup oil
2 cups flour
3 teaspoons baking powder
1 teaspoon salt

DESSERTS

Southern desserts are more rich than sweet—charlottes, custards, and molded creams. Home-grown riches—cream, fresh eggs, and fruits—endured here where family-run farms resisted industrialization, perhaps not to the benefit of the economy but certainly to the benefit of gastronomy. Blackberry cobbler requires a roadside berry patch for its principal ingredient, and charlotte russe is made sumptuous with cream so rich it is skimmed in blobs off the top of rich milk. Custard servers, a footed china bowl surrounded by cups, are treasured heirlooms in some homes. Custard is ladled ceremoniously from the bowl into cups to sip at holidays with thinly sliced fruitcake. Desserts today are simplified, but for grand occasions a charlotte or wine jelly pooled with soft-whipped cream melts the sternest resistance to such indulgence.

FIGS IN PORT WINE

Combine figs, lemon, and water in small saucepan. Bring to a boil, cover, and boil slowly until figs are tender, about 30 minutes. Remove from heat and add port. Cover and refrigerate several hours or overnight. Serve with sauce or sour cream. MAKES 4–6 SERVINGS.

1 pound dried figs
1 slice lemon with peel
1 cup water
1 cup ruby port
*Custard Sauce or sour cream

FLAMING BANANAS

Peel bananas. Heat butter in large skillet or blazer pan of chafing dish. Turn bananas in butter and cook 3 or 4 minutes, until golden-colored. Sprinkle with brown sugar and turn bananas until bubbling syrup is formed. Add 2 tablespoons rum and baste bananas with sauce. Finish immediately or set aside until ready to serve. Just before serving, warm bananas until sauce is bubbling. Warm remaining ¼ cup rum. Pour rum over bananas, ignite, and as flames flicker, serve bananas. Serve alone as dessert or as topping for vanilla or butter pecan ice cream. MAKES 6 SERVINGS.

6 bananas
2 tablespoons butter or margarine
¼ cup light brown sugar, packed
6 tablespoons light rum

FUDGE PIE À LA MODE

Preheat oven to 350°. Blend sugar with cocoa, flour, and salt. Add butter, eggs, and vanilla and mix well. Stir in walnuts. Turn into well-greased 8-inch pie plate. Bake 35 minutes or until a wood pick inserted in center comes out with moist crumbs clinging to it. Center should be moist, but not runny. Cool 30 minutes, cut into wedges, and serve with ice cream. Leftovers can be cut into squares to serve as brownies. MAKES 6–8 SERVINGS.

1 cup sugar
⅓ cup unsweetened cocoa
½ cup flour
¼ teaspoon salt
½ cup butter or margarine, melted
2 eggs
1 tablespoon vanilla extract
1½ cups coarsely chopped walnuts
Vanilla or butter pecan ice cream

AVOCADO CREAM

Cut avocados in halves, remove seeds, and peel. Cut into chunks and place in bowl, sprinkling in lemon or lime juice as avocado is added. Beat at medium-high speed of electric mixer, scraping sides of bowl with rubber spatula now and then, or mash with fork until smooth. Add sugar and beat until well blended. Pile into stemmed dessert glasses and chill 1–2 hours. Serve with lemon or lime wedges. MAKES 4–5 SERVINGS.

2 soft ripe avocados
Juice of 2 lemons or large limes
⅔ cup confectioners' sugar
Lemon or lime wedges

BERRY COBBLER

Preheat oven to 400°. If using fresh berries, wash, drain, and pick off any stems or leaves. Remove frozen berries from freezer just before mixing batter. Mix flour, sugar, baking powder, salt, and milk. Beat until smooth. Place butter in 10×6-inch or other shallow 1-quart baking dish and melt in oven. Turn batter into dish, then add berries. Bake 35–40 minutes for fresh berries or 45–50 minutes for frozen berries. Crust rises to top and browns. Serve warm with ice cream, milk, or cream. MAKES 4–6 SERVINGS.

3–4 cups blackberries, huckleberries, or blueberries, fresh or frozen
1 cup flour
1 cup sugar
2 teaspoons baking powder
¼ teaspoon salt
1 cup milk
2 tablespoons butter or margarine
Vanilla ice cream, milk, or cream

APRICOT BRANDY MOUSSE

Quarter marshmallows using scissors dipped periodically in hot water. Combine marshmallows and milk in saucepan. Cook and stir over low heat until marshmallows are melted and mixture smooth. Stir in brandy. Refrigerate until syrupy. Whip cream until stiff. Add brandy mixture and beat until very stiff. Beat in food color to tint a pale apricot shade if desired. Turn into 1-quart mold which has been rinsed in cold water or pile into dessert dishes. Chill until firm, at least 3 hours. Unmold and garnish with apricots or strawberry sauce. MAKES 4–6 SERVINGS.

1/4 pound marshmallows (about 20)
1/4 cup milk
1/4 cup apricot brandy
1 cup heavy cream
Red and yellow food color (optional)
Canned apricot halves or crushed
sweetened strawberries

Grasshopper Mousse: Substitute 2 tablespoons white crème de cacao and 2 tablespoons green crème de menthe for apricot brandy and tint a delicate green with food color if desired. Serve with chocolate sauce.

CHRISTMAS AMBROSIA

Puncture eyes of coconut with ice pick and drain out water. Place coconut in shallow baking pan and bake at 350° until shell begins to crack, about 30 minutes. Cool, crack shell apart, and pry out meat with a thin-bladed knife. Peel off brown skin and shred coconut meat.

Place 1/3 of coconut in glass dessert bowl. Peel and cut oranges in 1/4-inch slices or cut oranges in halves and remove pulp with orange spoon, holding over coconut to catch juices. Layer 1/2 the oranges over coconut in bowl, add another 1/3 of coconut, then the remaining oranges and remaining coconut. Sprinkle each layer lightly with sugar if oranges are not sweet. Average oranges need about 1/4 cup sugar. Cover and refrigerate 1 or 2 hours. Garnish with cherries and, if desired, more orange slices. MAKES 4–6 SERVINGS.

1 coconut or 2 1/2 cups frozen shredded
coconut, thawed
4 oranges
Confectioners' sugar (optional)
Maraschino cherries (optional)

QUEEN OF ALL PUDDINGS

Preheat oven to 350°. Pour milk over bread cubes and let stand until mixture has formed a thick dough. Beat vigorously with a wooden spoon, then beat in ¼ cup sugar and egg yolks. Stir in vanilla. Turn into greased 1½-quart baking dish. Set in pan of hot water and bake 50 minutes or until knife inserted near center comes out clean. Drop jelly by small spoonfuls on pudding. Return to oven while preparing meringue. Beat egg whites until soft peaks form. Beat in remaining sugar, 2 tablespoons at a time, and continue to beat until stiff. Starting at edge of baking dish, spread meringue over pudding, swirling top and sealing meringue to edge. Bake at 350° until lightly browned, 10–15 minutes. Cool 30 minutes before serving. MAKES 4–6 SERVINGS.

3 cups milk
2 cups stale bread cubes (Cuban, French, or Italian bread or Cuban crackers)
¼ cup sugar
4 eggs, separated
1 teaspoon vanilla extract
¼ cup guava jelly
6 tablespoons sugar

GRATED SWEET-POTATO PUDDING

Preheat oven to 350°. Combine milk and eggs in blender and process a few seconds to mix well. Add sweet-potato slices and blend at low speed until potato is shredded fine. Add sugar, cinnamon, nutmeg, cloves, and salt and blend well. Pour into well-greased 1½-quart baking dish. Bake 1 hour or until slightly puffed and knife inserted in center comes out clean. Serve warm with whipped cream or ice cream or cold with ice cream. MAKES 4 SERVINGS.

NOTE: Sweet-potato Pudding can also be served as a vegetable dish with meat or poultry. Some cooks add chopped raisins, dates, or nuts. If a blender is not available, peel and finely shred sweet potatoes and immediately mix with milk and eggs to prevent darkening.

1 cup milk
2 eggs
2 cups (mounded) thickly sliced peeled sweet potatoes (about 1 pound)
1 cup sugar
1 teaspoon cinnamon
1 teaspoon nutmeg
½ teaspoon ground cloves
¼ teaspoon salt

COFFEE CHANTILLY

Pour cream into small bowl of electric mixer and sprinkle with coffee. Refrigerate 1–2 hours. Whip at high speed until stiff. Add sugar 1 tablespoon at a time, and whip until very stiff. Whip in vanilla. Pile into dessert glasses and serve immediately or chill 1–2 hours. If desired, serve with whipped cream sprinkled with dry instant coffee or Chocolate Curls. MAKES 4 SERVINGS.

1 cup heavy cream
3 teaspoons instant coffee or 2 teaspoons instant espresso
2 tablespoons confectioners' sugar
½ teaspoon vanilla extract
Whipped cream (optional)
Additional instant coffee or *Chocolate Curls (optional)

CHOCOLATE MOUSSE

Combine chocolate and water in top of double boiler. Place over hot, not boiling, water until melted, stirring occasionally. Remove from heat and cool slightly. Whip cream until stiff. Add chocolate mixture and beat until well mixed. Add eggs 1 at a time and beat thoroughly. Beat in vanilla or rum. Turn into dessert glasses and chill 1–2 hours. If desired, serve with whipped cream and Chocolate Curls. MAKES 4 SERVINGS.

1 6-ounce package semisweet chocolate pieces
2 tablespoons water
½ cup heavy cream
2 eggs
1 teaspoon vanilla extract or 1 tablespoon rum
Whipped cream (optional)
*Chocolate Curls (optional)

CHOCOLATE COFFEE MOUSSE

Chill Chocolate Mousse and Coffee Chantilly until thick enough to mound on spoon. Drop a large spoonful of each in dessert glass or bowl, arranging side by side. Chill 2 hours or until ready to serve. Serve with whipped cream and Chocolate Curls. MAKES 6–8 SERVINGS.

1 recipe *Chocolate Mousse
1 recipe *Coffee Chantilly
Whipped cream
Chocolate Curls (see below)

CHOCOLATE CURLS

Chill a milk-chocolate candy bar. Warm chocolate bar in hand slightly. Shave from edge, using vegetable peeler, forming curls. Place on waxed paper and chill until ready to use.

CRUMBLE PUDDING

Let egg whites warm at room temperature for better volume. Preheat oven to 300°. Add baking powder to egg whites and beat until soft peaks form. Add sugar a few tablespoons at a time and salt and continue to beat until stiff. With rubber spatula, fold in crumbs, walnuts, and dates. Turn into well-greased 10×6-inch baking dish or 9-inch pie pan. Bake until lightly browned and crusty to the touch, about 1 hour 15 minutes. Serve warm or cooled. Cut into rectangles or wedges and serve with whipped cream. MAKES 4–6 SERVINGS.

3 egg whites
1 teaspoon baking powder
¾ cup sugar
¼ teaspoon salt
½ cup fresh bread crumbs (about 1 slice crumbled in blender)
½ cup chopped walnuts or pecans
½ cup chopped dates
Whipped cream, lightly sweetened and flavored with brandy

HUGUENOT TORTE

Preheat oven to 325°. Beat egg well, then beat in sugar, flour, baking powder, salt, and vanilla. Stir in apple and nuts. Turn into well-greased 10×6-inch baking dish. Bake 35–40 minutes, until a thin crisp layer forms on top. Top will be lightly browned. Serve warm with ice cream or whipped cream. MAKES 4–6 SERVINGS.

1 egg
¾ cup sugar
2 tablespoons flour
1½ teaspoons baking powder
⅛ teaspoon salt
1 teaspoon vanilla extract
½ cup chopped peeled tart apple
½ cup chopped walnuts or pecans

MIAMI FLAN

Preheat oven to 325°. Place ½ cup sugar in 8-inch skillet or other heavy 1-quart pan at least 2 inches deep. Stir with wooden spoon over moderate heat until sugar is melted and pale golden. Immediately remove from heat and stir to cool quickly and prevent burning. Tilt pan to coat sides with caramelized sugar. Set aside. Beat eggs with remaining ¼ cup sugar and salt. Stir in sherry and milk. Carefully pour into prepared pan. Bake 1 hour, until a knife inserted in center comes out clean. Cool and refrigerate several hours or overnight. Turn out on plate and cut in wedges to serve. MAKES 4–6 SERVINGS.

¾ cup sugar
5 eggs
½ teaspoon salt
2 tablespoons cream sherry or 2 teaspoons vanilla extract
2 cups milk, scalded

LEMON CREAM MOLD

Mix gelatin, ¼ cup sugar, and salt in heavy saucepan. Beat in egg yolks, water, and milk. Cook over low heat, stirring constantly, until mixture coats a metal spoon. Remove from heat and stir in lemonade concentrate. Chill until mixture mounds on spoon. Beat egg whites until stiff. Beat in 2 tablespoons sugar gradually. Continue beating until very stiff. Fold into gelatin mixture. Without washing beaters, whip cream until soft peaks form. Fold into gelatin mixture. Tint pale yellow with food color if desired. Turn into 5-cup mold which has been rinsed in cold water. Chill until firm, at least 4 hours. Unmold and garnish with mint and lemon slices. MAKES 6 SERVINGS.

1 envelope unflavored gelatin
¼ cup sugar
Dash salt
2 eggs, separated
¼ cup water
½ cup milk
1 6-ounce can frozen lemonade
*   concentrate, thawed*
2 tablespoons sugar
1 cup heavy cream
Yellow food color (optional)
Mint sprigs (optional)
Lemon slices (optional)

PINEAPPLE CLOUD DESSERT

Dissolve gelatin in boiling water and stir in cold water. Chill until syrupy. Drain pineapple thoroughly in a strainer over cup until almost dry. Pour undiluted evaporated milk into freezer tray or pan and freeze until ice crystals form at edges. Chill large bowl of mixer and beaters. Combine crumbs and nuts. Set aside ½ cup and spread remaining crumbs in 13×9-inch pan.

Turn semifrozen milk into chilled bowl. Beat at high speed until milk stands in soft peaks. Beat in lemon juice and peel. Beat syrupy gelatin at high speed until fluffy. Fold gelatin mixture and drained pineapple into whipped milk. Turn into prepared pan. Sprinkle with reserved crumbs. Chill several hours or overnight. Cut in squares. MAKES 18 SERVINGS.

NOTE: This dessert may be used to fill crumb pie shells. This amount is sufficient for 2 9-inch pies.

1 3-ounce package lemon gelatin
1 cup boiling water
¾ cup cold water
1 20-ounce can crushed pineapple, in syrup
*   for sweeter dessert, in juice for lighter*
*   dessert*
1 13-ounce can evaporated milk
2 cups fine graham cracker or vanilla
*   wafer crumbs*
½ cup finely chopped pecans or walnuts
Juice and grated peel of 1 lemon

NATCHEZ FLOATING ISLAND

Separate 4 eggs. Beat whites until foamy. Add cream of tartar and beat until soft peaks form. Beat in ½ cup sugar, 2 tablespoons at a time, and continue to beat until very stiff. Combine milk and 1 tablespoon sherry in wide skillet. Heat until bubbles appear at edge. Drop egg white mixture by heaping tablespoonfuls onto milk. Cook in 2 batches if necessary to keep egg whites separated. Cook over very low heat. Milk should not quite bubble. When meringues are set on bottom, carefully turn with 2 forks and cook 2–3 minutes longer, until tops feel moist but firm. Carefully lift out with forks and drain on towel. Strain milk used for poaching meringues and add more milk if needed to make 2 cups. Beat egg yolks and remaining whole egg in top of double boiler with remaining ¼ cup sugar and salt. Stir in milk. Cook over hot, not boiling water, stirring constantly until custard coats metal spoon. Remove from heat and set in cold water to cool promptly. Add remaining sherry. Pour into dessert bowl. Float meringues on custard. Cover and chill several hours. MAKES 4–5 SERVINGS.

NOTE: If desired, decorate with sugar threads. Heat ⅓–½ cup sugar in heavy skillet until syrupy and golden brown. Swirl over tops of meringues with tines of wooden fork.

5 eggs
¼ teaspoon cream of tartar
¾ cup sugar
2½ cups (approximately) milk
2 tablespoons cream sherry or 2 teaspoons
  vanilla extract
⅛ teaspoon salt

FILLED BAKED APPLES

Preheat oven to 375°. Wash and core apples and peel about ⅓ down from the stem ends. Arrange in greased 10×6-inch or 9-inch round baking dish. Snip dates and stuff lightly into core cavities. Squeeze lemon juice over apples. Drop a squeezed lemon half into dish to flavor apples. Sprinkle sugar over apples and add boiling water. Dot with butter. Bake uncovered until tender, 30–45 minutes. Baste 2 or 3 times with syrup in baking dish. Serve warm or chilled. MAKES 6 SERVINGS.

6 baking apples such as Rome Beauty
¼ pound pitted dates or raisins
1 lemon
6 tablespoons sugar, granulated or brown
½ cup boiling water
1 tablespoon butter or margarine

MRS. HARMON'S CHARLOTTE

This recipe originally called for 2 quarts cream, a dozen eggs, and four times the other ingredients, a rich concoction for Christmas or grand occasions.

Line sides of dessert dish or charlotte mold (about 1½ quarts) with ladyfingers, trimming ends if necessary. Sprinkle gelatin on water in cup. Soften 3 or 4 minutes. Place in pan of boiling water and stir until dissolved. Cool slightly. Beat egg whites until foamy, add cream of tartar, and beat until soft peaks form. Add 2 tablespoons sugar and beat until stiff. Set aside. Beat egg yolks with remaining sugar until light-colored. Add sherry and beat well. Whip cream in chilled bowl until stiff. Stir gelatin mixture into egg yolks. Fold egg yolk and white mixtures into cream. Spoon in prepared mold. Chill until set, several hours or overnight. If in mold, loosen edges, dip quickly in hot water, and turn out on plate. MAKES 6–8 SERVINGS.

4 ounces (approximately) ladyfingers, split
1 envelope unflavored gelatin
¼ cup cold water
3 eggs, separated
⅛ teaspoon cream of tartar
3 tablespoons sugar
1 tablespoon cream sherry, oloroso sherry, or brandy or 2 teaspoons vanilla extract
1 pint heavy cream

PUMPKIN SPANISH CREAM

Blend ½ cup brown sugar and gelatin in saucepan. Stir in egg yolks, cinnamon, ginger, nutmeg, and 1 cup milk until smooth. Cook and stir over low heat until slightly thickened and gelatin is dissolved. Remove from heat and stir in remaining 1 cup milk and pumpkin. Chill until mixture mounds on a spoon. Beat egg whites until foamy throughout. Add remaining ¼ cup brown sugar and continue to beat until stiff peaks form. Fold into pumpkin mixture. Spices darken pumpkin color, so if desired tint with food color. Turn into 5-cup mold or loaf pan which has been rinsed in cold water. Chill until firm, at least 4 hours. Unmold and garnish with whipped cream. MAKES 6–8 SERVINGS.

¾ cup brown sugar, packed
2 envelopes unflavored gelatin
2 eggs, separated
½ teaspoon cinnamon
½ teaspoon ginger
¼ teaspoon nutmeg
2 cups milk
1 cup canned pumpkin
Red and yellow food color (optional)
Whipped cream (optional)

SOUTHERN BANANA PUDDING

Blend sugar, flour, nutmeg, and salt in heavy saucepan or top of double boiler. Beat in eggs, then milk. Cook over low heat or simmering water in double boiler, stirring constantly, until custard coats spoon. Cool promptly by setting pan in cold water. Add vanilla and chill. Layer vanilla wafers and ⅔ of the bananas in 1-quart dessert bowl, ending with wafers. Stir remaining bananas into custard and mix to coat bananas thoroughly. Carefully pour custard over banana-wafer layers in bowl and spread custard-coated bananas on top. Cover closely with plastic film and refrigerate 2–3 hours. Serve with whipped cream if desired. MAKES 4–6 SERVINGS.

¼ cup sugar
1 tablespoon flour
¼ teaspoon nutmeg
¼ teaspoon salt
2 eggs
1½ cups milk
1 teaspoon vanilla extract
3 dozen (approximately) vanilla wafers
1½–2 pounds bananas, peeled and sliced
Whipped cream (optional)

TROPICAL FRUIT COMPOTE

Peel and section or cube fruits, reserving any juice. Combine guava jelly and reserved fruit juices in small saucepan. Stir over moderate heat until melted. Combine fruits and jelly syrup in bowl. Cover and refrigerate several hours. Just before serving, sprinkle with rum if desired. MAKES 6 SERVINGS.

½ pineapple
1 large tangelo or navel orange
1 grapefruit
½ cup guava jelly
Light or dark rum (optional)

STRAWBERRY SHERBET

Wash, drain, and hull strawberries. Add sugar and mash. Add lemon juice and slowly stir in buttermilk. Pour into 2 ice cube trays or 9-inch square pan. Freeze until mushy. Turn into bowl and beat until fluffy. Return to pan or trays and freeze until firm. Serve within a few hours or cover with plastic wrap to store. MAKES 6 SERVINGS.

1 basket strawberries (about 2½ cups)
1 cup sugar
1 tablespoon lemon juice
1 cup buttermilk

SYLLABUB

Syllabub can be mixed at the table, and traditionally is beaten with a syllabub churn, although a wire whisk can be used.

Pour sherry and sugar into glass serving bowl or 1½-quart pitcher and stir until sugar is dissolved. Cover and chill. When ready to serve, add milk slowly, beating rapidly with churn or whisk. Slowly beat in cream, beating to a froth. Ladle or pour into small wineglasses, dessert dishes, or stemmed glasses. Serve as a beverage or dessert. MAKES 6–8 SERVINGS.

½ cup cream sherry
½ cup sugar
2 cups milk, well chilled
1 pint heavy cream, well chilled

LIME BUTTERMILK SHERBET

Beat eggs until foamy. Gradually add sugar and continue to beat until thick and light. Beat in syrup, buttermilk, and lime juice. Tint pale green with food color if desired. Turn into 2 ice cube trays or 9-inch square metal pan. Freeze until firm at edges and thick in center. Turn into chilled bowl and beat at high speed until creamy. Return to tray and freeze until firm. When frozen, cover closely with plastic film. Let soften 5–10 minutes at room temperature before serving. This sherbet is refreshing served with sliced peaches, other summer fruits, or berries. MAKES 6–8 SERVINGS.

3 eggs
¾ cup sugar
½ cup light corn syrup
2 cups buttermilk
⅓ cup lime juice, preferably Key limes
Green food color (optional)

LEMON SAUCE

Blend cornstarch and sugar in small saucepan. Add hot water and stir over low heat until blended. Bring to a boil, stirring occasionally, and simmer 5 minutes. Remove from heat and stir in butter, lemon juice and peel. Serve warm or at room temperature with gingerbread or other desserts. MAKES 1¼ CUPS, 4–6 SERVINGS.

1 tablespoon cornstarch
½ cup sugar
1 cup very hot tap water
2 tablespoons butter or margarine
Juice and grated peel of 1 lemon

APRICOT NUT MOLD

Cook apricots in ½ cup water in covered saucepan until tender and most of water is absorbed, about 20 minutes. Purée in blender or by beating at high speed with mixer. Heat remaining 1½ cups water to a boil. Add gelatin and stir until dissolved. Mix well with apricots. Chill until thickened. Purée cottage cheese in sieve or blender or beat vigorously until almost smooth. Stir in gelatin mixture. Fold in nuts. Transfer 4- or 5-cup mold which has been rinsed in cold water. Chill until firm. Unmold and garnish with whipped cream to serve as dessert or with lettuce and mayonnaise to serve as salad. MAKES 4–6 SERVINGS.

½ cup dried apricots (about ¼ pound)
2 cups water
1 3-ounce package orange gelatin
1 cup cottage cheese
½ cup chopped nuts

TARPON SPRINGS RICE PUDDING

Combine rice and boiling water in saucepan. Add salt. Cover, bring again to a boil, and simmer 10 minutes or until rice is almost tender. Add milk and butter. Bring to a boil and cook uncovered 10 minutes longer, stirring often. Stir in sugar and lemon peel. Beat egg and stir in about 1 cup of rice mixture. Return to rice mixture and cook and stir 2 minutes. Cool and turn into dessert glasses. Sprinkle with cinnamon. MAKES 4 CUPS.

¼ cup rice
½ cup boiling water
⅛ teaspoon salt
1¾ cups milk
2 tablespoons butter or margarine
¼ cup sugar
Grated peel of ½ lemon
1 egg
Cinnamon

PEACH ICE CREAM

Peel and pit peaches. Mash with potato masher or sturdy fork. Add lemon juice and sugar and mix well. Whip cream until very stiff. Fold into peaches. Turn into 9-inch square baking pan or 2 ice cube trays. Freeze 1 hour or until set at edges. Stir until smooth, return to freezer, and freeze until firm. Remove from freezer 10 minutes before serving. Top with raspberries for added glamour. MAKES 6 SERVINGS.

2 pounds soft ripe peaches
3 tablespoons lemon juice
½ cup sugar
2 cups heavy cream
Raspberries, crushed and sweetened
  (optional)

PORT WINE JELLY

Sprinkle gelatin over ¼ cup water in bowl. Shave lemon peel off in thin strips, using vegetable peeler. Combine peel, remaining water, and sugar in small saucepan. Bring to boil. Strain boiling liquid over softened gelatin and stir until dissolved. Add lemon juice and wine. Mix well. Pour into dessert bowl or 3-cup mold which has been rinsed in cold water. Chill until firm. Unmold if desired, and serve with whipped cream. MAKES 4 SERVINGS.

NOTE: Recipe can be doubled, but use 3 envelopes instead of 2 envelopes gelatin.

1 envelope unflavored gelatin
¾ cup water
Peel of 1 lemon
⅓ cup sugar
Juice of 1 lemon
1 cup ruby port or cream sherry
Softly whipped cream

CUSTARD SAUCE OR POUR CUSTARD

Blend egg yolks, egg, sugar, and salt in heavy saucepan until smooth. Stir in milk. Cook over low heat, stirring constantly with spoon or wire whisk, until thick enough to coat a metal spoon without sliding off. Remove from heat and immediately set pan in cold water. Stir to cool promptly. Once the mixture is at room temperature, stir in vanilla. Chill well. Serve on fruits, puddings, or as a dessert. MAKES 8 SAUCE SERVINGS OR 3-4 DESSERT SERVINGS.

2–3 egg yolks
1 whole egg
¼ cup sugar
Dash salt
1½ cups milk (can use half-and-half or part cream)
1 teaspoon vanilla extract or 1 tablespoon sherry, brandy, or dark rum

QUICK STRAWBERRY MOUSSE

Pour gelatin into blender, add boiling water, and blend until gelatin is dissolved. Add strawberries, cover blender, and blend until strawberries are broken. Add lemon juice and cream and blend a few seconds, until smooth. Do not blend too long, as cream may become butter. Turn into 6-cup mold which had been rinsed in cold water. Chill until firm, 4 hours. Unmold and garnish with whole berries and whipped cream if desired. MAKES 4-6 SERVINGS.

1 3-ounce package strawberry gelatin
¾ cup boiling water
1 10-ounce package frozen strawberries
Juice of ½ lemon
1 cup heavy cream
Strawberries (optional)
Whipped cream (optional)

GRAPEFRUIT SHERBET

Soften gelatin in ½ cup water in large saucepan. Stir over moderate heat until dissolved. Stir in sugar. Add grapefruit concentrate and juice can of water. Chill until syrupy. Beat egg whites until foamy. Add cream of tartar and beat until stiff. Fold egg whites and salt into grapefruit mixture. Freeze in mechanical ice cream freezer, 2 ice cube trays, or shallow metal pan. Freeze until mushy and mix with rubber spatula or wooden spoon. Freeze until firm at edges. Turn into chilled bowl and beat at high speed until slightly fluffy. Return to freezer trays and freeze until firm. Cover with plastic film to store more than a few hours. MAKES 6–8 SERVINGS.

1 envelope unflavored gelatin
½ cup cold water
1½ cups sugar
2 6-ounce cans frozen grapefruit juice
  concentrate, thawed
1 juice can water
2 egg whites
¼ teaspoon cream of tartar
¼ teaspoon salt

PIES AND
PASTRY

A choice of pies, traditional pumpkin and mince among them, finishes off Thanksgiving feasts in the South, as everywhere. Pies are also family fare. Women who "have a light hand with pastry" take pride in their talent and find pies unbeatable as family pleasers. The American specialties—apple, cherry, fresh berry, and lemon meringue—are served, but the southern pies—buttery chess, pecan, and Osgood, (sometimes called Oh So Good)—are distinctive.

What would a drive through Georgia be without a stop at a roadside diner for a wedge of pecan pie and a cup of steaming-hot coffee? Roadside diners may have fallen on bad gastronomic times, but home-baked pecan pie remains a culinary triumph.

CRUMB PIE SHELL

Blend crumbs, butter, and sugar with fingers or back of wooden spoon in 9-inch pie pan. Press against bottom and sides of pie pan. Chill at least 1 hour before filling or bake at 375° 8–10 minutes, until slightly crusty. MAKES 1 9-INCH PIE SHELL.

1½ cups fine graham cracker, vanilla wafer, gingersnap, or chocolate wafer crumbs
⅓ cup butter or margarine, softened
2 tablespoons sugar (optional)

SOUTHERN SHORT PASTRY

Preheat oven to 450° if baking pie shell. Mix flour and salt. Add lard and cut in with 2 knives or pastry blender. Add water 1 tablespoon at a time and blend in with fork. Use just enough to make dough cling together. Shape in a ball, wrap in waxed paper, and refrigerate 1–2 hours. Roll out on floured surface. Gently fit into pie plate, being careful not to stretch. Flute edge. Prick in several places with fork if to be baked before filling. Bake 10–12 minutes, until just golden. Cool. Or fill unbaked pie shell and bake as directed for each pie. MAKES SUFFICIENT PASTRY FOR 1 8-INCH DOUBLE-CRUST OR 1 9-INCH SINGLE-CRUST PIE.

1½ cups flour
½ teaspoon salt
½ cup lard, cut into 4 or 6 pieces
3 tablespoons (approximately) cold water

TENNESSEE CHESS PIE

Preheat oven to 375°. Cream together butter and sugar until fluffy. Beat in corn meal and salt. Add eggs 1 at a time and beat well. Beat in lemon juice and peel. Turn into pie shell. Bake on lowest shelf of oven 35 minutes, until filling is golden brown. It should not be firm. Cool to room temperature. Serve in small wedges, as this pie is very rich. MAKES 10–12 SERVINGS.

½ cup butter or margarine, softened
2 cups sugar
2 tablespoons corn meal
¼ teaspoon salt
4 eggs
¼ cup lemon juice (2 lemons)
1 tablespoon grated lemon peel (2 lemons)
1 9-inch unbaked pie shell

BOURBON PUMPKIN PIE

Preheat oven to 375°. Combine pumpkin, milk, sugar, eggs, cinnamon, salt, allspice, ginger, nutmeg, and Bourbon. Beat together until well blended. Set pie shell on lowest shelf of oven and carefully pour in filling. Slide in oven shelf and bake 50 minutes or until a knife inserted near center comes out clean. Cool to room temperature or serve warm. Garnish with whipped cream if desired. MAKES 6–8 SERVINGS.

1 16-ounce can pumpkin
1 13-ounce can evaporated milk
⅔ cup sugar
3 eggs
1 teaspoon cinnamon
½ teaspoon salt
½ teaspoon allspice
¼ teaspoon ginger
¼ teaspoon nutmeg
¼ cup Bourbon (optional)
1 9-inch unbaked pie shell
Whipped cream (optional)

LIMEADE STRAWBERRY PIE

Whip cream until stiff but not buttery. Mix condensed milk and undiluted limeade. If desired tint pale green with food color. Fold limeade mixture into whipped cream. Chill while preparing strawberries. Wash and hull strawberries and drain on paper towel. Slice ½ the berries and fold into limeade filling. Spoon into pie shell and swirl top. Freeze 2–3 hours. Pie will keep in freezer several weeks if covered with plastic wrap after freezing. To serve, thaw slightly and garnish with remaining sliced strawberries. MAKES 6–8 SERVINGS.

1 cup heavy cream
1 14-ounce can sweetened condensed milk
1 6-ounce can frozen limeade concentrate; thawed
Green food color (optional)
1 12-ounce basket strawberries
1 9-inch *Crumb Pie Shell

CRANBERRY ORANGE PIE

Mix gelatin and sugar thoroughly in saucepan. Add orange juice. Stir over low heat until gelatin dissolves. Cool and gently stir in yogurt. Chill until very thick but not set. Fold in relish. Spoon into pie shell. Chill 2 or 3 hours or until set. Garnish with whipped cream and orange slices. MAKES 6–8 SERVINGS.

2 envelopes unflavored gelatin
¼ cup sugar
¾ cup orange juice
½ pint orange or orange-pineapple yogurt
1 14-ounce jar cranberry-orange relish
1 9-inch baked or crumb pie shell
Whipped cream
Orange slices (optional)

SWEET-POTATO PIE

Preheat oven to 375°. Drain potatoes and mash in large bowl of electric mixer before measuring. Return to mixer bowl and beat in sugar, eggs, milk, nutmeg, cinnamon, and butter until smooth. Spoon filling into pie shell, swirling top slightly. Bake on lowest shelf of oven 40–45 minutes, until crust is golden and filling set. Serve warm with whipped cream sweetened lightly and flavored with sherry or brandy if desired. MAKES 6–8 SERVINGS.

NOTE: Thin-skinned red sweet potatoes, sometimes called yams, make better-flavored pie filling.

3 cups (approximately) mashed cooked sweet potato (2½ pounds cooked and peeled or 2 24-ounce cans, drained)
½ cup sugar
3 eggs
½ cup milk
½ teaspoon nutmeg
¼ teaspoon cinnamon
2 tablespoons butter or margarine, melted
1 9-inch unbaked pie shell, rim crimped high
Whipped cream (optional)

FRENCH CHOCOLATE PIE

Combine chocolate and water in top of double boiler or heavy saucepan. Heat over hot, not boiling, water or very low heat until chocolate is melted, stirring occasionally. Cool slightly. Add vanilla. Whip 1 cup cream until stiff. Fold in chocolate mixture. Turn into pie shell. Chill 2 or 3 hours or until firm. Whip remaining cream and serve on pie. MAKES 6–8 SERVINGS.

1 4-ounce package sweet cooking chocolate
3 tablespoons water
1 teaspoon vanilla extract
1½ cups heavy cream
1 8- or 9-inch baked or crumb pie shell

LIME CHIFFON PIE

Sprinkle gelatin on cold water and let soften. Beat egg yolks with spoon in top of double boiler or heavy saucepan. Mix in lime juice, ½ cup sugar, and salt. Stir over hot water or very low heat, until thickened, 3–5 minutes. Remove from heat and stir in gelatin until dissolved. And lime peel. Beat egg whites until stiff. Gradually beat in remaining sugar. Fold egg white mixture into filling. Fold in whipped cream. Turn into pie shell and chill until firm. Garnish with additional whipped cream, piped through a pastry tube, if desired. MAKES 6–8 SERVINGS.

1 envelope unflavored gelatin
¼ cup cold water
4 eggs, separated
½ cup lime juice (about 4 limes)
1 cup sugar
¼ teaspoon salt
1 teaspoon grated lime peel
½ cup heavy cream, whipped
1 9-inch baked pie shell
Additional whipped cream (optional)

BUTTERMILK RAISIN PIE

Preheat oven to 375°. Beat together eggs and sugar until light. Beat in salt, cinnamon, nutmeg, cloves, and buttermilk until well mixed. Spread raisins in pie shell. Pour custard over raisins. Bake 35 minutes or until knife inserted near center comes out clean. Serve warm or cooled. MAKES 6–8 SERVINGS.

3 eggs
¾ cup sugar
¼ teaspoon salt
1 teaspoon cinnamon
½ teaspoon nutmeg or mace
¼ teaspoon ground cloves
1 cup buttermilk
1 cup raisins
1 9-inch unbaked pie shell

HOLIDAY RUM PIE

Mix gelatin, sugar, egg yolks, water, and milk in small saucepan. Cook and stir over medium heat until custard comes to a boil and gelatin is dissolved. Remove from heat and place pan in larger pan of cold water to cool promptly. Add rum and mix well. Chill until mixture mounds on spoon. Beat egg whites until foamy, add salt, and beat until stiff. Fold into custard. Whip cream until soft peaks form and fold into filling. Chill until mixture mounds when lifted with spoon. Pile into pie shell. Chill several hours. Garnish with Chocolate Curls or sprinkles and whipped cream. MAKES 8 SERVINGS.

1 envelope unflavored gelatin
½ cup sugar
3 eggs, separated
¼ cup water
¾ cup milk
¼ cup light or dark rum
⅛ teaspoon salt
½ cup heavy cream, whipped
1 9-inch baked pie shell
*Chocolate Curls or sprinkles
Additional whipped cream (optional)

SOUTHERN COCONUT PIE

Preheat oven to 350°. Melt butter in 1½- or 2-quart saucepan. Brush bottom of pie shell with butter. To remaining butter in saucepan add coconut, milk, eggs, sugar, vanilla and almond extracts. Mix well. Turn into pie shell. Bake on lowest rack of oven 1 hour or until crust and filling are golden and filling is set. Cool before serving. MAKES 6–8 SERVINGS.

1 9-inch unbaked pie shell
3 tablespoons butter or margarine
1 4-ounce can moist shredded coconut
1 cup milk
2 eggs, beaten
1 cup sugar
1 teaspoon vanilla extract
¼ teaspoon almond extract (optional)

GEORGIA PECAN PIE

Preheat oven to 375°. Combine sugar and butter. Beat in corn syrup, eggs, vanilla, and salt. Spread pecans in pie shell. Pour filling over pecans. Bake on lowest shelf of oven 40 minutes or until knife inserted near center comes out clean. Cool to room temperature and garnish with whipped cream if desired. MAKES 8 SERVINGS.

½ cup sugar
1 tablespoon melted or very soft butter or margarine
1 cup light corn syrup
3 eggs
1 teaspoon vanilla extract
⅛ teaspoon salt
1½ cups coarsely chopped pecans (5½ ounces)
1 9-inch unbaked pie shell
Whipped cream (optional)

SODA CRACKER PIE

Let egg whites stand at room temperature at least 1 hour. Preheat oven to 325°. Mix crumbs, dates, and pecans. Set aside. Beat egg whites until foamy throughout, add baking powder, and beat until soft peaks form. Add sugar gradually and continue to beat until very stiff and sugar is completely dissolved. Fold in crumb mixture and almond extract. With rubber spatula, spread in well-greased 9-inch pie pan. Bake 30 minutes or until golden and crusty to the touch. Cool in pan on wire rack. Cut into wedges and serve with whipped cream. MAKES 6–8 SERVINGS.

3 egg whites
14 saltines rolled into crumbs (about ¾ cup)
½ cup chopped dates
½ cup chopped pecans
½ teaspoon baking powder
1 cup sugar
1 teaspoon almond or vanilla extract
Whipped cream

PUMPKIN PRALINE RIBBON PIE

Press ¼ cup pecans into bottom of pie shell and bake on lower shelf of oven at 475° 8–10 minutes, until golden brown. Cool.

Blend gelatin and ⅓ cup granulated sugar in saucepan. Stir in egg yolks, water, and ½ cup pumpkin until blended. Cook and stir over low heat until slightly thickened and gelatin dissolves. Remove from heat and stir in remaining pumpkin, ½ cup sour cream, salt, cinnamon, ginger, and nutmeg. Cool thoroughly.

Beat egg whites until foamy throughout. Gradually add ¼ cup granulated sugar and continue to beat until stiff peaks form. Fold into pumpkin mixture. Spoon ½ the mixture into pie shell. Chill until almost set. Spread with remaining sour cream and sprinkle with remaining ¼ cup pecans and brown sugar. Spoon remaining filling over sour cream layer. Chill until firm, 2–3 hours. Garnish with whipped cream and pecan halves. MAKES 6–8 SERVINGS.

½ cup chopped pecans
1 9-inch unbaked pie shell
1 envelope unflavored gelatin
⅓ cup granulated sugar
3 eggs, separated
¼ cup cold water
1¼ cups canned pumpkin
1 cup sour cream
½ teaspoon salt
1 teaspoon cinnamon
½ teaspoon ginger
¼ teaspoon nutmeg or mace
¼ cup granulated sugar
2 tablespoons brown sugar
Whipped cream
Pecan halves (optional)

OSGOOD PIE

Preheat oven to 350°. Rinse raisins, drain on paper towel, then chop with sharp knife on board. Cream together butter, 1¼ cups sugar, cinnamon, and nutmeg until fluffy. Beat in egg yolks and vinegar. Stir in raisins and nuts. Beat egg whites until foamy throughout. Add remaining sugar gradually and continue to beat until stiff but not dry. Fold into raisin mixture. Turn into pie shell and bake on lower shelf of oven 40–45 minutes, until top is golden. Cool before serving. Filling will fall slightly while cooling. Serve with whipped cream if desired. MAKES 6–8 SERVINGS.

1 cup raisins
½ cup butter or margarine, softened
1½ cups sugar
1 teaspoon cinnamon
1 teaspoon nutmeg
3 eggs, separated
2 teaspoons vinegar
½ cup chopped pecans or walnuts
1 9-inch unbaked pie shell
Whipped cream (optional)

FRESH PEACH ROLL

Preheat oven to 400°. Mix flour, salt, and baking powder in bowl. Cut in ¼ cup butter and lard with pastry blender or 2 knives until particles are like meal. Gradually stir in water with fork to make dough that clings together. Shape into ball, wrap in waxed paper, and chill 1–2 hours. Roll pastry out to 12×9-inch rectangle, trimming edges even, if necessary. Spread peaches over pastry. Sprinkle with ½ cup sugar, dot with 1 tablespoon butter, and sprinkle with cinnamon. Carefully roll up from long side, pressing in peaches lightly as pastry is rolled. Seal edge by dampening with water and pressing to roll. Place seam side down in shallow pan. Sprinkle remaining ¼ cup sugar over roll. Bake 20 minutes or until golden brown. Pour boiling water over roll, reduce oven temperature to 350°, and bake 30 minutes or until roll is lightly browned. Slice and serve warm with some of the syrup in pan and ice cream.
MAKES 6–8 SERVINGS.

2 cups flour
½ teaspoon salt
½ teaspoon baking powder
¼ cup butter or margarine, cut in small pieces
½ cup lard or shortening
5–6 tablespoons cold water
3 cups diced peeled peaches (about 1½ pounds)
¾ cup sugar
1 tablespoon butter or margarine
½ teaspoon cinnamon
½ cup boiling water
Vanilla ice cream or whipped cream (optional)

MINCEMEAT TURNOVERS

Preheat oven to 450°. Roll out ½ the pastry to a thickness of ¼ inch on a floured surface and cut in 6 circles about 5 inches in diameter. (Use a saucer as a pattern and cut around it with floured knife.) Mix mincemeat, apple, nuts, and brandy. Place a rounded tablespoon filling in center of each circle. Fold over to form a half circle and press edges together firmly with fork. Place on baking sheet and prick or slit each in several places to allow steam to escape. Brush with egg and sprinkle with sugar. Repeat with remaining pastry and filling. Bake 15 minutes or until lightly browned. Serve warm. Turnovers can be reheated 15 minutes in a 375° oven.
MAKES 12 TURNOVERS.

Pastry for 2-crust 9-inch pie
⅔ cup prepared mincemeat
⅔ cup chopped unpeeled apple (1 small apple)
⅓ cup chopped pecans or walnuts
3 tablespoons brandy, dark rum, or orange juice
1 egg beaten with a little water
Sugar

CAKES, FILLINGS, AND FROSTINGS

Sumptuous cakes are the most elaborate part of the southern culinary heritage. Even modest kitchens afford a fruitcake for Christmas, and the fruitier and nuttier the better. Christmas, Thanksgiving, birthdays, anniversaries, and any grand occasion bring out towering layer cakes in awesome array—*Coconut, *Devil's Food, the famous *Alabama Lane Cake, *Japanese Fruitcake, and *Lady Baltimore Cake. Rich poundcakes are expensive to bake, but beautiful to serve because of superior slicing quality. In the fifties and sixties cakes baked in Bundt pans came to the rescue of women too busy to practice the fine art of frosting and stacking layers. These easy, almost foolproof, cakes such as the *Oatmeal Shape Cake can be showpieces, too.

NOTE: Unless otherwise specified, the following recipes call for all-purpose flour.

AMBROSIA UPSIDE-DOWN CAKE

Preheat oven to 350°. Place ½ cup butter in 8- or 9-inch square baking pan and heat in oven. When butter is melted, sprinkle in brown sugar, then coconut. Arrange orange slices overlapping in butter mixture. Let stand while preparing batter. Cream together remaining butter and granulated sugar until fluffy. Beat in eggs. Stir in ½ cup flour, ¼ cup milk, remaining flour, baking powder, salt, and remaining milk. Stir in lemon peel. Turn into prepared pan. Bake until wood pick inserted in center comes out clean, 30–35 minutes. Let stand 10 minutes on wire rack. Loosen edges with spatula and invert on cake plate. Serve warm with whipped cream or ice cream. MAKES 6–9 SERVINGS.

⅔ cup butter or margarine
½ cup brown sugar, packed
½ cup shredded or flaked coconut
1 large or 2 medium oranges, peeled and thinly sliced
⅔ cup granulated sugar
2 eggs
1½ cups flour
½ cup milk
2 teaspoons baking powder
¼ teaspoon salt
Grated peel of 1 lemon

ALABAMA LANE CAKE

Preheat oven to 350°. Beat egg whites until foamy throughout. Gradually add ½ cup sugar and beat until stiff. Set aside. Cream together butter and remaining sugar until fluffy. Beat in vanilla. Stir in some of the flour and milk alternately, then add baking powder and salt, and stir in remaining flour and milk. Fold in egg white mixture gently but thoroughly. Turn into 3 greased and floured 9-inch layer cake pans. Bake 20–25 minutes, until skewer inserted in center comes out clean. Cool in pans on racks 5 minutes, turn out, and cool completely. Spread filling between layers and frost top and sides. Cake can be filled, wrapped in foil or plastic, and stored in a cool cupboard for several days, then frosted a few hours before serving.

8 egg whites
2 cups sugar
1 cup butter or margarine, softened
1½ teaspoons vanilla extract
3 cups flour
1 cup milk
3 teaspoons baking powder
¼ teaspoon salt
*Lane Cake Filling
*Divinity Frosting

FLORIDA ORANGE CAKE

Preheat oven to 350°. Combine orange juice and ½ cup sugar and let stand while mixing and baking cake. Cream together butter and remaining 1 cup sugar until fluffy. Beat in eggs 1 at a time. Stir in soda, baking powder, salt, add ½ the flour, then add ½ the buttermilk, remaining flour, and lemon juice. Fold in dates, nuts, and peel. Turn into greased and floured 12-cup Bundt pan or 10-inch tube pan. Bake 50–55 minutes, until a pick inserted near center comes out clean. Stir orange juice mixture until sugar is dissolved. Remove cake from oven. Slowly pour syrup over cake and let stand in pan until cool. Loosen edges, turn out cake. This rather heavy, moist cake can be served with whipped cream.

Juice of 1 orange
1½ cups sugar
½ cup butter or margarine, softened
2 eggs
½ teaspoon soda
½ teaspoon baking powder
¼ teaspoon salt
2 cups flour
1 cup buttermilk
2 tablespoons lemon juice
1 cup chopped dates
½ cup chopped pecans
Peel of 1 orange, slivered

AUNT FANNY'S WHITE CAKE

This delicate cake was served for birthdays, anniversaries, or almost every grand occasion when I was a child.

Preheat oven to 350°. Beat egg whites until soft peaks form. Add ½ cup sugar gradually and continue to beat until stiff. Set aside. Without washing beaters, cream together shortening and remaining sugar until fluffy. Stir in flour, baking powder, and salt, alternating with water. Stir in flavoring. Fold in egg whites and turn into 3 well-greased and floured or waxed-paper-lined 8- or 9-inch layer cake pans. Bake 35–40 minutes, until tops spring back when lightly pressed. Cool in pans on racks 10 minutes. Turn out on racks, peel off paper, if used, and cool completely. Fill and frost as desired.

Fresh Coconut Cake: Puncture eyes of 1 coconut with ice pick and drain out liquid. Place coconut in shallow pan and roast at 350° 30 minutes or until shell cracks. Rap shell sharply with hammer to open in several pieces, pry out meat with thin-bladed knife, peel off brown skin, and shred coconut. Fill and frost cake with *Lavish White Mountain Frosting or *Divinity Frosting, sprinkling coconut between layers, on top, and pressing into sides.

Lady Baltimore Cake: Combine ½ cup each golden or dark raisins, finely chopped pecans, and finely chopped dried figs in bowl. Add ¼ cup cream sherry and mix well. Cover and let stand 1 hour or longer. Just before assembling cake, stir 1 cup *Lavish White Mountain Frosting into fruit mixture. Fill cake with fruit mixture and frost top and sides with remaining frosting.

4 egg whites
2 cups sugar
¾ cup white vegetable shortening
3 cups flour
4 teaspoons baking powder
1 teaspoon salt
1½ cups plus 1 tablespoon water
1½ teaspoons vanilla extract or 1 teaspoon lemon and ½ teaspoon almond extract

BLACKBERRY JAM CAKE

Preheat oven to 350°. Cream together butter and sugar until fluffy. Beat in eggs 1 at a time. Add cloves, cinnamon, and allspice and mix well. Stir in ½ the flour. Add baking powder, soda, jam, and ½ the buttermilk and mix lightly. Stir in remaining flour and buttermilk. Turn into 2 very well greased and floured or waxed-paper-lined 8-inch layer cake pans. Bake 45 minutes or until tops spring back when lightly pressed. Cool in pans 10 minutes, loosen edges with narrow-bladed spatula, turn out on wire rack, and cool thoroughly. Fill and frost with Penuche Frosting.

½ cup butter or margarine, softened
1 cup sugar
3 eggs
1 teaspoon ground cloves
1 teaspoon cinnamon
1 teaspoon allspice
2 cups flour
1 teaspoon baking powder
1 teaspoon soda
1 12-ounce jar blackberry jam (1 cup)
½ cup buttermilk
*Penuche Frosting

BETTY'S FUDGE CAKE

Preheat oven to 350°. Melt chocolate and cool slightly. Cream together shortening and sugar until fluffy. Beat in eggs until creamy and smooth. Stir in chocolate, ½ the flour, buttermilk, soda, salt, and remaining flour. Add vanilla and hot water and mix lightly but thoroughly. Turn into greased and floured 13×9-inch baking pan. Bake 35–40 minutes, until top springs back when lightly pressed and cake shrinks from sides of pan. Remove from oven. Snip marshmallows in halves with kitchen shears moistened in cold water. Arrange marshmallows over cake and return to oven until marshmallows are soft, 3–4 minutes. Remove from oven and press marshmallows flat with fingers or fork. Cool cake in pan. Frost with Fudge Frosting. Cut in squares to serve.

4 squares unsweetened chocolate
½ cup shortening
1¾ cups sugar
2 eggs
2 cups flour
½ cup buttermilk
1 teaspoon soda
½ teaspoon salt
1 teaspoon vanilla extract
¾ cup hot water
10 marshmallows
*Fudge Frosting

CARROT CAKE

Preheat oven to 350°. Combine flour, sugar, soda, salt, and oil in bowl. Mix well. Beat in eggs 1 at a time. Stir in carrots and vanilla. Turn into greased and lightly floured 9-inch square baking pan. Bake 35–40 minutes, until cake shrinks from side of pan and top springs back when lightly pressed. Cool in pan 10 minutes. Turn out on wire rack and cool completely. Serve in squares with whipped cream or Lemon Sauce or frost with Creamy Praline Frosting.

1 cup flour
1 cup sugar
1 teaspoon soda
½ teaspoon salt
½ cup oil
2 eggs
1½ cups shredded carrots
1 teaspoon vanilla extract
Whipped cream, *Lemon Sauce, or
  *Creamy Praline Frosting

BRIDE'S CAKE

This firm-textured, delicate-flavored layer cake slices neatly and resists crumbling on the carpet when eaten from a small plate, so is an ideal party cake.

Preheat oven to 350°. Cream together butter and sugar until fluffy. Beat in ½ cup flour. Beat in egg whites 2 at a time, beating in 1 egg white at the last. Stir in remaining flour ½ cup at a time. Stir in baking powder and vanilla. Turn into 3 greased and floured 9-inch layer cake pans. Bake 35–40 minutes. Cool in pans 10 minutes, turn out on wire racks, cool, and frost as desired.

1 cup butter or margarine, softened
1¾ cups sugar
2½ cups flour
9 egg whites
1 teaspoon baking powder
1½ teaspoons vanilla extract or
  2 teaspoons grated lemon peel

Bride's Cake: Frost and decorate with *Ornamental Frosting.

Louisville Rum Cake: Fill vanilla-flavored cake with *Rum Filling and frost with *Divinity Frosting flavored with rum.

Lemon Cake: Fill lemon-flavored cake with *Lemon Cream Filling and frost with *Lemon Seven-minute Frosting.

Orange-filled White Cake: Fill with *Orange Filling and frost with *Divinity Frosting or *Lavish White Mountain Frosting.

MARIE'S JELLY ROLL

Preheat oven to 375°. Bring eggs to room temperature. Beat egg whites until foamy throughout, add salt, and beat until stiff. Add sugar 2 tablespoons at a time and beat until very stiff. Set aside. Beat egg yolks until well blended. Stir in flour, baking powder, and vanilla. Fold into egg whites. Spread in well-greased and lightly floured 15×10-inch jelly-roll pan. Bake 12 minutes or until top springs back when lightly pressed. Dust a clean towel heavily with confectioners' sugar. Turn cake out on towel. Trim off crisp edges. Roll cake with towel from short end. Wrap towel tightly around roll and cool cake. Carefully unroll and spread cake with jelly. Remove from towel and place on plastic wrap or waxed paper. Roll up again and twist wrap firmly around jelly roll to hold securely. Unwrap, place on platter, and sprinkle with more confectioners' sugar. Slice and serve with whipped cream. MAKES 6–8 SERVINGS.

4 eggs, separated
¼ teaspoon salt
½ cup granulated sugar
½ cup flour
½ teaspoon baking powder
1 teaspoon vanilla extract
Confectioners' sugar
¾ cup (approximately) guava jelly
Whipped cream (optional)

DEVIL'S FOOD CAKE

Preheat oven to 375°. Cream together butter and sugar until fluffy. Beat in chocolate. Add eggs 1 at a time and beat thoroughly. Stir in flour, salt, and soda in 4 or 5 additions alternately with buttermilk. Stir in vanilla. Turn into 3 greased and lightly floured 9-inch layer cake pans. Bake 30–35 minutes, until tops spring back when lightly pressed. Cool in pans 10 minutes, loosen edges with spatula, and turn out on racks. Cool thoroughly; fill and frost.

1 cup butter or margarine, softened
2 cups sugar
3 1-ounce squares unsweetened chocolate, melted and cooled
5 eggs
2½ cups flour
¼ teaspoon salt
1 teaspoon soda
1 cup buttermilk
1 teaspoon vanilla extract
*Lavish White Mountain Frosting or
  *Divinity Frosting

FRESH APPLE CAKE

Beat together eggs, granulated sugar, and vanilla in large bowl until sugar is dissolved. Beat in oil until smooth. Stir in flour, soda, and salt. Fold in walnuts and apples. Batter will be thick. Turn into greased and floured 11×7-inch baking dish (2 quarts) or 12-cup Bundt pan. Bake 1 hour for baking dish or 1 hour 25 minutes for Bundt pan until top springs back when lightly pressed. Cool cake in baking dish on rack or 10 minutes in Bundt pan, turn out, and cool on rack. Dust cake with confectioners' sugar or frost with Lemon Cheese Icing.

2 eggs, beaten
2 cups granulated sugar
1 teaspoon vanilla extract
½ cup oil
2 cups flour
2 teaspoons soda
½ teaspoon salt
1 cup chopped walnuts or pecans
4 cups chopped peeled tart apples
Confectioners' sugar or *Lemon Cheese
  Icing

GRAHAM SPICE CAKE

Preheat oven to 350°. Cream together butter and sugar until fluffy. Beat in eggs 1 at a time, then beat in vanilla. Mix graham cracker crumbs, flour, salt, baking powder, soda, nutmeg, and cinnamon. Stir in crumb mixture alternately with milk. Turn into 2 well-greased 8-inch layer cake pans or 12×8-inch pan. Bake 35–40 minutes or until top springs back when lightly pressed. Cool in pan on rack 10 minutes, turn out, and cool thoroughly. Fill and frost layers or frost tops and sides of sheet cake. This cake is also good with sliced peaches or bananas and whipped cream.

½ cup butter or margarine, softened
1 cup sugar
2 eggs
1 teaspoon vanilla extract
1¾ cups fine graham cracker crumbs
  (about ⅓ pound)
½ cup flour
½ teaspoon salt
1½ teaspoons baking powder
¼ teaspoon soda
¼ teaspoon nutmeg
½ teaspoon cinnamon
⅔ cup milk
*Penuche Frosting or *Mocha Whipped
  Cream

BANANA CHIFFON CAKE

Preheat oven to 325°. Mix flour, sugar, baking powder, and salt in large bowl of mixer. Make a well in center and add in order: oil, egg yolks, bananas, and lemon juice. Beat until smooth. Add cream of tartar to egg whites in large bowl. Beat until they form very stiff peaks. Do not underbeat. Gradually fold banana mixture into egg whites, just until blended. Turn into ungreased 10-inch tube pan. Bake 1 hour and 5 minutes or until skewer inserted halfway between edge of pan and tube comes out clean. Immediately invert pan with tube over bottle neck or funnel so cake is elevated at least 1 inch above table. Let cake hang until cool. Loosen edges and remove from pan. Spread cake with *Rum Whipped Cream or any favorite frosting or serve plain with ice cream.

2 cups flour
1½ cups sugar
3 teaspoons baking powder
1 teaspoon salt
½ cup oil
7 medium egg yolks, unbeaten
1 cup mashed bananas (2 or 3 bananas)
1 tablespoon lemon juice
½ teaspoon cream of tartar
1 cup egg whites (7 or 8 whites)

JAPANESE FRUITCAKE

Preheat oven to 350°. Beat egg whites until soft peaks form. Gradually beat in ½ cup granulated sugar and beat until stiff. Cream butter with remaining granulated sugar until fluffy. Beat in egg yolks and vanilla. Stir in flour, baking powder, and salt, alternating with milk. Fold in egg whites gently but thoroughly. Turn ⅓ of the batter into greased and floured 9-inch layer cake pan. Add cinnamon, raisins, and pecans to remaining batter and mix lightly. Turn into 2 greased and floured 9-inch layer cake pans. Bake 25 minutes or until skewer inserted in center comes out clean. Cool in pans 5 minutes, turn out, and cool on wire racks. Fill layers with Raisin Brandy Filling, stacking spice layer, white layer, then spice layer. Frost tops and sides with Butter Cream Frosting. Or omit frosting and dust with confectioners' sugar.

4 eggs, separated
2 cups granulated sugar
1 cup butter or margarine, softened
1 teaspoon vanilla extract
3 cups flour
3 teaspoons baking powder
1 teaspoon salt
1 cup milk
1 teaspoon cinnamon
1½ cups raisins
½ cup chopped pecans
*Raisin Brandy Filling
*Butter Cream Frosting flavored with brandy or confectioners' sugar

MOTHER'S WHITE FRUITCAKE

Preheat oven to 300°. Combine raisins, citron, pineapple, and cherries in large bowl. Add sherry, mix, and let stand while mixing batter. Prepare almonds and add to fruit. Beat egg whites until foamy. Add ½ cup sugar and beat until stiff. Set aside. Cream together butter and remaining sugar until fluffy. Stir in salt, baking powder, and flour. Batter will be very stiff. Fold in egg whites. Pour batter over fruit mixture and mix thoroughly but lightly. Pans should be well greased on bottoms and sides and lined on the bottoms with a double thickness of waxed paper, which should also be greased. Pack batter lightly into pans, filling no more than ½ full. Bake until a wood pick inserted in center comes out clean, about 1 hour for miniature loaves, about 2 hours for 8×4-inch loaves, or 3 hours for a spring-form or charlotte mold. Cool in pans on rack. Carefully loosen edges, turn out, and peel off paper liners. Wrap and store a week or longer before slicing. MAKES ABOUT 5 POUNDS.

1 15-ounce package golden raisins
½ pound citron, chopped (1 cup)
¼ pound candied pineapple, slivered
  (½ cup)
½ pound candied cherries, chopped
  (1 cup) (optional)
½ cup cream sherry or water and
  1 teaspoon vanilla extract
2 cups blanched almonds, chopped (about
  11 ounces)
6 egg whites
1 cup sugar
¾ cup butter or margarine, softened
1 teaspoon salt
1 teaspoon baking powder
2 cups flour

APRICOT BRANDY CAKE

Preheat oven to 300°. Let butter, eggs, and sour cream stand at room temperature 1–2 hours before mixing cake. Cream butter and sugar until fluffy. Beat in eggs 1 at a time and beat until well blended. Beat in lemon peel. Gradually stir in flour, soda, and salt alternating with sour cream and brandy. Turn into greased and floured 10-inch tube pan or 12-cup Bundt pan. Bake 1¼–1½ hours, until skewer inserted near center comes out clean. Cool in pan 10–15 minutes. Loosen with thin-bladed spatula around edges and tube and turn out on wire rack and cool. Slice thin to serve.

½ cup butter or margarine
7 eggs
½ pint sour cream
2⅔ cups sugar
1½ teaspoons grated lemon peel
2⅔ cups flour
½ teaspoon soda
½ teaspoon salt
½ cup apricot-flavored brandy

HEIRLOOM FRUITCAKE

Prepare fruits, using scissors dipped periodically in hot water to prevent sticking, or sharp knife. Combine in large bowl. Add Bourbon, mix well, and let stand 30 minutes or longer. Add pecans and mix. Preheat oven to 275°. Cream together butter and brown sugar. Beat in eggs 2 at a time, then beat 2 or 3 minutes longer. Mix ½ cup flour with fruits. Stir spices, remaining flour, and jelly into batter. Pour batter over fruit and mix well, using large spoon or hands. Pack into pans which have been greased, lined on the bottom with 2 layers of waxed paper, and greased again. Bake until wood pick inserted in center comes out clean. Check occasionally and if tops become dry, cover loosely with foil. Approximate baking times will be 2½ hours for 8×4-inch loaf pans, 3 hours 15 minutes for 9×5-inch loaf pans, and 4 hours 10 minutes for 7-inch round charlotte mold. Cool cakes in pans on rack. Carefully loosen edges with spatula, turn out, and peel off paper liners. Place on plastic wrap, if desired sprinkle liberally with Bourbon, wrap tightly, and store at least 3 weeks before serving.

NOTE: This cake should be sliced very thin. Refrigerating facilitates slicing.

1½ 15-ounce packages seedless raisins (about 4½ cups)
1 11-ounce package currants (about 2 cups)
¼ pound chopped citron (½ cup)
¼ pound chopped candied lemon peel (½ cup)
¼ pound chopped candied orange peel (½ cup)
¾ pound chopped candied cherries (2 cups)
½ pound slivered candied pineapple (1 cup)
1 pound pitted dates, chopped
½ cup Bourbon, grape juice, or orange juice
2 cups shelled chopped pecans (½ pound)
2 cups butter or margarine, softened
2½ cups dark brown sugar, packed
12 eggs
4 cups flour
2 tablespoons cinnamon
1 tablespoon ground cloves
1 tablespoon nutmeg
½ cup blackberry or grape jelly

SOUR CREAM POUNDCAKE

Have all ingredients at room temperature. Preheat oven to 325°. Cream together butter and granulated sugar until fluffy. Beat in eggs 1 at a time. Add nutmeg and mix well. Stir in flour by thirds alternating with sour cream. Stir in soda. Turn into well-greased 12-cup Bundt pan or 10-inch tube pan. Bake 1 hour 40 minutes or until skewer inserted halfway between tube and edge comes out clean. Cool in pan 10 minutes, loosen at edges with thin-bladed spatula, turn out on rack, and cool completely. Cake falls slightly as it cools. Dust with confectioners' sugar if desired. Slice thin.

1 cup butter or margarine, softened
3 cups granulated sugar
6 eggs
1½ teaspoons nutmeg or mace or
* 1 teaspoon grated lemon peel*
3 cups flour
1 cup sour cream
¼ teaspoon soda
Confectioners' sugar (optional)

SOUTHERN RIGHTS CAKE

Preheat oven to 350°. Cream together butter and sugar until fluffy. Beat in eggs 1 at a time. Add spices and beat until well blended. Mix in molasses and brandy. Stir in flour and soda. Turn into 2 well-greased and lightly floured 8-inch layer cake pans. Bake 25–30 minutes, until tops spring back when lightly pressed. Cool 10 minutes in pans, then turn out on rack, and cool completely. Frost with any favorite frosting.

1 cup butter or margarine, softened
1 cup sugar
3 eggs
1½ teaspoons cinnamon
1½ teaspoons ginger
1½ teaspoons allspice
½ cup molasses
¼ cup brandy
2 cups flour
½ teaspoon soda

MARBLE CAKE

Preheat oven to 350°. Cream together butter and sugar until fluffy. Beat in egg and vanilla. Stir in flour, baking powder, and salt (pour in ⅓ at a time), alternating with milk (pour in ½ at a time). Turn ⅔ of the batter into well-greased 8-inch square baking pan. Stir cinnamon and cloves into remaining batter. Drop by spoonfuls over batter in pan and cut in with rubber spatula. Bake 35 minutes or until skewer inserted in center comes out clean. Cool in pan 10 minutes, turn out, and cool completely. Frost with *Penuche or other frosting—or dust with confectioners' sugar.

½ cup butter or margarine, softened
¾ cup sugar
1 egg
1 teaspoon vanilla extract
1¾ cups flour
1 teaspoon baking powder
½ teaspoon salt
1 cup milk
½ teaspoon cinnamon
¼ teaspoon ground cloves

SYLVIA'S BUTTERMILK LEMON CAKE

Preheat oven to 325°. Mix flour, soda, and salt. Cream together butter and sugar until fluffy. Beat in eggs 1 at a time, beating thoroughly after each. Stir in flour mixture, alternating with buttermilk. Stir in lemon juice. Turn into well-greased and floured 12-cup Bundt pan or 10-inch tube pan. (Do not use a loose-bottom tube pan.) Bake 1 hour or until skewer inserted halfway between tube and edge comes out clean. Cool in pan about 10 minutes, until cake shrinks from sides slightly. Puncture deeply with skewer in several places. Slowly pour on glaze and let soak into cake and seep down along edges. Cover with plastic wrap and cool. Loosen edges with thin-bladed spatula and turn out on cake plate. Slice thin and serve plain, with fruit, ice cream, or whipped cream.

3½ cups flour
1 teaspoon soda
½ teaspoon salt
1½ cups butter or margarine, softened
2½ cups sugar
4 eggs
1 cup buttermilk
Juice of 1 lemon
Lemon Orange Glaze (see below)

LEMON ORANGE GLAZE

Grate peels and add to juice and sugar in small bowl. Stir until sugar is dissolved and let stand while baking cake. Stir again before pouring on cake.

Peel and juice of 2 lemons
Peel and juice of 1 medium orange
1½ cups sugar

OATMEAL SHAPE CAKE

Preheat oven to 350°. Pour boiling water over rolled oats and let stand while mixing batter. Cream butter, brown and granulated sugars in large bowl until fluffy. Beat in eggs 1 at a time. Stir in flour, salt, soda, cinnamon, and nutmeg. Stir in oat mixture. Turn into greased and floured 12-cup Bundt pan. Bake 1 hour and 10 minutes or until skewer inserted near center comes out clean. Cool in pan 15 minutes, then carefully loosen edges with spatula. Turn out on wire rack and cool completely. Dust with confectioners' sugar or spread thin sugar icing on top and let run down sides.

2½ cups boiling water
2 cups quick-cooking rolled oats
1 cup butter or margarine, softened
1 cup brown sugar, packed
2 cups granulated sugar
4 eggs
2⅔ cups flour
1 teaspoon salt
2 teaspoons soda
2 teaspoons cinnamon
2 teaspoons nutmeg
Confectioners' sugar or sugar icing

PRUNE NUT CAKE

Preheat oven to 325° for sheet cake or 350° if using deeper pan. Combine flour, soda, cinnamon, nutmeg, allspice, and salt. Set aside. Combine sugar, oil, and eggs. Blend well. Add dry ingredients alternating with buttermilk. Stir in prunes and nuts. Turn into greased and lightly floured 13×9-inch pan, 12-cup Bundt, or 10-inch tube pan. Bake sheet cake 1 hour or, if using deeper pan, 1 hour 15 minutes until top springs back when lightly pressed or wood pick inserted in center comes out clean. Cool in pan 10 minutes. Turn out on rack and cool completely. Dust with confectioners' sugar or spread Creamy Praline Frosting over cake.

2 cups flour
1 teaspoon soda
1 teaspoon cinnamon
1 teaspoon nutmeg
1 teaspoon allspice
½ teaspoon salt
1½ cups granulated sugar
1 cup oil
3 eggs
1 cup buttermilk
1 cup chopped moisturized or pitted
  cooked prunes (about 6 ounces)
1 cup chopped nuts
Confectioners' sugar or *Creamy Praline
  Frosting

RICH STRAWBERRY SHORTCAKE

Preheat oven to 425°. Combine baking mix, sugar, and nutmeg in bowl or on board. Add sour cream and egg and blend with fork or fingertips until dough clings together. Turn out on board and knead a few strokes. Pat out ½ the dough in ungreased 8-inch layer cake pan. Brush with ½ the melted butter. On board, pat out remaining dough to an 8-inch circle. Place over layer in pan and brush with remaining melted butter. Bake 25 minutes or until wood pick inserted in center comes out clean. Cool in pan or serve warm.

Meanwhile, wash and hull berries. Set aside 6 of the most attractive for garnish. Slice remaining berries and sprinkle with sugar. Let stand 20 or 30 minutes.

Carefully split shortcake layers. Spread ¾ of the sugared berries on bottom layer. Cover with top layer, add remaining sugared berries, whipped cream, and whole berries. Cut in wedges. MAKES 6 SERVINGS.

2½ cups buttermilk baking mix
2 tablespoons sugar
⅛ teaspoon nutmeg or mace
½ cup sour cream
1 egg
2 tablespoons melted butter or margarine
1 pint strawberries
2–4 tablespoons sugar
½ pint heavy cream, whipped

GEORGIA PECAN CAKE

Preheat oven to 275°. Cream together butter and sugar until fluffy. Beat in eggs, 2 at a time. Beat in nutmeg. Mix pecans, raisins, and cherries on large piece of waxed paper. Add ½ cup flour and mix well with hands. Stir remaining flour and baking powder in alternately with brandy. Fold in pecan mixture. Batter will be very stiff. Turn into well-greased and lightly floured 12-cup Bundt pan, 10-inch tube pan, or 2 9×5-inch loaf pans. Bake 2–2½ hours for Bundt or tube pans, 1½ hours for loaf pans, until skewer inserted in center comes out clean. Cool in pans on wire rack 15 minutes, loosen edges with narrow spatula, turn out on rack, and cool completely.

1 cup butter or margarine, softened
2 cups sugar
6 large eggs
4 teaspoons nutmeg
4 cups coarsely chopped pecans
5 cups golden raisins (about 2 pounds)
½ pound candied cherries, sliced
  (optional)
4 cups flour
1 teaspoon baking powder
½ cup brandy, Bourbon, or orange juice

QUEEN ELIZABETH CAKE

Preheat oven to 325°. Place dates in bowl, add 1 teaspoon soda and boiling water. Let stand while mixing batter. Cream together butter and sugar until fluffy. Beat in egg. Add flour, baking powder, and remaining soda, mixing lightly. Stir in the date mixture, vanilla and nuts. Turn into greased and floured 12 × 9-inch baking pan. Bake 55–60 minutes, until top springs back when lightly pressed. Cool cake in pan while making glaze. Pour glaze over cake and spread evenly, then sprinkle with coconut. Cool in pan and cut in squares to serve. MAKES 24 PIECES.

1 cup pitted dates, chopped
1¼ teaspoons soda
1 cup boiling water
¼ cup butter or margarine, softened
1 cup sugar
1 egg
1½ cups flour
1 teaspoon baking powder
1 teaspoon vanilla extract
⅔ cup chopped nuts
Caramel Glaze (see below)

CARAMEL GLAZE

Combine butter, cream, and sugar in saucepan. Bring to a boil and boil 3 minutes. Pour and spread over cake. Sprinkle with coconut and press into glaze lightly.

3 tablespoons butter or margarine
3 tablespoons cream or undiluted
  evaporated milk
½ cup brown sugar, packed
½ cup shredded coconut

LANE CAKE FILLING

Combine egg yolks, sugar, raisins, coconut, and butter in top of double boiler. Cook and stir over very hot, not boiling, water until thick enough to mound when dropped from spoon, at least 15 minutes. Remove from heat and stir in brandy. Cool and use to fill *Alabama Lane Cake.

8 egg yolks
1 cup sugar
1 cup raisins
1 cup shredded coconut
½ cup butter or margarine, softened
¼ cup brandy, light rum, or Bourbon

LEMON CREAM FILLING

Beat egg yolks in top of double boiler. Add sugar, cornstarch, water, lemon juice and peel. Mix well. Cook over boiling water, stirring often, about 15 minutes or until thickened. Stir in butter. Cool and spread between cake layers. MAKES ENOUGH FOR 3 8- OR 9-INCH LAYERS.

2 egg yolks
1 cup sugar
1¼ cups cornstarch
1 cup water
½ cup lemon juice
½ teaspoon grated lemon peel
1 tablespoon butter or margarine

ORANGE FILLING

Thoroughly mix sugar, cornstarch, and salt in small heavy saucepan. Stir in milk until smooth. Cook and stir over moderate heat until smooth and thickened. Sauce will look translucent. Stir a spoonful of hot sauce into egg yolks, stir egg yolks into sauce, and cook and stir over heat until smooth and thickened. Do not boil. Remove from heat and beat in butter, orange and lemon juices, and peel. Cool. Use to fill cake layers. MAKES ENOUGH FOR 2 LAYERS OR A THIN FILLING FOR 3 LAYERS.

½ cup sugar
2 tablespoons cornstarch
¼ teaspoon salt
¾ cup milk
2 egg yolks, beaten
1 tablespoon butter or margarine
¼ cup orange juice
1 tablespoon lemon juice
1 teaspoon grated orange peel

RUM FILLING

Beat butter until fluffy. Beat in egg yolk, then ½ the sugar. Add salt and rum. Beat in remaining sugar or enough to thicken to spreading consistency. MAKES ENOUGH TO FILL 3 9-INCH LAYERS GENEROUSLY OR FILL AND FROST 2 8-INCH LAYERS.

½ cup butter or margarine, softened
1 egg yolk (optional)
4 cups (approximately) confectioners'
  sugar
Pinch salt
¼ cup rum, preferably dark

RAISIN BRANDY FILLING

Blend sugar, cornstarch, and salt in small saucepan. Stir in water. Cook and stir over moderate heat until sauce boils and looks transparent. Stir into beaten eggs. Return to very low heat and beat briskly for 1 minute. Remove from heat and beat in brandy and raisins. Cool thoroughly and use to fill *Japanese Fruitcake.

1 cup sugar
7 tablespoons cornstarch
¼ teaspoon salt
2 cups water
2 eggs, beaten
¼ cup brandy or light rum
1½ cups chopped raisins

CREAMY PRALINE FROSTING

Combine sugar, buttermilk, butter, soda, and corn syrup in 3-quart saucepan. Bring to a boil over moderate heat and cook over moderately low heat to 234° on a candy thermometer (thread stage). Remove from heat and cool to about 180°. Add vanilla. Beat with sturdy wooden spoon or electric beater until thick and creamy and slightly lighter in color. Spread on cake. MAKES ENOUGH FOR TOP OF 13×9-INCH LOAF OR 2 LAYERS.

1 cup sugar
½ cup buttermilk
½ cup butter or margarine
1 teaspoon soda
1 tablespoon light or dark corn syrup
1 teaspoon vanilla extract

JELLY FROSTING

Combine egg white, jelly, and salt in top of double boiler or bowl that can be placed in pan of boiling water. Place over boiling water. Beat at high speed of mixer or rotary beater until frosting stands in stiff peaks. Add lemon juice, remove from heat, and beat until thick enough to spread. Use to fill and frost cakes or cupcakes. MAKES ENOUGH FOR 2 8- OR 9-INCH LAYERS OR 24 CUPCAKES.

NOTE: This frosting is best if prepared 24 hours or less before serving.

2 egg whites
1 10- or 12-ounce jar currant jelly (about 1 cup)
Dash salt
1 teaspoon lemon juice

FUDGE FROSTING

Melt chocolate. Cream butter in small bowl of electric mixer. Stir in chocolate and instant coffee. Add 2 cups sugar and mix well. Stir in hot water, vanilla, and more hot water or confectioners' sugar as needed to achieve spreading consistency. Stir in nuts. Spread on *Betty's Fudge Cake. MAKES ENOUGH FOR TOP OF 13×9-INCH LOAF OR 2 8- OR 9-INCH CAKE LAYERS.

3 ounces unsweetened chocolate
¼ cup butter or margarine
1 teaspoon instant coffee
2–2¼ cups confectioners' sugar
3–4 tablespoons hot water
1 teaspoon vanilla extract
½ cup chopped pecans or walnuts

DIVINITY FROSTING

Combine sugar, corn syrup, water, and salt in saucepan. Stir gently over moderate heat until sugar is dissolved. Bring to a boil, cover, and boil slowly 2 minutes. Uncover and cook to 245° on candy thermometer (firm-ball stage). Meanwhile, beat egg whites in small bowl of electric mixer until stiff. Turn into large mixer bowl. Add hot syrup in fine stream, beating at high speed. Beat in vanilla and continue to beat until thick enough to spread and frosting begins to lose shiny appearance. MAKES ENOUGH TO FILL AND FROST 2 8- OR 9-INCH LAYERS GENEROUSLY, 3 LAYERS THINLY.

2½ cups sugar
¼ cup light corn syrup
½ cup water
¼ teaspoon salt
2 egg whites
2 teaspoons vanilla extract or 1 tablespoon dark rum

LEMON SEVEN-MINUTE FROSTING

Combine egg whites, sugar, lemon juice, corn syrup, peel, and salt in top of double boiler. Beat using hand mixer or rotary beater, to blend well. Place over boiling water and beat at high speed until peaks form when beater is raised, about 7 minutes. Remove from heat and continue beating until thick enough to spread. Tint pale yellow with food color if desired. MAKES ENOUGH TO FILL AND FROST 2 8- OR 9-INCH CAKE LAYERS OR FROST 3 8- OR 9-INCH LAYERS.

2 egg whites
1½ cups sugar
3 tablespoons lemon juice
1 tablespoon white corn syrup
½ teaspoon grated lemon peel
⅛ teaspoon salt
Yellow food color (optional)

BUTTER CREAM FROSTING

Beat butter until fluffy, then beat in sugar, flavoring, and enough milk to thin sufficiently to spread. MAKES ENOUGH FOR 3 8-INCH LAYERS OR TOPS AND SIDES OF 3 9-INCH LAYERS.

2½ tablespoons butter or margarine, softened
2 cups confectioners' sugar
1 tablespoon lemon juice or brandy or 1 teaspoon vanilla extract
2 teaspoons (approximately) milk

PENUCHE FROSTING

Combine sugars, milk, corn syrup, and salt in large saucepan and bring to a boil over moderate heat, stirring until sugars are dissolved. Boil to 232° on candy thermometer (thread stage). Remove from heat, add butter and vanilla, and cool to about 130°. Beat until creamy and spread on cake. If frosting hardens too much while beating, beat in a few drops of hot water. MAKES ENOUGH FOR 2 8-INCH LAYERS.

1 cup granulated sugar
1 cup light brown sugar, packed
1 small can evaporated milk (⅔ cup)
1 tablespoon light or dark corn syrup
Dash salt
1 tablespoon butter or margarine
1 teaspoon vanilla extract

LEMON CHEESE ICING

Beat together cream cheese and butter until fluffy, using mixer or sturdy spoon. Beat in sugar, salt, lemon juice and peel until well blended. Add a little more sugar if frosting is not thick enough to spread. Tint pale yellow with food color if desired. Spread on cake. MAKES ENOUGH FOR TOP OF 11×7-INCH CAKE OR 2 8-INCH LAYERS.

1 3-ounce package cream cheese, softened
½ cup butter or margarine, softened
1 pound confectioners' sugar (4½ cups)
Dash salt
1 tablespoon lemon juice
2 teaspoons grated lemon peel
Yellow food color (optional)

ORNAMENTAL FROSTING

Beat egg whites until foamy throughout, add ¼ cup sugar, and beat until well blended. Beat in cream of tartar, then remaining sugar, a little at a time. Add enough sugar to achieve a thin spreading consistency. Beat in lemon peel. Spread a thin layer on cake and between layers. Beat remaining frosting until very stiff and spread on cake. Make a second recipe and beat very stiff for decorating. Press through pastry tube to form borders or other decorations. MAKES ENOUGH FOR 2 8- OR 9-INCH LAYERS.

3 egg whites
1 pound (approximately) confectioners' sugar
½ teaspoon cream of tartar
½ teaspoon grated lemon peel or vanilla extract

LAVISH WHITE MOUNTAIN FROSTING

Combine 3 cups sugar, corn syrup, and water in saucepan. Stir gently over low heat to prevent splashing sides of pan until sugar is dissolved. Bring to a boil, cover, and boil 3 minutes. Uncover and cook to 238° on candy thermometer (soft-ball stage). Meanwhile, beat egg whites in large bowl of electric mixer until soft peaks form. Gradually beat in 3 tablespoons sugar and continue to beat until stiff. Add hot syrup in fine stream, beating at high speed. Add salt and vanilla and continue to beat until thick enough to spread. MAKES ENOUGH TO FILL AND FROST 3 8- OR 9-INCH LAYERS.

NOTE: This frosting remains moist for 2 or 3 days after spreading on cake.

3 cups sugar
2 tablespoons white corn syrup
1 cup water
5 egg whites
3 tablespoons sugar
⅛ teaspoon salt
2 teaspoons vanilla extract

WHIPPED CREAM FROSTING

Chill bowl and beaters in refrigerator at least 1 hour before whipping cream and have cream well chilled. Pour cream into chilled bowl and whip at high speed until soft peaks form. Whip in sugar and continue to whip until stiff, but not buttery. Whip in vanilla. Refrigerate cake after spreading with this frosting. Double recipe to frost sides. MAKES ENOUGH TO FILL AND FROST TOP OF 2 8- OR 9-INCH LAYERS.

1 cup heavy cream
2 tablespoons confectioners' sugar
1 teaspoon vanilla extract

Rum Whipped Cream: Omit vanilla in Whipped Cream Frosting and whip in 1 tablespoon dark rum.

Mocha Whipped Cream: Reduce vanilla to ¼ teaspoon and whip in 1 tablespoon unsweetened cocoa and 1 teaspoon instant coffee powder or crystals with sugar.

COOKIES AND
CANDIES

One of my earliest childhood memories is of my plump little grandmother rolling out and cutting tea cakes in her pantry, the room off the kitchen which accommodated an ever-ready pastry board. Tea cakes are a plain, crisp cookie, very lightly sweetened, which children and grown-ups ate with iced tea, lemonade, or milk. More lavish cookies were baked for receptions, the party that far antedated the cocktail party, and for holidays. *Pecan Cocoons (known elsewhere as butterballs, butter crescents, or Mexican wedding cakes), *Shortening Bread (shortbread to the Scotch), and *Bourbon Balls are still made today. The most famous confection of the South is pralines. There are two distinct kinds—examples of both are here, along with *Peanut Brittle, beloved to the peanut growers of the South. The recipes that follow cover a wide spectrum, ranging from the simplest to the most elaborate of southern cookies and confections.

NOTE: The cookie recipes in this chapter call for all-purpose flour.

PEANUT BRITTLE

Oil a 15×10-inch jelly-roll pan or 2 large shallow baking pans and set aside.

Combine sugar, corn syrup, and water in large heavy saucepan. Bring to a boil, stirring until sugar is dissolved, and boil to 260° on candy thermometer (very hard-ball stage). Add butter and peanuts. Continue boiling to 310°, stirring constantly with long-handled wooden spoon. Syrup will turn a dark golden color.

Remove from heat and add vanilla and soda. Stir quickly, as candy becomes very foamy. Immediately pour in prepared pan and spread as thin as possible with spoon. Cool thoroughly, crack with meat mallet or sturdy rolling pin, turn out, and break into desired pieces. Store in tightly covered tin or jar. MAKES ABOUT 2 POUNDS.

2 cups sugar
1 cup white corn syrup
½ cup water
2 tablespoons butter or margarine
2 cups salted Virginia peanuts (1 12-ounce can)
1 teaspoon vanilla extract
1 tablespoon soda

CHRISTMAS DROP MINTS

Combine water, sugar, and corn syrup or cream of tartar in heavy 2- or 3-quart saucepan. Stir gently over moderate heat so no syrup splashes on sides of pan until sugar is dissolved. Bring to a boil. Cover and boil 3 minutes. Uncover, place candy thermometer in boiling syrup, and boil without stirring to 238° (soft-ball stage). Pour on large platter which has been rinsed in cold water. Cool to lukewarm. Stir with sturdy spoon until clear syrup forms a creamy liquid. Continue to stir until thick and white. Scrape from platter into heavy plastic bag and knead in bag until very creamy and pliable. Seal bag with a twist tie and store at room temperature to ripen 2 days up to 6 or 7 days. Transfer candy to top of double boiler. Melt slowly over hot, not boiling, water, stirring now and then. Stir in peppermint extract and food color to tint medium green. Mix well. Drop from tip of teaspoon on trays lined with waxed paper or place wooden spoon handle in spout of 1-pint funnel and pour hot candy around spoon. Drop mints by lifting spoon handle for a moment and plunging back into spout. Let mints dry 2 or 3 hours. Decorate each with a tiny star of red frosting in center. Cover with plastic film to store. MAKES ABOUT ¾ POUND, 3–4 DOZEN 1-INCH MINT PATTIES.

⅔ cup water
2 cups sugar
2 tablespoons white corn syrup or
⅛ teaspoon cream of tartar
½ teaspoon peppermint extract
Green food color
*Ornamental Frosting tinted red or
frosting in pressurized can

TEXAS PRALINES

Combine sugar, buttermilk, soda, and salt in large saucepan (4–6 quarts). Cook over moderate heat to thread stage, 230° on a candy thermometer. Add pecans and continue to cook to the soft-ball stage, 238° on thermometer, stirring constantly. Remove from heat and beat in butter and vanilla. Let cool slightly, then beat until mixture begins to lose its sheen. Working rapidly to prevent candy from setting, drop by teaspoonfuls onto waxed paper. When set, remove pralines to a tray. MAKES ABOUT 3 DOZEN.

3 cups sugar
1 cup buttermilk
1 teaspoon soda
⅛ teaspoon salt
2 cups chopped pecans
2 tablespoons butter or margarine
1½ teaspoons vanilla extract

JAMES MERRICK SMITH'S CREOLE PRALINES

Combine 3½ cups sugar, milk, and soda in large kettle. Place over moderate heat and stir to dissolve sugar. Cook until foamy. Meanwhile, heat remaining sugar in heavy skillet over moderately high heat until sugar forms a golden brown syrup, stirring now and then with wooden spoon. Carefully pour caramelized sugar into milk and sugar mixture, stirring with a long-handled wooden spoon. Cook to 236° on candy thermometer (soft-ball stage). Remove from heat and cool to 140° (very warm). Beat until creamy, then add pecans. Work quickly and be careful not to beat too long, as candy will harden and cannot be dropped. Drop by dessert spoonfuls on tray lined with waxed paper. When set, remove to serving dish or covered tin, separating layers with waxed paper. MAKES 2–3 DOZEN.

4½ cups sugar
1 cup milk
Pinch soda
2–2½ cups coarsely chopped pecans

BOURBON, RUM, OR BRANDY BALLS

Blend sugar and cocoa, mashing out lumps with back of spoon. Work in crumbs, pecans, honey, and Bourbon. Mix well. Oil hands and shape mixture into balls 1 inch in diameter. Let ripen overnight or longer. Roll in confectioners' sugar if desired. MAKES 4–5 DOZEN.

1 cup confectioners' sugar
2 tablespoons unsweetened cocoa
1 cup fine vanilla wafer crumbs (about ½ 12-ounce package)
1 cup finely chopped pecans
2 tablespoons honey or white corn syrup
¼ cup Bourbon, rum, or brandy
Additional confectioners' sugar (optional)

WALNUT FINGERS

Preheat oven to 300°. Beat egg whites until stiff. Beat in brown sugar a few tablespoons at a time. Gradually beat in flour, baking powder, salt, and vanilla. Fold in walnuts. Spread in well-greased 8-inch square baking pan. Bake 1 hour or until wood pick inserted in center comes out clean. Cool in pan 10–15 minutes. Cut in strips 1 inch wide, then cut strips into thirds. Carefully remove from pan and cool on wire rack. MAKES 2 DOZEN FINGERS.

3 egg whites
1 cup brown sugar, packed
1 cup flour
½ teaspoon baking powder
⅛ teaspoon salt
1 teaspoon vanilla extract
1½ cups coarsely chopped walnuts

APPLESAUCE REFRIGERATOR COOKIES

Preheat oven to 375°. Cream together butter and sugar until fluffy. Beat in egg. Mix flour, soda, and salt. Mix nuts into flour mixture. Stir in flour mixture alternately with applesauce. Stir in vanilla. Shape dough into rolls, flouring hands if too sticky to handle. It is easier to handle 3 or 4 rolls than 1 long roll. Wrap rolls in waxed paper and refrigerate overnight or up to a week. Slice rolls ¼ inch thick. Place on greased cookie sheets and bake 10–12 minutes. Remove from pans and cool on wire racks. MAKES 5 OR 6 DOZEN 2-INCH COOKIES.

¾ cup butter or margarine, softened
1 cup sugar
1 egg
2½ cups flour
½ teaspoon soda
¼ teaspoon salt
½ cup finely chopped nuts
½ cup applesauce
1½ teaspoons vanilla extract

LEMON REFRIGERATOR COOKIES

Cream butter with sugar until fluffy. Beat in egg, lemon juice, and peel. Stir in flour and salt. Turn dough onto large sheet of waxed paper. Knead to blend thoroughly. Shape into a roll 1½ inches in diameter. Wrap in waxed paper and twist ends closed. Chill at least 4 hours. Preheat oven to 400°. Cut dough into slices ⅛ inch thick. Place on cookie sheets and bake 8–10 minutes, until lightly browned at edges. Cool on wire racks. MAKES 4 DOZEN.

½ cup butter or margarine, softened
½ cup sugar
1 egg
1 tablespoon lemon juice
2 teaspoons grated lemon peel
1½ cups flour
½ teaspoon salt

BROWN SUGAR REFRIGERATOR COOKIES

Cream together butter and sugar until fluffy. Add egg and beat until smooth. Stir in ½ the flour, baking powder, and salt, then remaining flour. Add vanilla and nuts and mix well. Flour a sheet of waxed paper lightly or chill dough about 30 minutes to facilitate shaping. Place dough in center of waxed paper and shape into a roll about 2 inches in diameter. Wrap in waxed paper and twist ends. Refrigerate overnight or until ready to bake. Preheat oven to 375°. Cut dough into slices ⅛ inch thick and place on ungreased cookie sheet. Bake 10–12 minutes, until lightly browned. Remove from cookie sheet and cool on wire racks. MAKES 3½–4 DOZEN.

¼ cup butter or margarine, softened
½ cup brown sugar, packed
1 egg
1 cup flour
½ teaspoon baking powder
Dash salt
½ teaspoon vanilla extract
⅓ cup finely chopped pecans or walnuts

BENNE SEED COOKIES

Preheat oven to 350°. Toast sesame seeds in shallow pan in oven, stirring 2 or 3 times until golden, 12–15 minutes. Cool. Cream together butter, brown sugar, and egg until fluffy. Add flour, baking powder, and salt and mix well. Stir in sesame seeds and vanilla. Drop by half-teaspoonfuls 2 inches apart on greased cookie sheets. Bake at 350° 8–10 minutes, until edges are brown. Remove from cookie sheet and cool on wire racks. MAKES 6–7 DOZEN.

½ cup sesame seeds (2¼–2¾ ounces)
½ cup butter or margarine, softened
1 cup brown sugar, packed
1 egg
1 cup flour
½ teaspoon baking powder
¼ teaspoon salt
1 teaspoon vanilla extract

UNBAKED COCOA OATMEAL DROPS

Blend sugar and cocoa in saucepan. Add milk and butter. Bring to a boil, stirring now and then. Boil 1 minute. Stir in peanut butter, oatmeal, vanilla, and nuts. Drop by teaspoonfuls on tray lined with waxed paper. Let stand until cold and firm. MAKES ABOUT 3½ DOZEN.

1 cup sugar
3 tablespoons unsweetened cocoa
¼ cup milk
¼ cup butter or margarine
¼ cup peanut butter, smooth or crunchy
1½ cups quick-cooking oatmeal
1 teaspoon vanilla extract
½ cup chopped salted peanuts (optional)

OLD-FASHIONED RAISIN DROPS

Preheat oven to 400°. Cover raisins with boiling water, let stand 10–15 minutes, and drain well. This step can be eliminated if raisins are very moist. Measure flour, add soda and salt, and mix well. Cream brown sugar, shortening, and egg in large bowl of mixer until fluffy. Beat in buttermilk. Stir in flour mixture lightly but thoroughly. Stir in raisins. Drop by rounded teaspoonfuls 2 inches apart on ungreased cookie sheet. Bake 10 minutes or until a light imprint remains when cookie is pressed. Remove from cookie sheet and cool on wire rack. MAKES 3 DOZEN 2½-INCH COOKIES.

NOTE: On a warm humid day dough may be soft. If so, refrigerate 1 hour or longer.

½ cup raisins
Boiling water (optional)
1½ cups flour
½ teaspoon soda
¼ teaspoon salt
1 cup brown sugar, packed
½ cup shortening
1 egg
2 tablespoons buttermilk or water

PECAN COCOONS

Butterfingers, butterballs, pecan fingers, Russian tea cakes, and Mexican wedding cakes are other names for this favorite holiday cookie.

Preheat oven to 400°. Cream butter with ¼ cup sugar until fluffy and smooth. Beat in vanilla. Stir in flour, salt, and pecans. Chill dough until stiff. Pinch off small pieces and roll between palms of hands into cocoons (small ovals) about 1½ inches long. Place on ungreased cookie sheets and bake 12–15 minutes, until beginning to brown at edges. Remove from cookie sheets and cool on wire racks. If desired, shake lightly in bag with more confectioners' sugar. MAKES ABOUT 4 DOZEN.

1 cup butter or margarine, softened
¼ cup sifted confectioners' sugar
1 teaspoon vanilla extract
2 cups flour
¼ teaspoon salt
½ cup finely chopped pecans
Additional confectioners' sugar (optional)

ENGLISH MATRIMONIAL BARS

Preheat oven to 350°. Mix brown sugar, flour, and oatmeal in bowl with fork. Cut butter in small pieces and add to flour mixture. Mix until crumbly, using fork, then fingertips. Press ½ the mixture in a greased 8-inch square baking pan. Drop jam by spoonfuls on layer in pan and spread lightly. Spread remaining crumb mixture over jam and press lightly. Bake 35–40 minutes, until lightly browned. Cool in pan on wire rack 15–20 minutes. Mark in 2-inch squares with spatula or knife. Cool completely, then carefully remove squares and cut each in halves to form 2 bars. These cookies are crumbly so should be served on small plates. MAKES 32 BARS.

1 cup brown sugar, packed
1 cup flour
1 cup oatmeal
½ cup butter or margarine, softened
¾ cup raspberry jam

LIZZIES (FRUITCAKE COOKIES, CHRISTMAS ROCKS, HERMITS)

Prepare fruit, using scissors dipped periodically in hot water to prevent sticking or sharp knife to cut. Combine fruit in large bowl. Add sherry, mix well, cover, and let stand 30 minutes. Add pecans and mix again. Preheat oven to 350°. Cream butter with sugar. Beat in eggs 1 at a time. Mix ½ cup flour with the fruit. Stir remaining flour, cinnamon, nutmeg, cloves, and soda into creamed mixture. Fold in fruit mixture. Drop by teaspoonfuls on ungreased cookie sheets, spacing 2 inches apart. Bake 15–18 minutes, until browned. Remove from pans and cool on wire racks. These cookies ripen as fruitcake does and are best if stored in tightly covered tins at least 10 days. MAKES 8–9 DOZEN 2½-INCH COOKIES.

1 15-ounce package seedless raisins
½ pound candied cherries, sliced
¼ pound dates, chopped
¼ pound chopped citron (½ cup)
¼ pound chopped candied orange peel
  (½ cup)
½ cup cream sherry or Bourbon
½ pound coarsely chopped pecans
  (2 cups)
¾ cup butter or margarine, softened
1½ cups brown sugar, packed
3 eggs
2 cups flour
1½ teaspoons cinnamon
½ teaspoon nutmeg
½ teaspoon ground cloves
1 teaspoon soda

SAND TARTS

Preheat oven to 375°. Cream butter and 1 cup sugar until fluffy. Beat in egg and vanilla. Stir in flour, baking powder, and salt. Shape dough into a ball, wrap in waxed paper or plastic wrap, and refrigerate at least 1 hour. Roll out ½ at a time on lightly floured surface to a thickness of ⅛ inch. Cut with floured cutter. Place on greased cookie sheets. Blend 1 tablespoon sugar with cinnamon. Brush cookies with egg white, sprinkle lightly with cinnamon sugar, and lightly press an almond half in the center of each. Bake 10 minutes or until edges of cookies turn golden. Remove from cookie sheets and cool on wire racks. MAKES ABOUT 3 DOZEN 3-INCH COOKIES.

½ cup butter or margarine, softened
1 cup sugar
1 egg
1 teaspoon vanilla extract
1½ cups flour
1 teaspoon baking powder
½ teaspoon salt
1 tablespoon sugar
¼ teaspoon cinnamon
1 egg white
36 (approximately) blanched almond
  halves

HAYSTACKS

Preheat oven to 325°. Mix coconut, ⅓ cup sugar, and 1 egg white in top of double boiler or heavy saucepan. Heat over boiling water or very low heat, stirring now and then, until sugar is blended in and mixture is warm. Beat remaining 2 egg whites until fluffy, gradually add remaining ⅓ cup sugar, and continue to beat until stiff. Beat in flour, baking powder, and salt. Fold flour mixture and almond extract into coconut mixture. Drop by tablespoonfuls into muffin cups lined with paper cups. Top each cookie with a half candied cherry if desired. Bake until pale golden and firm to the touch, though centers should be moist. Cool thoroughly and peel off papers carefully. MAKES 8–12 MACAROONLIKE COOKIES.

3 cups shredded coconut
⅔ cup sugar
3 egg whites
⅓ cup flour
½ teaspoon baking powder
Dash salt
½ teaspoon almond extract
Candied cherries (optional)

CREAM CHEESE COOKIES

Soften cream cheese and butter in bowl at room temperature. Cream together until well blended. Add salt and sugar and blend. Work in flour a few spoonfuls at a time. Turn dough out on sheet of waxed paper or foil. Roll in waxed paper to form a roll about 1½ inches in diameter. Wrap waxed paper around roll, seal ends, and refrigerate overnight or up to 3 or 4 days. Preheat oven to 400°. Cut dough into slices ¼ inch thick. Place on greased cookie sheet. Drop a dot of jelly from teaspoon in center of each cookie. Bake 15 minutes, just until edges of cookies brown lightly. Remove from cookie sheets and cool on wire rack. MAKES ABOUT 3½ DOZEN.

1 3-ounce package cream cheese
½ cup butter or margarine
Dash salt
1 teaspoon sugar
1 cup flour
Jelly, preserves, or marmalade

SPICED OATMEAL COOKIES

Preheat oven to 400°. Cream butter and sugar until fluffy. Add egg and beat vigorously until well blended and light in color. Add buttermilk and mix well. Stir in flour ½ cup at a time, adding salt, soda, cinnamon, cloves, and nutmeg after first ½ cup flour. Stir in oatmeal, nuts, and raisins. Drop by rounded teaspoonfuls on greased cookie sheets. Bake 10 minutes or until light imprint remains when top is lightly pressed. Remove from cookie sheets and cool on wire racks. MAKES 2 DOZEN 2-INCH COOKIES.

½ cup butter or margarine, softened
¾ cup brown sugar, packed
1 egg
*¼ cup buttermilk or 1 tablespoon vinegar
and sweet milk to make ¼ cup*
1 cup flour
½ teaspoon salt
½ teaspoon soda
½ teaspoon cinnamon
¼ teaspoon ground cloves
¼ teaspoon nutmeg
2½ cups oatmeal
½ cup chopped pecans or walnuts
½ cup raisins

LEMON CURD SQUARES

Preheat oven to 350°. Blend butter, 1 cup flour, and confectioners' sugar, working with fingers or back of sturdy spoon. Press firmly in ungreased 8-inch square pan. Bake 20 minutes or until pale brown at edges. Meanwhile, beat eggs. Beat in granulated sugar, 2 tablespoons flour, baking powder, salt, lemon juice, and peel. Pour over baked layer. Return to oven and bake 25–30 minutes, until golden brown but soft in center. Cool in pan 15 minutes on wire rack and cut into squares. Cool several hours or overnight to allow topping to set. MAKES ABOUT 3 DOZEN 1⅓-INCH SQUARES.

½ cup butter or margarine, softened
1 cup flour
¼ cup confectioners' sugar
2 eggs
1 cup granulated sugar
2 tablespoons flour
½ teaspoon baking powder
¼ teaspoon salt
2 tablespoons lemon juice
Grated peel of 1 lemon

DATE NUT SQUARES

Preheat oven to 350°. Cut up dates with kitchen scissors. Place in bowl, sprinkle with soda, and add boiling water. Let stand while preparing dough. Cream butter with sugar until fluffy. Gradually stir in flour, cocoa, and vanilla. Add date mixture and mix well. Turn into well-greased 13×9-inch pan. Sprinkle chocolate pieces and nuts over top. Bake 35–40 minutes, until wood pick inserted in center comes out clean. Cool slightly, cut in rectangles or squares, and serve with ice cream. Leftovers can be cut into bars or small squares and served as cookies. MAKES 12 DESSERT SERVINGS.

1 8-ounce package dates
1 teaspoon soda
1 cup boiling water
1 cup butter or margarine, softened
1 cup sugar
1¾ cups flour
2 teaspoons Dutch process cocoa
1 teaspoon vanilla extract
1 6-ounce package semisweet chocolate pieces
¾–1 cup chopped nuts
Vanilla, coffee, or chocolate ice cream

OATMEAL CRISPS

Preheat oven to 375°. Beat egg, then beat in sugar, butter, vanilla and almond extracts. Stir in oatmeal, baking powder, and salt. Drop by teaspoonfuls on well-greased cookie sheets. Space cookies 2 inches apart. Bake 15 minutes or until lightly browned. Cool on pan about 1 minute, remove with spatula, and cool on wire rack. MAKES 2–2½ DOZEN.

1 egg
½ cup sugar
1 tablespoon melted butter or margarine
1 teaspoon vanilla extract
½ teaspoon almond extract
1 cup oatmeal
½ teaspoon baking powder
½ teaspoon salt

BUTTERSCOTCH CHEWS

Preheat oven to 350°. Melt butter over moderate heat, stir in sugar until dissolved, then add egg, salt, baking powder, flour, and walnuts. Spread in well-greased 8-inch square baking pan. Bake 25 minutes or until wood pick inserted in center comes out moist but with no uncooked dough clinging to it. Do not overbake. Cool in pan 10–15 minutes. Cut in squares or bars and cool on wire rack. MAKES 16 2-INCH SQUARES.

½ cup butter or margarine
1 cup brown sugar, packed
1 egg
¼ teaspoon salt
1 teaspoon baking powder
1 cup flour
½ cup chopped walnuts

DARK RICH BROWNIES

Preheat oven to 350°. Melt butter and chocolate in saucepan over low heat, stirring constantly. Remove from heat and stir in sugar, eggs, vanilla, flour, and salt. Add nuts and mix. Spread in greased 8-inch square baking pan. Bake 30 minutes or until a dull crust forms on top but center holds an impression when pressed lightly. Cool in pan 10–15 minutes, then cut into 2-inch squares. MAKES 16 BROWNIES.

⅓ cup butter or margarine
3 squares unsweetened chocolate
1 cup sugar
2 eggs
1 teaspoon vanilla extract
¾ cup flour
⅛ teaspoon salt
½ cup chopped nuts

SUMMER COOKIES

Preheat oven to 350°. Combine butter, sugar, and egg and beat until well blended and creamy. Beat in lemon juice, vanilla, and peel. Add ½ cup flour, stir well, then stir in 1 tablespoon milk, remaining flour, soda, salt, and remaining milk. Chill dough 1–2 hours. Shape into balls ¾ inch in diameter. Place 2 inches apart on cookie sheet and bake 12–15 minutes, until barely golden at edges. Cool on wire racks. MAKES 2½ DOZEN.

½ cup butter or margarine, softened
½ cup sugar
1 egg
1 tablespoon lemon juice
½ teaspoon vanilla extract
1 teaspoon grated lemon peel
1¼ cups flour
2 tablespoons milk or water
¼ teaspoon soda
Dash salt

SHORTENING BREAD

Preheat oven to 325°. Cream butter with brown sugar until light and fluffy. Work in flour, using hands or back of spoon. Press dough into 8-inch square baking pan. Prick with fork in crisscross pattern in such a fashion that diamond shapes cut after cookies are baked will each have a fork mark. Bake 35 minutes or until firm but not hard. Cool 10–15 minutes, then cut in diamond shapes. Continue cooling in pan, then remove. Store in layers separated with waxed paper in tightly covered container. MAKES ABOUT 3 DOZEN PIECES.

1 cup butter or margarine, softened
½ cup light brown sugar, packed
2 cups flour

OLD-FASHIONED TEA CAKES

Preheat oven to 400°. Cream butter with ½ cup sugar until fluffy. Beat in egg and vanilla. Stir in flour, baking powder, salt, and milk. Roll out ¼ inch thick on well-floured surface. Cut with floured round cutter. Place on ungreased baking sheets. If desired, sprinkle with additional sugar or sugar mixed with nutmeg. Bake 10 minutes or until edges begin to turn golden. Remove from cookie sheets and cool on wire racks. MAKES 2 DOZEN 2¾-INCH COOKIES.

¼ cup butter or margarine, softened
½ cup sugar
1 egg
1 teaspoon vanilla extract
2 cups flour
1 teaspoon baking powder
⅛ teaspoon salt
2 tablespoons milk
*Additional sugar or sugar mixed with
    nutmeg (optional)*

THUMBPRINTS

Preheat oven to 350°. Cream butter with brown sugar until fluffy. Beat in egg yolk until smooth. Stir in flour. Beat egg white until foamy. With lightly floured hands, roll dough in 1-inch balls. Dip in egg white, then roll in pecans. Place on greased cookie sheets. Make a dent with thumb in center of each cookie. Bake 15 minutes or until lightly browned. Remove from pans and cool on wire rack. Place a dab of jelly in thumbprint in each cookie. MAKES 1½–2 DOZEN.

½ cup butter or margarine, softened
¼ cup brown sugar, packed
1 egg, separated
1 cup flour
1 cup finely chopped pecans
Jelly or jam

INDEX

244